C++ Programming for Linux Systems

Create robust enterprise software for Linux and Unix-based operating systems

Desislav Andreev

Stanimir Lukanov

BIRMINGHAM—MUMBAI

C++ Programming for Linux Systems

Group Product Manager: Gebin George

Publishing Product Manager: Kunal Sawant

Book Project Manager: Prajakta Sawant

Senior Editor: Rounak Kulkarni

Technical Editor: Shruti Thingalaya

Copy Editor: Safis Editing

Proofreader: Safis Editing

Indexer: Hemangini Bari

Production Designer: Shankar Kalbhor

DevRel Marketing Coordinator: Sonia Chauhan

Business Development Executive: Debadrita Chatterjee

First published: September 2023

Production reference: 2200923

Published by Packt Publishing Ltd.

Grosvenor House

11 St. Paul's Square

Birmingham

B3 1RB, UK.

ISBN 978-1-80512-900-4

www.packtpub.com

*To my beautiful and loving wife, Svetla-Maria, for her unconditional support,
tremendous energy, and endless ability to tolerate my character.
To my parents, Slaveika and Andrey, for giving me life,
teaching me to believe in myself, and motivating me to keep learning.*

– Dr. Desislav Andreev

*Dedicated to Vanya, Plami, and Teko, who fully supported me
in this adventurous journey – of writing my first book.*

– Stanimir Lukanov

Foreword

Desislav Andreev and Stanimir Lukanov are leading engineers in C++ programming. I have known and worked with Desislav for more than 12 years in my capacity as a Professor and Head of the Department - Computer Systems in the Faculty of Computer Systems and Technologies at the Technical University of Sofia, Bulgaria.

In the ever-evolving landscape of software development, certain principles remain timeless: the pursuit of excellence, the thirst for knowledge, and the audacity to innovate. In this book, *C++ Programming for Linux Systems: Create robust enterprise software for Linux and Unix-based operating systems*, the professional experience and skills of Desislav and Stanimir are used for presenting a unique combination of fundamental OS knowledge with programming skills. The authors have embraced the challenges of C++ and embarked on the ambitious quest to share their knowledge and insights with the broader community. In this age of rapid technological advancement, their passion and dedication to creating robust software solutions are nothing short of inspiring.

C++ has long been the language of choice for building powerful and efficient software systems, and it finds its natural home on Linux and Unix-based platforms. The authors' decision to focus on these operating systems is a testament to their understanding of the importance of crafting software that can withstand the rigors of enterprise-level demands. They guide you through the subtle of C++ language and demonstrate how to harness its full potential within the Linux environment.

One of the most compelling aspects of this book is its practicality. The authors don't just teach theory, but rather they provide knowledge and proper examples needed to tackle real-world challenges. From concurrent system programming and process management to process communication and process scheduling, you will gain a deep understanding of how C++ can be harnessed for building high-quality software.

In this book, Desislav and Stanimir, as two industry experts, have distilled their collective knowledge and experience into an invaluable resource for all those who seek to navigate the complex and exciting world of system programming on Linux and Unix-based platforms.

This book serves as both a comprehensive introduction for those new to system programming and software design in Linux environment and a valuable resource for experienced developers looking to expand their expertise.

Whether you are a student eager to embark on a journey of discovery or a professional seeking to sharpen your skills, *C++ Programming for Linux Systems* offers something for everyone.

Prof. Milena Lazarova

Head of Department "Computer Systems", Faculty Computer Systems and Technologies, Technical University of Sofia

Contributors

About the author(s)

Desislav Andreev is a software engineer with a Ph.D. in AI systems and quantum machine learning. He has several publications in software engineering and AI applications. In his 10 years in the field, he has worked in automotive software engineering and higher education. He is skilled in system and software architectures, operating systems, C/C++ development, autonomous driving, and computer graphics. He currently works as a Lead C++ Developer in VMware, developing its core infrastructure. He is also a lecturer at the Technical University of Sofia. He was previously a Technical Professional and software architect in the CRE and ADAS departments of Visteon Corp., working closely with both OEMs and development teams.

Stanimir Lukanov is a C++ expert, software tech lead and architect at VMware. He has over 15 years of experience creating efficient and robust C++ enterprise code. He is a member of the Bulgarian National Body, part of The C++ Standards Committee. His interests are in software security for distributed enterprise systems. Since 2017, Stanimir has worked at Vmware, where he currently leads a team developing core security functionality for one of the major products in the company's portfolio. Before joining, he held the position of senior software engineer at Visteon Corp. and JCI. He was responsible for the software architecture, code reviews, leading C++ trainings, and delivering high-quality C++ code for real-time automotive systems.

The authors want to thank their families and friends for their support and patience while writing their first book. They are also thankful to their colleagues and reviewers for their excellent work and constant dedication.

About the reviewer(s)

Lyubomir Koev has been programming with C++ for the past 10 years. He has worked on projects ranging from 3D graphics, raytracing, shaders, networking, and services. His main interests are in performance-aware programming - developing high-quality code made to run efficiently. He likes to explore different algorithms and data structures and their efficient implementation. In his spare time, he teaches C++ at Sofia University as well as outside courses.

Table of Contents

Part 2: Advanced Techniques for System Programming

6

7

8

Using Clocks, Timers, and Signals in Linux   185

9

Understanding the C++ Memory Model   205

10

Using Coroutines in C++ for System Programming   237

Index   255

Other Books You May Enjoy   266

Preface

Greetings, dear reader! You are among friends. Welcome to this journey of advanced skills, unexpected surprises, cunning knowledge, and novel programming tools. Suppose you are an experienced software engineer who knows how to write quality code and is aware of some build and operating systems. You have also met several computer architectures and fixed one or two bugs. And how about the following: You are a student who just learns how to do the job of a software engineer. You want to be a good professional someday. And you want to be the expert, whom others call, whenever the software behaves unpredictably. Or you just have picked up this book out of initial interest, still not knowing what to expect. Then perfect!

We challenge you to remember any situations in your practice, where, to this day, you have no explanation of what happened. No, we do not mean the supernatural – although this topic is rather arcane. We speak about the system and how we conduct its behavior as professional engineers. Our code is just an instrument that tells the machine what to do. So, let's say you have remembered that one bug that has been bugging you for some time – how do you proceed? What if it stands between you and your next promotion? How about when it disappoints a client that is important to you? Or you just want to impress your teacher. We get you! We are there, too.

Do not be fooled, though. We give you the opportunity to enrich the way you engineer through some fundamental pointers, but we do not have all the answers. We strongly believe that changing the way you see how code works will make you a more robust expert, no matter your professional field. And you should care because the world of technology is rapidly advancing. It is impossible to keep up with every innovation, algorithm, language, operating system, and architecture. But you could start asking yourself the right questions at the right moment. You have the possibility to know how to optimize further, design better, validate your environment, and encourage yourself to understand your own work thoroughly.

We challenge you again. This time to be more self-aware and efficient through our experience and expertise. There are some sophisticated real-world challenges that we so impatiently want to share with you. Please remember, it will take you some time. As friends, we hope you enjoy this book and share the exciting parts with others. Chop-chop... Let's go!

Who this book is for

This book is for programmers and developers who want to boost their programming knowledge in C++ for Linux and Unix-based operating systems. Whether you are a beginner looking to learn how to use C++ in such an environment or an experienced programmer looking to explore the latest C++20 features applicable to system programming, you'll find this book helpful.

What this book covers

Chapter 1, Getting Started with the Linux Systems and the POSIX Standard, introduces the reader to the reasoning behind the existence of different operating systems. The Linux specifics are discussed, and the reader proceeds to the fundamentals of Unix-based OS programming. The kernel space and user spaces are mentioned as the System Call Interface is explained thoroughly. Afterward, we use this opportunity to present POSIX and some standard function calls in order to let the reader grasp the benefits of the system programming.

Chapter 2, Learning More about Process Management, expands on learnings from the previous chapter and states that if the operating system is the main resource manager, then the process is the main resource user. It does so through a routine, which could get complex and needs to be well analyzed. Therefore, the chapter goes through the main process's life cycle - its startup, running, and final states. The nature of the thread is presented as well. We go through the OS's scheduling algorithms as well. A sample C++ application is introduced and its `main()` function is discussed as an entry point. In addition, different ways to initiate a process are presented: `fork()`, `vfork()`, and `exec()`. Other fundamental functions such as `wait()`, `exit()`, `pthread_create()`, and `pthread_join()` are discussed as well.

Chapter 3, Navigating through the Filesystems, shows how the file is the basic resource representation in Linux - both for data and access to I/O devices. This abstraction allows the user to manipulate streams or store data in the same manner, through the same system interfaces. The file system structure - metadata and inodes, is discussed. Examples of C++ file system operations are presented to the reader. We use this opportunity to introduce the pipes as an initial instrument for inter-process communication. The `string_view` C++20 object is offered as well. At the end, we mention signal handling as it will be required for later chapters.

Chapter 4, Diving Deep into the C++ Object, guides the reader through some core C++ features like the process of object creation and its initialization. We discuss lifetime object problems, temporaries, RVO, RAII pattern, and C++20. We also cover function objects and lambda expressions together with their specifics and guidance on how to use them. Next, we will get deeper into lambdas. In the end, we will focus on some specific examples of how to use lambdas in STL and multithreading.

Chapter 5, Handling Errors with C++, explores the different kinds of error reporting in C++ programming for Unix-based operating systems, such as error codes, exceptions, and asserts. We will discuss the best practices in exception handling and exception manipulation and what happens with uncaught exceptions in the system. We will discuss the exception specifications and why we prefer the `noexcept` keyword. We will go through the performance impact when using exceptions and the mechanics behind them. Next, we will discuss how we can use `std::optional` to handle errors. At the end, we will discuss what `std::uncaught_exceptions` functionality provides.

Chapter 6, Concurrent System Programming with C++, discusses the fundamentals and the theory behind processes and threads in Unix-based operating systems. We will go through the changes in the memory model of C++ in order to natively support concurrency. We will get acquainted with the C++ primitives which enable multithreading support - thread, jthread, and task. Next, we will learn how to synchronize the execution of parallel code using C++ synchronization primitives. We will also investigate what STL provides in the direction of parallel algorithms. In the end, we will learn how to write lock-free code.

Chapter 7, Proceeding with Inter-process Communication, guides readers through the basic IPC mechanisms in the Linux environment (as they already have the impression of the multithreading's challenges). It is important that the processes are able to communicate with each other easily, therefore, we go quickly through message queues. They allow the exchange of data without blocking processes. We will spend some time discussing synchronization mechanisms – semaphore and mutex- and then proceed with the shared memory. It provides quick access to some data and, at the same time, allows heterogeneous systems to have a common point for data exchange. At last, the sockets are frequently used, but mainly for their possibility to allow communication between computer systems on the network.

Chapter 8, Using Clocks, Timers, and Signals in Linux, introduces the signals and timers in Unix-based operating systems. We will initially present how the signaling system works and how the user can effectively manage the time of operations. We will cover what C++ language provides as functionality to handle clocks and timers. We will introduce the standard time API, `std::chrono`, predefined clocks and times. Next, we will cover how to use them correctly and what to expect from them. Next, we will focus on the duration capabilities that the standard provides and user-defined clocks. Ultimately, we will cover the calendar and time zone libraries introduced in C++20.

Chapter 9, Understanding the C++ Memory Model, explores some new C++20 features. It guides the reader through some crucial remarks on how and why to manage dynamic resources. It proceeds with a discussion on the conditional variables and mutex usages, as well as lazy initialization and cache friendliness. An introduction to the C++ memory order follows as we discuss ways to choose from different synchronization mechanisms. The spinlock/ticketlock techniques are also presented.

Chapter 10, Using Coroutines in C++ for System Programming, talks about coroutines, an already existing term with implementations in some programming languages, but now they are introduced in C++20. They are described as stackless functions suspended during execution and resumed later. The chapter discusses those exact valuable features in the area of system programming. Their disadvantages are also discussed, for example, keeping the suspended coroutine state on the heap. Some practical usages are presented.

To get the most out of this book

Some familiarity with the basics of the C++ language and POSIX programming in C language is required before starting with this book. Prior knowledge of the fundamentals of Linux and Unix will be helpful but not necessary.

Software covered in the book	Operating system requirements
C++20	Linux Mint 21
GCC12.2	
godbolt.org	

If you are using the digital version of this book, we advise you to type the code yourself or access the code from the book's GitHub repository (a link is available in the next section). Doing so will help you avoid any potential errors in copying and pasting code.

Each chapter has its respective Technical requirements. All examples are run through them. The code is system-dependent, so it might not work directly in your environment.

Download the example code files

You can download the example code files for this book from GitHub at `https://github.com/PacktPublishing/C-Programming-for-Linux-Systems`. If there's an update to the code, it will be updated in the GitHub repository.

We also have other code bundles from our rich catalog of books and videos available at `https://github.com/PacktPublishing/`. Check them out!

Conventions used

There are a number of text conventions used throughout this book.

`Code in text`: Indicates code words in text, database table names, folder names, filenames, file extensions, pathnames, dummy URLs, user input, and Twitter handles. Here is an example: "The example uses the `open()` and `close()` POSIX functions, which try to open and close a file from the filesystem of our Linux test environment."

A block of code is set as follows:

```
if (ecode.value() == EEXIST)
```

When we wish to draw your attention to a particular part of a code block, the relevant lines or items are set in bold:

```
std::for_each(v1.begin(), v1.end(),
                [&mean, sum{0.0}, count{0}, text](const double& val)
    mutable
```

Any command-line input or output is written as follows:

```
$ ./test
```

> **Tips or important notes**
> Appear like this.

Get in touch

Feedback from our readers is always welcome.

General feedback: If you have questions about any aspect of this book, email us at `customercare@ packtpub.com` and mention the book title in the subject of your message.

Errata: Although we have taken every care to ensure the accuracy of our content, mistakes do happen. If you have found a mistake in this book, we would be grateful if you would report this to us. Please visit `www.packtpub.com/support/errata` and fill in the form.

Piracy: If you come across any illegal copies of our works in any form on the internet, we would be grateful if you would provide us with the location address or website name. Please contact us at `copyright@packt.com` with a link to the material.

If you are interested in becoming an author: If there is a topic that you have expertise in and you are interested in either writing or contributing to a book, please visit `authors.packtpub.com`.

Share Your Thoughts

Once you've read *C++ Programming for Linux Systems*, we'd love to hear your thoughts! Scan the QR code below to go straight to the Amazon review page for this book and share your feedback.

`https://packt.link/r/1805129007`

Your review is important to us and the tech community and will help us make sure we're delivering excellent quality content.

Download a free PDF copy of this book

Thanks for purchasing this book!

Do you like to read on the go but are unable to carry your print books everywhere?

Is your eBook purchase not compatible with the device of your choice?

Don't worry, now with every Packt book you get a DRM-free PDF version of that book at no cost.

Read anywhere, any place, on any device. Search, copy, and paste code from your favorite technical books directly into your application.

The perks don't stop there, you can get exclusive access to discounts, newsletters, and great free content in your inbox daily

Follow these simple steps to get the benefits:

1. Scan the QR code or visit the link below

https://packt.link/free-ebook/9781805129004

2. Submit your proof of purchase

3. That's it! We'll send your free PDF and other benefits to your email directly

Part 1: Securing the Fundamentals

This part of the book will provide you with the necessary instruments to get into the advanced topics of system programming. Experienced readers will find it helpful, too, as some of the C++20 features are practically presented in the area of system programming. This part ensures that the readers are on the same page with the presented subjects and provides the opportunity to extract the best from the technical examples. At the same time, it notes important aspects of the Linux system development.

This part has the following chapters:

- *Chapter 1, Getting Started with Linux Systems and the POSIX Standard*

- *Chapter 2, Learning More about Process Management*

- *Chapter 3, Navigating through the Filesystems*

- *Chapter 4, Diving Deep into the C++ Object*

- *Chapter 5, Handling Errors with C++*

1

Getting Started with Linux Systems and the POSIX Standard

This book is about **Linux** and how we use **C++** in **Linux** environments to manage critical resources. The **C++** language is continuously improving, as you'll explore in the following chapters. Before we go there, we'd like to spend some time in this chapter developing a fundamental understanding of **operating systems** (**OSs**). You are going to learn more about the origins of some specific techniques, the **system call interface** and the **Portable Operating System Interface** (**POSIX**).

Your choice of OS matters. Although OSs were created with a single purpose, nowadays their roles differ. Much is expected of them as well. Each OS has its own strengths and weaknesses, which we are going to discuss briefly. **Linux** is in widespread use across multiple technological areas and has a huge community worldwide, so it is perfect for our practical purposes. In our experience, programming in Linux or other *Unix-based OS* environments is rather common. Wherever your expertise resides – from **Internet of Things** (**IoT**) devices and embedded software development to mobile devices, supercomputing, or spacecraft – there is a good chance that you will cross paths with a Linux distribution at some point.

Use this chapter as an introduction to system programming. Even if you are already familiar with the topic, take your time to revisit the terms and details. Most of them are covered by college courses or are taken as common knowledge, but it is nonetheless important for us to explain some of the fundamentals here to make sure we will be on the same page in the chapters to come.

In this chapter, we are going to cover the following main topics:

- Getting familiar with the concept of OSs
- Getting to know the Linux kernel

- Introducing the system call interface and system programming

- Navigating through files, processes, and threads

- Running services with `init` and `systemd`

- **Portable Operating System Interface (POSIX)**

Technical requirements

In order to get familiar with the programming environment, the reader must prepare the following:

- A Linux-based system capable of compiling and executing C++20 (for example, Linux Mint 21)

Getting familiar with the concept of OSs

So, what is an OS? You could probably provide at least one answer, but let's discuss this briefly as it is important to understand what our computer system truly is and how we manipulate it. Although you might be familiar with most of the information provided here, we are using this chapter to align with you on the matter of OSs and their uses. Some might say that the OS was created to make the hardware work as a whole. Others will argue that it is an aggregation of programs, dedicated to managing the system resources overall. It is crucial to utilize these resources, such as CPU and memory, efficiently. There is also the concept of the OS as an abstraction and an extension of the hardware. Ultimately, we can safely say that the modern OS is a complex entity. It also has additional functions, such as the collection of statistics, multimedia handling, system safety and security, overall stability, reliable error handling, and so on.

While the OS is obliged to execute all those tasks, it is still necessary for the programmer to pay attention to the system specifics and requirements. Working from a higher level of abstraction, through virtual machines, for example, does not mean discarding the need to understand how our code impacts the system's behavior. And programmers, who are closer to the OS layers, are required to manage the system's resources efficiently as well. This is one of the reasons that OSs provide **application programming interfaces**, or **APIs**. It is valuable expertise to know how to use such APIs and what kind of benefits they provide.

We believe that the ability to work closely with the OS is a skill that is not so common. Knowledge of how the OS and the computer architecture will behave is at the expert level of software engineering. We will discuss some types of OSs just to give you a broad picture, but the focus of the book is specifically on **POSIX-compliant** OSs. That said, let's get familiar with one of our main toolsets.

Types of OSs

If we do some quick research online, we will find many types of OSs, and the type definition will strictly be based on the criterion searched for. One example is the purpose of the OS: is it a general-purpose one, such as macOS and Windows, or more specific, such as **Embedded Linux** and **FreeRTOS**? Another example is OSs for PCs versus those for mobile devices. Likewise, the licensing could describe the OSs as open source, enterprise, or enterprise open source. Based on the number of active users at a time, Windows could be considered a *single-user* OS, as it constructs just one **Win32 API** for the current *user session*. On the other hand, Unix-like OSs are considered *multi-user*, as multiple users can work simultaneously on the system, where each *shell* or a *Terminal* instance is considered a separate user session.

So, the system's applications and their constraints are fundamental. Therefore, a key distinction to be aware of is the level of restrictions on the system's behavior. The **general-purpose operating systems (GPOSs)** started initially as *time-sharing* OSs. Historically, there is another type of OS, originating from the same period as the time-sharing ones – the **real-time operating systems (RTOSs)**. It is expected that system programmers understand the specifics of **GPOSs** and **RTOSs**. In the following chapters, we will discuss how properties such as task priorities, timer values, peripheral speeds, interrupt and signal handlers, multithreading, and dynamic memory allocation can lead to changes in system behavior. Sometimes these are unpredictable. That's why we recognize two types of **RTOSs**: hard and soft **RTOSs**. Hard **RTOSs** are usually strictly related to a given piece of hardware. The system developer is familiar with the end device requirements. The task execution times can be preliminary evaluated and programmed, although the device's input is still treated as asynchronous and unpredictable. Therefore, our focus in this book remains on **GPOS** programming with a bit of soft **RTOS** functions.

Let's set the stage like this: the user receives system resources in a cyclic manner so often that it creates the impression that the user is the only one relying on those resources. The user's work must not be disrupted, and quick response times are to be expected from an OS; theoretically, the smaller the procedures, the shorter the response times. We will discuss this further in *Chapter 2* as it is not completely true.

> **Important note**
> The user is the main *driver* of the system's functionality with a **GPOS**. The main job of the OS is maintaining active dialog with the users and the high availability of operations.

Here, each task and each request to the OS must be handled quickly within a strict time interval. The **RTOS** expects user input only during exceptional situations, errors, and unpredicted behavior.

> **Important note**
> Asynchronously working devices and additional peripheral electronics are the main *drivers* of the system's functionality in an RTOS. The main job of the OS remains process management and task scheduling.

As we said, there are two types of **RTOS**: *hard RTOS* and *soft RTOS*. In a hard **RTOS**, real-time tasks are guaranteed to be executed on time. System reaction deadlines are usually preliminarily defined, and the *mission-critical* data is stored in ROM, so it cannot be updated at runtime. Functionalities such as virtual memory are often removed. Some modern CPU cores provide the so-called **tightly coupled memory** (**TCM**), into which the frequently used data and code lines are loaded from the **non-volatile memory** (**NVM**) on system startup. The system's behavior is *scripted a priori*. The role of these OSs is related to machine control, where the user's input is forbidden.

A soft **RTOS** provides critical tasks with the highest priority until completion and without interruptions. Still, real-time tasks are expected to be completed in a timely manner and should not wait endlessly. It is obvious that this type of OS cannot be utilized for mission-critical tasks: factory machines robots, vehicles, and so on. But it can be used to control the overall system behavior, so this type of OS is found in multimedia and research projects, artificial intelligence, computer graphics, virtual reality devices, and more. As these **RTOSs** do not clash with the **GPOSs**, they can be integrated with them. Their functions can be found in some Linux distributions as well. An interesting realization of this is **QNX**.

Linux in short

There are a few misconceptions here, so let's settle them briefly. Linux is a *Unix-like OS*, meaning it provides similar (and occasionally the same) interfaces as Unix – its functions, especially APIs, are designed to match the ones from Unix. But it is not a *Unix-based* OS. Their functions are not implemented in the same way. A similar misconception exists in understandings of the FreeBSD-macOS relationship. Although both share a significant portion of code, their approach is completely different, including the way their kernels are structured.

It is important to bear these facts in mind as not all functions we are going to use in this book exist or are reachable on all Unix-like OSs. We are focusing on Linux, and our examples will work as long as the respective technical requirements for each chapter are met.

There are a few reasons for this decision. First, Linux is open-sourced, and you can easily check its kernel code: `https://github.com/torvalds/linux`. You should be able to read it easily as it is written in C. Even though C is not an object-oriented language, the Linux kernel follows many **object-oriented programming** (**OOP**) paradigms. The OS itself consists of many independent design blocks, called *modules*. You could easily configure, integrate, and apply them specifically for your system's needs. Linux gives us the ability to work with real-time systems (described later in the chapter) and do parallel code executions (discussed in *Chapter 6*). In short – Linux is easily adaptable, expandable, and configurable; we could easily use this to our advantage. But *where*, exactly?

Well, we could develop applications that are close to the OS, or we could even produce some modules ourselves, which can be loaded or unloaded at runtime. Such an example is a filesystem or device driver. We are going to revisit this topic in *Chapter 2*, when deep diving into the *process* entity. For now, let's say that the modules pretty much look like an OOP design: they are constructible and destructible; sometimes, based on the kernel's needs, common code could be generalized into one module, and these modules have hierarchical dependencies. Nevertheless, the Linux kernel is considered *monolithic*; for example, it has complex functionality, but the entire OS runs in *kernel space*. In contrast, there are *micro-kernels* (QNX, MINIX, or L4), which constitute the bare minimum of a running OS. Additional functionality in this case is provided through modules that work outside the kernel itself. This leads to a slightly chaotic but overall clear picture of the possibilities of the Linux kernel.

Getting to know the Linux kernel

Figure 1.1 illustrates an example of a Linux kernel. Based on your needs, the system architecture could look different, but you can observe the three main layers we expect to see in any given Linux system.

These are the *user space* (running processes and their threads), the *kernel space* (the running kernel itself, usually a process of its own), and the *computer* – this could be any kind of computing device, such as a PC, tablet, smartphone, supercomputer, IoT device, and so on. One by one, all the terms observed in the diagram will fall into place as we explain them in the following chapters, so don't worry if you are not familiar with all of them right now.

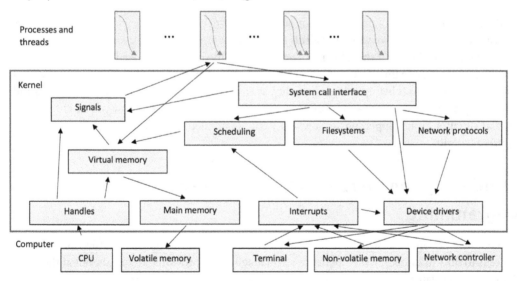

Figure 1.1 – Overview of the Linux kernel and the neighboring layers

Some interdependencies in the preceding diagram have probably made an impression on you already. For example, see how the *device drivers*, the *respective devices*, and the *interrupts* are related. The device drivers are a generalization of *character device drivers*, *block device drivers*, and *network device drivers*. Note how the interrupts are related to the *scheduling* of the tasks. This is a trivial but fundamental mechanism, used heavily in the implementation of drivers. It is an initial *communication and control* mechanism of the OS and the hardware.

Just one example: let's say you want to restore and read a file from the disk (**NVM**), and you request it through some standard programming function. A `read()` call will be executed under the hood, which is then translated to a *filesystem* operation. The filesystem calls the device driver to find and retrieve the content behind the given file descriptor, which is then related to an address known by the filesystem. This will be discussed further in *Chapter 3*. The required device (**NVM**) starts to search for the piece of data – a file. Until the operation is finished, if the caller process is a single-threaded process and has nothing else to do, it will be stopped. Another process will start to work until the device *finds* and *returns a pointer* to the file's address. Then an interrupt is triggered, and this helps the OS to invoke the *scheduler*. Our initial process will be started again using the newly loaded data, and the second process will now be stopped.

This task example demonstrates how you can impact the system's behavior with just a small, insignificant operation – and this is one you will have learned to code in your first programming classes. In most cases, nothing bad will happen, of course. Many processes will be rescheduled all the time during the lifespan of your system. It is the OS's job to make this happen without disruptions.

But the interrupt is a heavy operation that could lead to needless memory accesses and useless application state switches. We will discuss this in *Chapter 2*. For now, just think about what happens if the system is overloaded – the CPU is at 99% usage, or the disk has received many requests and cannot handle them in a timely manner. And what if that system was part of an airplane's embedded devices? Of course, this is highly unlikely in reality, as airplanes have strict technical requirements and high-quality standards to meet. But just for the sake of argument, consider how you might prevent a similar situation from happening, or how you would guarantee the code's successful execution in any user scenario.

Introducing the system call interface and system programming

Of course, the example that we just saw is simplified but gives us some idea about the work that the OS needs to do – in essence, it is responsible for managing and providing resources, but at the same time remains available for other processes' requests. This is a messy job on modern OSs. Rarely can we do anything about it. So, to have better control and predictability of system behavior, programmers might directly use the OS's API, called the **system call interface**.

> **Important note**
>
> The NVM data request is a procedure that benefits from the **system call interface**, as the OS will be obliged to turn this request into an **application binary interface** (**ABI**) call, referring to the respective device driver. Such an operation is known as a *system call*. Using system calls to implement or execute functions provided by the OS is known as *system programming*. The system calls are the only entry points to the kernel's services. They are generally wrapped by libraries such as `glibc` and are not invoked directly.

In other words, the system calls define the programmer's interface through which all kernel services are made available. The OS can be considered as more of a mediator between the kernel service and the hardware. Unless you like to play with hardware pins and low-level platform instructions, or you are a module architect yourself, you should bravely leave the details to the OS. It is the OS's responsibility to handle the specific computer physical interface operations. It is the application's responsibility to use the correct system calls. And it is the software engineer's task to be aware of their impact on the system's overall behavior. Bear in mind that using system calls comes with a price.

As observed in the example, the OS will do a lot while retrieving a file. And even more will be done when memory is allocated dynamically, or a single memory chunk is accessed by multiple threads. We will discuss this further in the following chapters, and will emphasize using systems calls sparingly, with awareness, whether voluntarily or involuntarily, wherever possible. Simply said, system calls are not trivial function calls as they are not executed in user space. Instead of going to the next procedure in your program's stack, the system call triggers a mode switch, which leads to a jump to a routine in the kernel's memory stack. Reading from a file can be visualized as follows:

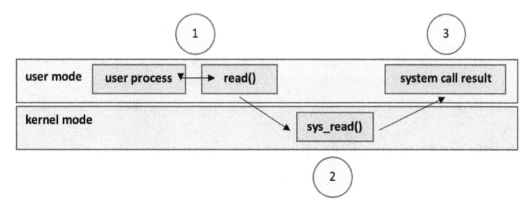

Figure 1.2 – System call interface representation of reading from a file

When should we use system calls then? Put simply, when we want to be very precise about some OS tasks, often related to **device management**, **file management**, **process control**, or **communication infrastructure**. We are going to present many examples of these roles in the later chapters, but in brief, you are welcome to read more and get familiar yourself with the following:

```
syscall()
fork()
exec()
exit()
wait()
kill()
```

> **Important links**
>
> The right place to start is the **Linux man-pages project**, linked here: `https://www.kernel.org/doc/man-pages/`.
>
> A brief list of the useful system calls can be found at the following link: `https://man7.org/linux/man-pages/man2/syscalls.2.html`.

We strongly encourage you to do more research on system calls used in your own projects. Are there any, and what kind of job do they do? Are there any alternatives in your implementations?

You have probably already guessed that using the **system call interface** involves a security risk for the system, too. Being that close to the kernel and the device control provides a great opportunity for malicious software to infiltrate your software. While your software is impacting system behavior, another program might sniff around and gather valuable data. The least you could do is design your code in such a way that the user's interface is well isolated from the crucial procedures, especially system calls. It is impossible to be 100% safe, and while there are many comprehensive books on the matter of security, the art of securing a system is a constantly evolving process itself.

Speaking about processes, let's proceed to the next topic: the fundamental entities of a Linux system.

Navigating through files, processes, and threads

If you made it to here – great job! We are going to cover processes and threads thoroughly in *Chapter 2*, and filesystems in *Chapter 3*. In the meantime, we will take a short detour here, just to paint a better picture for you, through the definition of three important terms: **files**, **processes**, and **threads**. You probably already noticed two of these in the kernel overview earlier, so we will explain them briefly now in case you are not familiar with them.

File

In short, we require files to represent multiple kinds of resources on our system. The programs we write are files as well. The compiled code, for example, the executable binaries (`.bin`, `.exe`), and the libraries are all files (`.o`, `.so`, `.lib`, .dll, and so on). Additionally, we need them for communication mechanisms and for storage management. Do you know what types of files are recognizable on Linux? Let's brief you on that quickly:

- **Ordinary or regular files**: Almost all files storing data on the system are treated as regular files: text, media, code, and so on.

- **Directories**: Used for building the hierarchical structure of the filesystem. Instead of storing data, they store the locations of other files.

- **Special (device) files**: You can find them under your `/dev` directory, representing all your hardware devices.

- **Links**: We use these to allow access to another file at a different location. Actually, they are substitutions of real files, and through them those files are accessed directly. This is different than Windows' shortcuts. They are specific file types, and an application is required to support them – first to handle the shortcut metadata, then to point at the resource, so the file is not accessed in one go.

- **Sockets**: This is the communication endpoint for a process to exchange data, including with other systems.

- **Named pipes**: We use named pipes to exchange bidirectional data between two processes currently running on the system.

In *Chapter 3*, we will play around with these through some practical examples. You will see the usage of every file type there, except sockets, which will be explained in great detail later in the book. What we need now is a program to run.

Process and thread

A process is an *instance of a program,* an executing instance, to be precise. It has its own address space and remains isolated from other processes. This means that each process has a range of (usually virtual) addresses that the OS assigns to it. Linux treats them as *tasks*. They are not observable by the general user. This is just how the kernel does its job. Each task is described through the `task_struct` entity, defined in `include/linux/sched.h`. System administrators and system programmers observe processes through the process table, hashed through each process's specific process identifier – `pid`. This method is used for a quick lookup of a process – use the `ps` command in Terminal to see the process status on the system and then type the following command to see the specific info for a single process:

```
ps -p <required pid>
```

For example, let's start some program, called `test`, and let it run:

```
$ ./test
```

You can open a separate Terminal and see `test` in the list of running processes as follows:

```
$ ps
PID TTY              TIME CMD
...
56693 ttys001    0:00.00 test
```

And if you know the `PID` already, then just do the following:

```
$ ps -p 56693
56693 ttys001    0:00.00 test
```

A new process is created via a copy of the current process's attributes and will belong to a *process group*. One or more groups create a *session*. Each session is related to a *terminal*. Both groups and sessions have *process leaders*. The *cloning* of attributes is used mainly for resource sharing. If two processes share the same virtual memory space, they are treated and managed as two *threads* in a single process, but they are not as heavyweight as processes. What is a thread, then?

> **Important note**
>
> Overall, there are four entities we care about: first is the executable file as it is the unit-carrier of the instructions to be executed. Second is the process – the worker unit executing those instructions. Third – we need these instructions as instruments to handle and manage system resources. And fourth is the thread – the smallest sequence of instructions, managed independently by the OS, and part of a process. Bear in mind that the implementations of processes and threads are different for every OS, so do your research before using them.

From the kernel's point of view, the main thread of the process is the *task group leader*, identified in the code as `group_leader`. All threads spawned by the group leader are iterable through `thread_node`. Actually, they are stored in a singly linked list and `thread_node` is its head. The spawned threads carry a pointer to the `group_leader` tool. The *process creator*'s `task_struct` object is pointed by it. You probably already guessed correctly that it is the same as the `task_struct` of the group leader.

> **Important note**
>
> If a process spawns another process, for example, through `fork()`, the newly created processes (known as *child processes*) know about their creator through the `parent` pointer. They are also aware of their siblings through the `sibling` pointer, which is a list node to some other child process of the parent. Each parent knows about its children through `children` – a pointer to the list head, storing the children and providing access to them.

As we can see in the following figure, the threads do not define any other data structures:

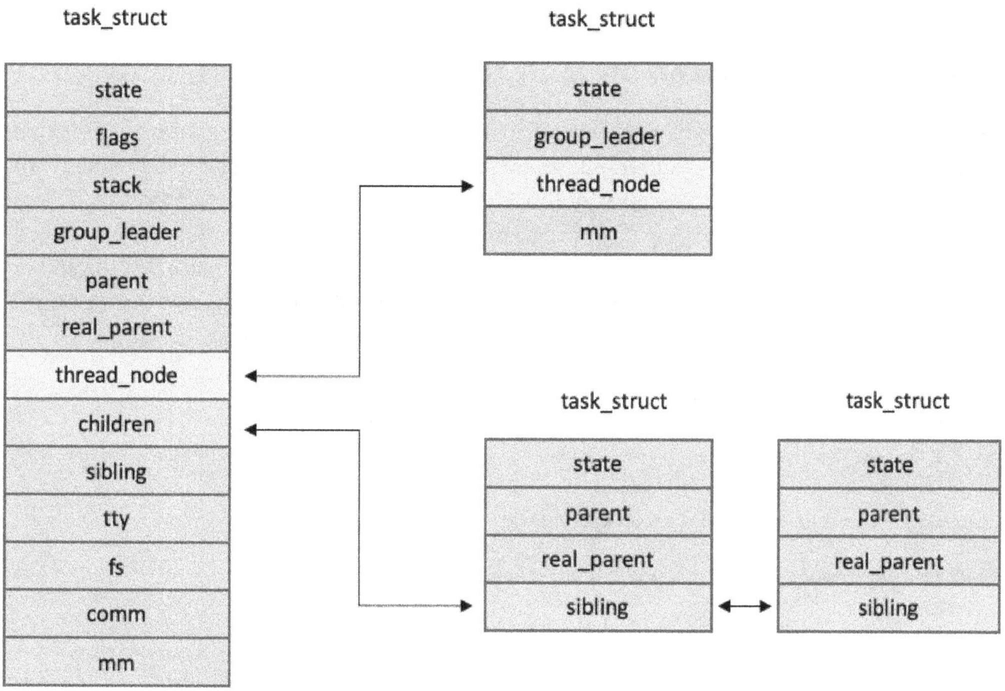

Figure 1.3 – Structures of processes and threads through task_structs

We've mentioned fork() already a couple of times, but what is it? Well, put simply, it is a system function that creates a process copy of the process caller. It provides the parent with the new process's ID and initiates the execution of the child. We are going to provide some code examples in the next chapter, so you could take a look there for more details. There's something important we should mention now, as we are on the topic of Linux environments.

Behind the scenes, fork() is replaced with clone(). Different options are provided through flags, but if all are set to zero, clone() behaves like fork(). We advise you to read more here: https://man7.org/linux/man-pages/man2/clone.2.html.

You're probably asking yourself why this implementation is preferable. Think about it this way: when the kernel does a switch between the processes, it checks the address of the current process in the virtual memory, the *page directory* to be exact. If it is the same as the newly executed process, then they share the same address space. Then, the switch is only a simple pointer jump instruction, usually to the entry point of the program. This means a faster rescheduling is to be expected. Be careful – the processes might share the same address space, but not the same program stack. clone() takes care of creating a different stack for each process.

Now that the process is created, we must take a look at its *running mode.* Note that this is not the same as the *process state.*

Types of processes based on their running mode

Some processes require user interaction to be initiated or interacted with. They are known as *foreground processes.* But as you've probably figured out, there are some processes that run independently of our, or any other user's, activity. Processes of this kind are known as *background processes.* Unless instructed otherwise, the terminal inputs as program execution calls or user commands are treated as foreground processes by default. To run a process in the background, simply place & at the end of the command line that you use to start the process. For example, let's call the already known test, and after it finishes, we see the following in Terminal:

```
$ ./test &
[1] 62934
[1]  + done        ./test
```

You can easily stop it using its pid when calling the kill command:

```
$ ./test &
[1] 63388
$ kill 63388
[1]  + terminated./test
```

As you can see, killing a process and letting it terminate by itself are two different things, and killing the process could lead to unpredictable system behavior or the inability to access some resource, such as a file or a socket left unclosed. This topic will be revisited later in the book.

Other processes run unattended. They are known as *daemons* and run constantly in the background. They are expected to be always available. Daemons are usually started through the system's startup scripts and run until it's shut down. They usually provide system services and multiple users rely on them. Therefore, the daemons on startup are usually initiated by the user with ID 0 (usually root) and might run with root privileges.

> **Important note**
>
> The user with the highest privileges on a Linux system is known as the root user, or simply root. This privilege level allows the performing of security-related tasks. This role has a direct impact on the system's integrity, therefore all other users must be set with the least-possible privilege level until a higher one is required.

A *zombie process* is a process that has been terminated, but is still recognized through its `pid`. It has no address space. Zombie processes continue to exist for as long as their parent processes run. This means that until we exit the main process, shut down the system, or restart it, the zombie process will still appear as `<defunct>` when listed by `ps`:

```
$ ps
   PID TTY            TIME CMD
...
64690 ttys000     0:00.00 <defunct>
```

You can see zombie processes through `top` as well:

```
$ top
t-p - 07:58:26 up 100 days,  2:34, 2 users,   load average: 1.20, 1.12,
1.68
Tasks: 200 total,   1 running, 197 sleeping,   1 stopped,   1 zombie
```

Getting back to the discussion on background processes, there is another way to execute specific procedures without explicitly starting background processes. Even better – we can manage such processes running on system startup or on different system events. Let's look at this in the next section.

Running services with init and systemd

Let's use this opportunity to discuss the `init` and the `systemd` process daemons. There are others as well, but we've decided to retain our focus on these two. The first one is the initial process, executed on a Linux system by the kernel, and its `pid` is always 1:

```
$ ps -p 1
PID TTY            TIME CMD
1 ?          04:53:20 systemd
```

It is known as the parent of all processes on the system as it is used to initialize, manage, and track other services and daemons. The first `init` daemon for Linux is called `Init` and it defines six system states. All system services are mapped to those states, respectively. Its script is used to start processes in a pre-defined order, which is occasionally used by system programmers. One possible reason to use this is to reduce the startup duration of the system. To create a service or edit the script, you could modify `/etc/init.d`. As this is a directory, we could list it with the `ls` command and see all the services that could be run through `init`.

This is what we have on our machine:

```
$ ls /etc/init.d/
acpid
alsa-utils
anacron
...
ufw
unidd
x11-common
```

Each of these scripts follows the same code template for its execution and maintenance:

```bash
#!/bin/bash
# chkconfig: 2345 20 80
# description: Description comes here....

# Source function library.
. /etc/init.d/functions

start() {
    # code to start app comes here
    # example: daemon program_name &
}

stop() {
    # code to stop app comes here
    # example: killproc program_name
}

case "$1" in
    start)
        start
        ;;
    stop)
        stop
        ;;
    restart)
        stop
        start
        ;;
    status)
        # code to check status of app comes here
        # example: status program_name
        ;;
    *)
        echo "Usage: $0 {start|stop|status|restart}"
esac

exit 0
```

Figure 1.4 – init.d script, representing the possible service actions

You can generate the same template yourself and read more about the `init` script source code through the following command:

```
$ man init-d-script
```

You can list the status of the available services through the following command:

```
$ service --status-all
 [ + ]   acpid
 [ - ]   alsa-utils
 [ - ]   anacron
...
 [ + ]   ufw
 [ - ]   uuidd
 [ - ]   x11-common
```

We could stop the firewall service – `ufw`:

```
$ service ufw stop
```

Now, let's check its status:

```
$ service ufw status
● ufw.service - Uncomplicated firewall
Loaded: loaded (/lib/systemd/system/ufw.service; enabled; vendor
preset: enabled)
Active: inactive (dead) since Thu 2023-04-06 14:33:31 EEST; 46s ago
Docs: man:ufw(8)
Process: 404 ExecStart=/lib/ufw/ufw-init start quiet (code=exited,
status=0/SUCCESS)
Process: 3679 ExecStop=/lib/ufw/ufw-init stop (code=exited, status=0/
SUCCESS)
Main PID: 404 (code=exited, status=0/SUCCESS)
Apr 06 14:33:30 oem-virtual-machine systemd[1]: Stopping Uncomplicated
firewall...
Apr 06 14:33:31 oem-virtual-machine ufw-init[3679]: Skip stopping
firewall: ufw (not enabled)
Apr 06 14:33:31 oem-virtual-machine systemd[1]: ufw.service:
Succeeded.
Apr 06 14:33:31 oem-virtual-machine systemd[1]: Stopped Uncomplicated
firewall.
```

Now, let's start it again and check its status once more:

```
$ service ufw start
$ service ufw status
● ufw.service - Uncomplicated firewall
Loaded: loaded (/lib/systemd/system/ufw.service; enabled; vendor
preset: enabled)
Active: active (exited) since Thu 2023-04-06 14:34:56 EEST; 7s ago
Docs: man:ufw(8)
Process: 3736 ExecStart=/lib/ufw/ufw-init start quiet (code=exited,
status=0/SUCCESS)
Main PID: 3736 (code=exited, status=0/SUCCESS)
Apr 06 14:34:56 oem-virtual-machine systemd[1]: Starting Uncomplicated
firewall...
Apr 06 14:34:56 oem-virtual-machine systemd[1]: Finished Uncomplicated
firewall.
```

In a similar fashion, you could create your own service and use the `service` command to start it. An important remark is that `init` is considered an outdated approach on modern, full-scale Linux systems. Still, it can be found on every Unix-based OS, unlike **systemd**, so system programmers would anticipate its use as a common interface to services. Therefore, we use it more as a simple example and an explanation for where services are coming from. If we want to use the latest approach, we must turn to **systemd**.

systemd is an **init** daemon that represents the modern approach to running services on Linux systems. It provides a parallel system services startup feature, which additionally speeds up the initialization procedure. Each service is stored in a `.service` file under the `/lib/systemd/system` or `/etc/systemd/system` directory. The services found in `/lib` are definitions for system startup services and those in `/etc` are for the services that start during system runtime. Let's list them:

```
$ ls /lib/systemd/system
accounts-daemon.service
acpid.path
acpid.service
...
sys-kernel-config.mount
sys-kernel-debug.mount
sys-kernel-tracing.mount
syslog.socket
$ ls /etc/systemd/system
bluetooth.target.wants
display-manager.service
...
timers.target.wants
vmtoolsd.service
```

Before we continue with an example, let's put one disclaimer here – systemd has a much more complex interface than init. We encourage you to spend time examining it separately as we cannot summarize it in short here. But if you list your systemd directories, you will probably observe many types of files. In the context of the daemon, they are known as units. Each of them provides a different interface as they each relate to a certain entity managed by systemd. The script inside each file describes what options are set and what the given service does. The units names are eloquent. .timer is for timer management, .service is for how a given service will be initiated and what it depends on, .path describes the path-based activation of a given service, and so on.

Let's make a simple systemd service that will have the purpose of monitoring whether a given file is being modified. One example is monitoring some configuration: we wouldn't want to limit its permissions for file update, but we'd still like to know whether someone has changed it.

First, let's create some dummy file through a simple text editor. Let's imagine it's a real configuration. Printing it out gives the following:

```
$ cat /etc/test_config/config
test test
```

Let's prepare a script that describes the procedure we require to be executed when the file is changed. Again, just for the purposes of this example, let's create it through a simple text editor – it will look like this:

```
$ cat ~/sniff_printer.sh
echo "File /etc/test_config/config changed!"
```

When the script is called, there will be a message that the file has changed. Of course, you could put any program here. Let's call it sniff_printer, because we are sniffing for a file change through the service, and we will print some data.

How does this happen then? First, we define our new service through the required unit – myservice_test.service – implementing the following script:

```
[Unit]
Description=This service is triggered through a file change

[Service]
Type=oneshot
ExecStart=bash /home/oem/sniff_printer.sh

[Install]
WantedBy=multi-user.target
```

Second, we describe the file path we're monitoring through another unit called myservice_test. path, implemented via the following code:

```
[Unit]
Description=Path unit for watching for changes in "config"

[Path]
PathModified=/etc/test_config/config
Unit=myservice_test.service

[Install]
WantedBy=multi-user.target
```

Combining all these pieces together, we get a service that will print out a simple message. It will be triggered whenever the provided file is updated. Let's see how it goes. As we are adding a new file to the service directory, we must execute a reload:

```
$ systemctl daemon-reload
```

Now, let's enable and start the service:

```
$ systemctl enable myservice_test
$ systemctl start myservice_test
```

We need to update the file through some text editor, such as the following:

```
$ vim /etc/test_config/config
```

In order to see the effect we've triggered, we have to go through the service status:

```
$ systemctl status myservice_test
● myservice_test.service - This service is for printing the "config".
Loaded: loaded (/etc/systemd/system/myservice_test.service; enabled;
vendor preset: enabled)
Active: inactive (dead) since Thu 2023-04-06 15:37:12 EEST; 31s ago
Process: 5340 ExecStart=/bin/bash /home/oem/sniff_printer.sh
(code=exited, status=0/SUCCESS)
Main PID: 5340 (code=exited, status=0/SUCCESS)
Apr 06 15:37:12 oem-virtual-machine systemd[1]: Starting This service
is for printing the "config"....
Apr 06 15:37:12 oem-virtual-machine bash[5340]: File /etc/test_config/
config changed!
Apr 06 15:37:12 oem-virtual-machine systemd[1]: myservice_test.
service: Succeeded.
Apr 06 15:37:12 oem-virtual-machine systemd[1]: Finished This service
is for printing the "config"..
```

You can validate that the service has been triggered as our message is present:

```
Apr 06 15:37:12 oem-virtual-machine bash[5340]: File /etc/test_config/
config changed!
```

We also see the code that was executed and its successful status:

```
Process: 5340 ExecStart=/bin/bash /home/oem/sniff_printer.sh
(code=exited, status=0/SUCCESS)
Main PID: 5340 (code=exited, status=0/SUCCESS)
```

But the process is no longer active as the service unit is of type oneshot, therefore only another file update will retrigger it. We believe this example offers a simple explanation of how a daemon could be created and started during system runtime. Feel free to experiment yourself and try different unit types or options.

The process daemon and the startup procedures are a large area of expertise in system administration, programming, monitoring, and obtaining execution flow information. These topics as well as that of the next section deserve books of their own.

Portable Operating System Interface (POSIX)

The **POSIX** standard has the main task of maintaining compatibility between different OSs. Therefore, POSIX is frequently used by both standard application software developers and system programmers. Nowadays, it can be found not only on Unix-like OSs, but in Windows environments as well – for example, **Cygwin**, **MinGW**, and **Windows Subsystem for Linux** (**WSL**). POSIX defines both the system- and the user-level APIs with one remark: using POSIX, the programmer doesn't need to distinguish between system calls and library functions.

The POSIX API is frequently used in the C programming language. Thus, it is compilable with C++. Additional functions are provided to the **system call interface** in a few important areas of system programming: **file operations**, **memory management**, **process and thread control**, **networking and communications**, and **regular expressions** – as you can see, it pretty much covers everything that the already existing system calls do. Just don't get confused and think that this is always the case.

As with every standard, POSIX has multiple versions, and you must be aware of which one is present in your system. It also could be a part of some environment subsystem, such as the **Microsoft POSIX subsystem** for Windows. This is a key remark as it is possible that the environment itself doesn't expose the entire interface to you. One reason could be the security assessment of the system.

With the evolution of POSIX, rules for code quality have been established. Some of them are related to **multithreaded memory access**, **synchronization mechanisms** and **concurrent executions**, **security** and **access restrictions**, and **type safety**. A famous concept in POSIX's software requirements is *write once, adopt everywhere*.

The standard defines and targets four main areas of its application, called volumes:

- **Base definitions**: Main definitions for the specification: syntax, concepts, terms, and service operations
- **System interfaces**: Interface descriptions and definitions' availability
- **Utilities**: Shell, command, and utility descriptions
- **Rationale**: Versioning information and historical data

With all that said, in this book our focus is mainly on POSIX as a different approach to system calls. In the following chapters, we will see the benefit of the general pattern for using objects such as message queues, semaphores, shared memory, or threads. A significant improvement is the simplicity of the function calls and their naming conventions. For example, `shm_open()`, `mq_open()`, and `sem_open()` are used to create and open a shared memory object, a message queue, and a semaphore, respectively. Their similarity is obvious. Similar ideas in POSIX are welcomed by system programmers. The API is public, too, and there are substantial community contributions. Additionally, POSIX provides an interface to objects such as the mutex, which is not trivially found and used on Unix. However, in later chapters, we will advise readers to focus more on the C++20 features and for good reason, so bear with us.

Using POSIX allows software engineers to generalize their OS-related code and declare it as *not-OS-specific*. This allows easier and faster reintegration of the software, thus reducing the time to market. System programmers can also easily switch from one system to another while still writing the same type of code.

Summary

In this chapter, we have covered the definitions of basic concepts related to OSs. You have learned about Linux's main kernel structure and its expectations of software design. Real-time OSs were briefly introduced, and we covered the definitions of system calls, the system call interface, and POSIX as well. We've also laid the foundations of multiprocessing and multithreading. In the next chapter, we will discuss the process as the main resource user and manager. We will start with some C++20 code. Through this, you will learn about the Linux's process memory layout, the OS's process-scheduling mechanism, and how multiprocessing operates plus the challenges it brings. You will also learn some interesting facts about atomic operations.

2

Learning More about Process Management

You became familiar with the concept of processes in the previous chapter. Now, it's time to get into details. It is important to understand how process management is related to the system's overall behavior. In this chapter, we will emphasize fundamental OS mechanisms that are used specifically for process control and resource access management. We will use this opportunity to show you how to use some C++ features too.

Once we've investigated the program and its corresponding process as system entities, we are going to discuss the states that one process goes through during its lifetime. You are going to learn about spawning new processes and threads. You are also going to see the underlying problems of such activities. Later we are going to check out some examples while slowly introducing the multithreaded code. By doing so, you will have the opportunity to learn the basics of some POSIX and C++ techniques that are related to asynchronous execution.

Regardless of your C++ experience, this chapter will help you to understand some of the traps that you could end up in at the system level. You can use your knowledge of various language features to enhance your execution control and process predictability.

In this chapter, we are going to cover the following main topics:

- Investigating the nature of the process

- Continuing with the process states and some scheduling mechanisms

- Learning more about process creation

- Introducing the system calls for thread manipulation in C++

Technical requirements

To run the code examples in this chapter, you must prepare the following:

- A Linux-based system capable of compiling and executing C++20 (for example, **Linux Mint 21**)

- The GCC12.2 compiler (`https://gcc.gnu.org/git/gcc.gitgcc-source`) with the `-std=c++2a` and `-lpthread` flags

- Alternatively, for all the examples, you can use `https://godbolt.org/`

- All code examples in this chapter are available for download from: `https://github.com/PacktPublishing/C-Programming-for-Linux-Systems/tree/main/Chapter%202o2.`

Disassembling process creation

As we mentioned in the previous chapter, a process is a running instance of a program that contains its respective metadata, occupied memory, opened files, and so on. It is the main job executor in the OS. Recall that the overall goal of programming is to transform one type of data into another type of data, or count. What we do via programming languages is provide instructions to the hardware. Often, we *tell* the CPU what to do, including moving pieces of data throughout different portions of memory. In other words, the computer must *compute*, and we must tell it how to do this. This understanding is crucial and independent of the programming languages or OSs that are used.

With this, we have come back to the topic of system programming and understanding system behavior. Let's immediately state that process creation and execution is neither simple nor fast. And neither is the process switching. It is rarely observable through the naked eye, but if you must design a highly scalable system or have a strict timeline for events during the system's execution, then you will get to process interaction analysis sooner or later. Again, this is how the computer works and this knowledge is useful when you get into resource optimization.

Speaking of resources, let's remind ourselves of the fact that our process was initially just a program. It is usually stored on **non-volatile memory** (**NVM**). Depending on the system, this could be a hard drive, SSD, ROM, EEPROM, Flash, and so on. We have mentioned these devices as they have different physical characteristics, such as speed, storage space, write access, and fragmentation. Each of these is an important factor when it comes to the system's durability, but for this chapter, we care mostly about speed.

Again, as we already mentioned in the previous chapter, a program, just like all other OS resources, is a file. The C++ program is an executable object file, which contains the code – for example, the instructions – that must be given to the CPU. This file is the result of a compilation. The compiler is another program that converts the C++ code into machine instructions. It is crucial to be aware of what instructions our system supports. The OS and the compiler are prerequisites for the integrated standards, libraries, language features, and so on, and there is a good chance that the compiled object file is not going to run on another system that's not exactly matching ours. Moreover, the same code, compiled on another system or through another compiler, would most probably have a different executable object file size. The bigger the size, the longer the time to load the program from **NVM** to the **main memory (Random Access Memory (RAM)** is used the most). To analyze the speed of our code and optimize it as best as possible for a given system, we will look at a generic diagram regarding the full path along which our data or an instruction goes along. This is slightly off-topic, so bear with us:

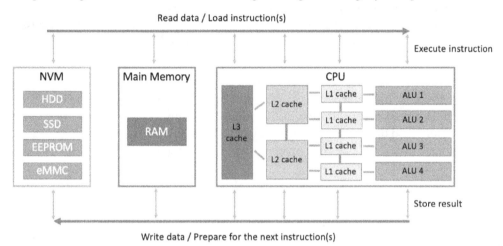

Figure 2.1 – Loading a program and its sequence of instruction execution events

A generalized CPU overview has been provided here as different architectures will have different layouts. L1 and L2 caches are **Static RAM (SRAM)** elements, making them extremely fast, but expensive. Therefore, we must keep them small. We also keep them small to achieve small CPU latency. The L2 cache has a bigger capacity to make a shared space between the **Arithmetic Logic Units (ALUs)** – a frequent example is two hardware threads in a single core, where the L2 cache plays the shared memory role. The L3 cache doesn't always exist, but it's usually based on **Dynamic RAM (DRAM)** elements. It is slower than the L1 and the L2 caches but allows the CPU to have one more level of cache, just for speed-up purposes. One example would be instructing the CPU to guess and prefetch data from the RAM, thus sparing time in RAM-to-CPU loads. Modern C++ features can use this mechanism a lot, leading to significant speed-ups in process execution.

In addition, depending on their roles, three types of caches are recognized: the **instruction cache**, **data cache**, and **Translation Lookaside Buffer (TLB)**. The first two are self-explanatory, whereas the **TLB** is not directly related to CPU caches – it is a separate unit. It's used for addresses of both data and instructions, but its role is to speed up virtual-to-physical address translation, which we'll discuss later in this chapter.

RAM is often used, and mostly involves **Double Data Rate Synchronous Dynamic RAM (DDR SDRAM)** memory circuits. This is a very important point because different DDR bus configurations have different speeds. And no matter the speed, it is still not as fast as CPU internal transfers. Even with a 100%-loaded CPU, the DDR is rarely fully utilized, thus becoming our *first significant bottleneck*. As mentioned in *Chapter 1*, NVM is way slower than DDR, which is its *second significant bottleneck*. We encourage you to analyze your system and see the speed differences.

> **Important note**
>
> Your programs' sizes matter. The process of optimizing the sequence of events for executing program instructions or loading data is a permanent and continuous balancing act. You must be aware of your system's hardware and OS before thinking of code optimization!

If you're still not convinced, then think about the following: if we have a program to visualize some data on some screen, it might not be an issue for a desktop PC user if it's there after 1 second or 10 seconds. But if this is a pilot on an airplane, then showing data within a strict time window is a safety compliance feature. And the size of our program matters. We believe the next few sections will give you the tools you'll need to analyze your environment. So, what happens with our program during execution? Let's find out.

Memory segments

Memory segments are also known as *memory layouts* or *memory sections*. These are just areas of memory and should not be mistaken for segmented memory architecture. Some experts prefer to use *sections* when the compile-time operations are discussed and *layout* for the runtime. Choose whatever you like, so long as it describes the same thing. The main segments are **text** (or **code**), **data**, **BSS**, **stack**, and **heap**, where **BSS** stands for **Block Started by Symbol** or **Block Starting Symbol**. Let's take a closer look:

- **Text**: This is the code that will be executed on the machine. It is created at compile time. When it gets to runtime, it is the read-only portion of the process. The current machine instructions are found there, and depending on the compiler, you could find the const variables there as well.

- **Data**: This segment is created at compile time as well and consists of initialized global, static, or both global and static data. It is used for preliminary allocated storage, whenever you don't want to depend on runtime allocation.

- **BSS**: In contrast to the **data** segment, **BSS** does not allocate space in the object file – it only marks the required storage if the program gets to runtime. It consists of uninitialized global, static, or both global and static data. This segment is created at compile time. Its data is considered initialized to 0, theoretically as per the language standard, but it is practically set to 0 by the OS's program loader during process startup.

- **Stack**: The program stack is a memory segment that represents the running program routines – it holds their local variables and tracks where to continue from when a called function returns. It is constructed at runtime and follows the **Last-in, First-Out** (**LIFO**) policy. We want to keep it small and fast.

- **Heap**: This is another runtime-created segment that is used for dynamic memory allocation. For many embedded systems, it is considered forbidden, but we are going to explore it further later in this book. There are interesting lessons to be learned and it is not always possible to avoid it.

In *Figure 2.1*, you can observe two processes that are running the same executable and are being loaded to the main memory at runtime. We can see that for Linux, the **text** segment is copied only once since it should be the same for both processes. The **heap** is missing as we are not focusing on it right now. As you can see, the **stack** is not endless. Of course, its size depends on many factors, but we guess that you've already seen the *stack overflow* message a few times in practice. It is an unpleasant runtime event as the program flow is ungracefully ruined and there's the chance of it causing an issue at the system level:

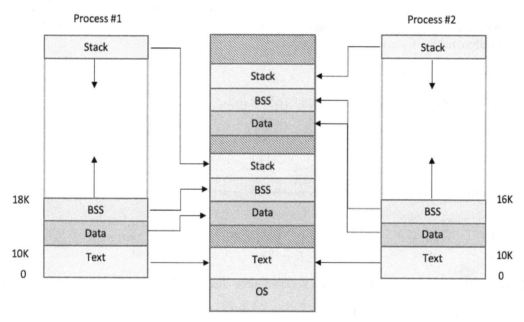

Figure 2.2 – The memory segments of two processes

The main memory at the top in *Figure 2.2* represents the **virtual address space**, where the OS uses a data structure, called a **page table**, to map the process's memory layout to the physical memory addresses. It is an important technique to generalize the way the OS manages memory resources. That way, we don't have to think about the device's specific characteristics or interfaces. At an abstract level, it is quite like the way we accessed files in *Chapter 1*. We will get back to this discussion later in this chapter.

Let's use the following code sample for analysis:

```
void test_func(){}
int main(){
    test_func(); return 0;
}
```

This is a very simple program, where a function is called right after the entry point. There's nothing special here. Let's compile it for C++20 without any optimizations:

```
$ g++ mem_layout_example.cpp -std=c++2a -O0 -o test
```

The resulting binary object is called test. Let's analyze it through the size command:

```
$ size test
   text       data        bss        dec        hex    filename
   2040        640          8       2688        a80    test
```

The overall size is 2,688 bytes, 2,040 of which are the instructions, 640 are the **data**, and 8 are for **BSS**. As you can see, we don't have any global or static data, but still, 648 bytes have gone there. Keep in mind that the compiler is still doing its job, so there are some allocated symbols there, which we could analyze further when required:

```
$ readelf -s test
```

Now, let's focus on something else and edit the code as such:

```
void test_func(){
    static uint32_t test_var;
}
```

A static variable that's not initialized must cause **BSS** to grow:

```
$ size test
   text       data        bss        dec        hex    filename
   2040        640         16       2696        a88    test
```

So, **BSS** is bigger – not by 4 bytes, but with 8. Let's double-check the size of our new variable:

```
$ nm -S test | grep test_var
0000000000004018 0000000000000004 b _ZZ9test_funcvE8test_var
```

Everything is fine – the unsigned 32-bit integer is for 4 bytes, as expected, but the compiler has put some extra symbols there. We can also see that it is in the **BSS** section, which is indicated by the letter b in front of the symbol. Now, let's change the code again:

```
void test_func(){
    static uint32_t test_var = 10;}
```

We have initialized the variable. Now, we expect it to be in the **data** segment:

```
$ size test
text        data        bss         dec         hex     filename
2040         644           4        2688         a80     test
$ nm -S test | grep test_var
0000000000004010 0000000000000004 d _ZZ9test_funcvE8test_var
```

As expected, the **data** segment has been enlarged by 4 bytes and our variable is there (see the letter d in front of the symbol). You can also see that the compiler has shrunk **BSS** usage to 4 bytes and that the overall object file size is smaller – just 2688 bytes.

Let's make a final change:

```
void test_func(){
    const static uint32_t test_var = 10;}
```

Since const cannot be changed during the program's execution, it has to be marked as read-only. For this, it could be put into the **text** segment. Note that this is system implementation-dependent. Let's check it out:

```
$ size test
 text        data        bss         dec         hex     filename
 2044         640           8        2692         a84     test
$ nm -S test | grep test_var
0000000000002004 0000000000000004 r _ZZ9test_funcvE8test_var
```

Correct! We can see the letter r in front of the symbol and that the **text** size is 2044 and not 2040, as it was previously. It seems rather funny that the compiler has generated an 8-byte **BSS** again, but we can live with it. What would happen to the sizes if we removed static from the definition? We encourage you to try this out.

At this point, you've probably made the connection that the bigger compile-time sections generally mean a bigger executable. And a bigger executable means more time for the program to be started because copying the data from NVM to the main memory is significantly slower than copying data from the main memory to the CPU's caches. We will get back to this discussion later when we discuss context switching. If we want to keep our startup fast, then we should consider smaller compile-time sections, but larger runtime ones. This is a balancing act that is usually done by the software architects, or someone who has a good system overview and knowledge. Prerequisites such as NVM read/write speed, DDR configuration, CPU and RAM loads during system startup, normal work and shutdown, the number of active processes, and so on must be considered.

We will revisit this topic later in this book. For now, let's focus on the meaning of the memory segments in the sense of new process creation. Their meaning will be discussed later in this chapter.

Continuing with process states and some scheduling mechanisms

In the previous section, we discussed to how initiate a new process. But what happens with it under the hood? As mentioned in *Chapter 1*, processes and threads are considered tasks in Linux's scheduler. Their states are generic, and their understanding is important for correct procedure planning. A task, when expecting a resource, might have to wait or even stopped. We can affect this behavior through synchronization mechanisms as well, such as semaphores and mutexes, which we'll discuss later in this chapter. We believe that understanding these fundamentals is crucial for system programmers as bad task state management can lead to unpredictability and overall system degradation. This is strongly observable in large-scale systems.

For now, let's step aside for a bit and try to simplify the code's goals – it needs to instruct the CPU to perform an operation and modify the data. Our task is to think about what the correct instructions would be so that we can save time in rescheduling or doing nothing by blocking resources. Let's look at the states our process could find itself in:

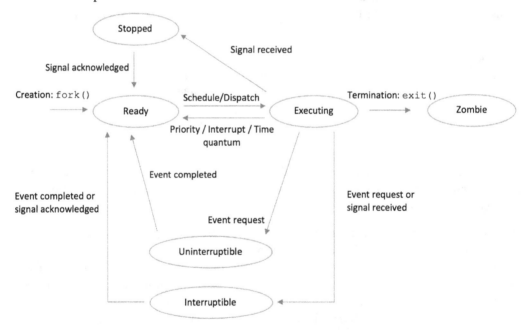

Figure 2.3 – Linux task states and their dependencies

The states in the preceding figure are detailed, but Linux presents them to the user in four general letter denotations:

- **Executing (R – Running and Runnable)**: A processor (core or thread) is provided for the instructions of the process – the task is running. The scheduling algorithm might force it to give the execution. Then, the task becomes runnable, and it's added to a queue of *runnables*, waiting their turn. Both states are distinct but are denoted as *processes in execution*.

- **Sleeping (D – Uninterruptible and S – Interruptible)**: Remember the example with file read/write from the previous chapter? That was a form of uninterruptable sleeping that was caused by waiting for external resources. Sleep cannot be interrupted through signals until the resource is available and the process is available for execution again. Interruptible sleep is not only dependent on resource availability but allows the process to be controlled by signals.

- **Stopped (T)**: Have you ever used *Ctrl + Z* to stop a process? That's the signal putting the process in a stopped state, but depending on the signal request, it could be ignored, and the process will continue. Alternatively, the process could be stopped until it is signaled to continue again. We will discuss signals later in this book.

- **Zombie (Z)**: We saw this state in *Chapter 1* – the process is terminated, but it is still visible in the OS's task vector.

Using the `top` command, you will see the letter S on the top row of the process information columns:

```
$ top
. . .
PID USER PR NI VIRT RES SHR S %CPU %MEM TIME+ COMMAND
```

It will show you the letter denotation for the state of each process. Another option is the ps command, where the STAT column will give you the current states:

```
$ ps a
PID TTY STAT TIME COMMAND
```

With that, we know what states the tasks end up in, but not how and why they switch between them. We'll continue this discussion in the next section.

Scheduling mechanisms

Modern Linux distributions provide many scheduling mechanisms. Their sole purpose is to help the OS decide which task must be executed next in an optimized fashion. Should it be the one with the highest priority or the one that will finish fastest, or just a mix of both? There are other criteria as well, so don't fall under the false apprehension that one will solve all your problems. Scheduling algorithms are especially important when there are more processes in the **R** state than the available processors on the system. To manage this task, the OS has a **scheduler** – a fundamental module that every OS implements in some form. It is usually a separate kernel process that acts like a load balancer, which means it keeps the computer resources busy and provides service to multiple users. It can be configured to aim at small latency, fair execution, max throughput, or minimal wait time. In real-time OSs, it must guarantee that deadlines are met. These factors are obviously in conflict, and the scheduler must resolve these through a suitable compromise. System programmers can configure the system's preferences based on the users' needs. But how does this happen?

Scheduling at a high level

We request the OS to start a program. First, we must load it from NVM. This scheduling level considers the execution of the **program loader**. The destination of the program is provided to it by the OS. The **text** and **data** segments are loaded into the main memory. Most modern OSs will load the program *on demand*. This enables a faster process startup and means that only the currently required code is provided at a given moment. The **BSS** data is allocated and initialized there as well. Then, the virtual address space is mapped. The new process, which carries the instructions, is created and the required fields, such as process ID, user ID, group ID, and others, are initialized. The **program counter** is set to the entry point of the program and control is passed to the loaded code. This overhead is considerably significant in the process's lifetime because of the hardware constraints of **NVM**. Let's see what happens after the program reaches the RAM.

Scheduling at a low level

This is a collection of techniques that try to provide the best order of task execution. Although we don't mention the term **scheduling** much in this book, be sure that every manipulation we do causes tasks to state switch, which means we cause the scheduler to act. Such an action is known as a **context switch**. The switch takes time too as the scheduling algorithm may need to reorder the queue of tasks, and newly started task instructions must be copied from the RAM to the CPU cache.

> **Important note**
> Multiple running tasks, parallel or not, could lead to time spent in rescheduling instead of procedure executions. This is another balancing act that depends on the system programmer's design.

Here is a basic overview:

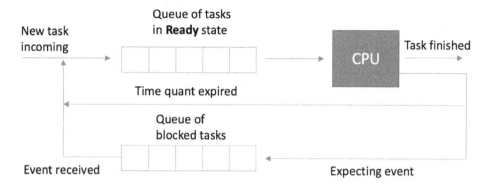

Figure 2.4 – Ready /blocked task queues

The algorithm must pick a task from the queue and place it for execution. At a system level, the basic hierarchy is as (from highest priority to lowest) scheduler -> block devices -> file management -> character devices -> user processes.

Depending on the queue's data structure implementation and the **scheduler's** configuration, we could execute different algorithms. Here are some of them:

- **First-come-first-serve (FCFS)**: Nowadays, this is rarely used because longer tasks might stall the system's performance and important processes might never be executed.

- **Shortest job first (SJF)**: This provides a shorter time to wait than FCFS, but longer tasks may never be called. It lacks predictability.

- **Highest priority first (HPF)**: Here, tasks have priority, where the highest one will be executed. But who sets the priority value and who decides if an incoming process will cause rescheduling or not? The Kleinrock rules are one such discipline where priority is increased linearly, while the task stays in the queue. Depending on the run-stay ratio, different orders are executed – FCFS, Last-CFS, SJF, and so on. An interesting article on this matter can be found here: https://dl.acm.org/doi/10.1145/322261.322266.

- **Round-robin**: This is a resource starvation-free and preemptive algorithm, where each task gets a time quantum in an equal portion. Tasks are executed in circular order. Each of them gets a CPU time slot, equal to the time quantum. When it expires, the task is pushed to the back of the queue. As you have probably deduced, the queue's length and the quantum's value (usually between 10 and 300ms) are of great significance. An additional technique to maintain fairness is to enrich this algorithm in modern OS schedulers.

- **Completely fair scheduling** (**CFS**): This is the current Linux scheduling mechanism. It applies a combination of the aforementioned algorithms, depending on the system's state:

```
$ chrt -m
SCHED_OTHER    the standard round-robin time-sharing policy
SCHED_BATCH    for "batch" style execution of processes
SCHED_IDLE     for running very low priority background jobs.
SCHED_FIFO     a first-in, first-out policy
SCHED_RR       a round-robin policy
```

This approach is complex and deserves a book on its own.

What we care about here is the following:

- **Priority**: Its value is the actual task priority, and it's used for scheduling. Values between 0 and 99 are dedicated to real-time processes, whereas values between 100 and 139 are for user processes.

- **Nice**: Its value is meaningful at the user-space level and adjusts the process's priority at runtime. The root user can set it from -20 to +19 and a simple user could set it from 0 to +19, where a higher **nice** value means lower priority. The default is 0.

Their dependency is that priority = nice + 20 for user processes and priority = -1 – real_time_priority for real-time processes. The higher the priority value, the lower the scheduling priority. We cannot change the base priority of a process, but we can start it with a different **nice** value. Let's call ps with a new priority:

```
$ nice -5 ps
```

Here, -5 means 5. Making it 5 requires **sudo** permissions:

```
$ sudo nice -5 ps
```

Changing the priority of a process runtime can be done with the renice command and pid:

```
$ sudo renice -n -10 -p 9610
```

This will set the nice value to -10.

To start a real-time process or set and retrieve the real-time attributes of pid, you must use the chrt command. For example, let's use it to start a real-time process with a priority of 99:

```
$ sudo chrt --rr 99 ./test
```

We encourage you to take a look at other algorithms, such as **Feedback**, **Adaptive Partition Scheduling** (**APS**), **Shortest Remaining Time** (**SRT**), and **Highest Response Ratio Next** (**HRRN**).

The topic of scheduling algorithms is wide and not only concerns the OS task's execution but other areas, such as network data management. We cannot go through its entirety here, but it was important to illustrate how to initially handle it and learn about your system's strengths. That said, let's continue by looking at process management.

Learning more about process creation

A common practice in system programming is to follow a strict timeline for process creation and execution. Programmers use either daemons, such as `systemd` and other in-house developed solutions, or startup scripts. We can use the Terminal as well but this is mostly for when we repair the system's state and restore it, or test a given functionality. Another way to initiate processes from our code is through system calls. You probably know some of them, such as `fork()` and `vfork()`.

Introducing fork()

Let's look at an example; we'll discuss it afterward:

```cpp
#include <iostream>
#include <unistd.h>
using namespace std;
void process_creator() {
    if (fork() == 0) // {1}
        cout << "Child with pid: " << getpid() << endl;
    else
        cout << "Parent with pid: " << getpid() << endl;
}
int main() {
    process_creator();
    return 0;
}
```

Yes, we are aware that you've probably seen a similar example before and it's clear what should be given as output – a new process is initiated by `fork()` [1] and both `pid` values are printed out:

```
Parent with pid: 92745
Child with pid: 92746
```

In `Parent`, `fork()` will return the ID of the newly created process; that way, the parent is aware of its children. In `Child`, 0 will be returned. This mechanism is important for process management because `fork()` creates a duplicate of the calling process. Theoretically, the compile-time segments (**text**, **data**, and **BSS**) are created anew in the main memory. The new **stack** starts to unwind from the same entry point of the program, but it branches at the fork call. Then, one logical path is followed by the parent, and another by the child. Each uses its own **data**, **BSS**, and **heap**.

You're probably thinking that large compile-time segments and stacks will cause unnecessary memory usage because of duplication, especially when we don't change them. And you're correct! Luckily for us, we are using a virtual address space. This allows the OS to have extra management and abstraction over the memory. In the previous section, we discussed that processes with the same **text** segments will share a single copy as it is read-only. There is an optimization that Linux adapts, where **data** and **BSS** will be *shared* through their single instances. If none of the processes update them, duplication is deferred until the first write. Whoever does this initiates copy creation and works with it. This technique is called **copy-on-write**. So, the only penalty for process creation would be the time and memory for the child's metadata and the parent's page tables. Still, make sure your code doesn't fork() endlessly as this will cause a so-called **fork bomb**, leading to a denial of system service and resource starvation. The next section will cover creating a child process in its own address space through exec.

exec and clone()

The exec function call is not really a system call, but a group of system calls with the execXX(<args>) pattern. Each has a specific role, but most importantly, they create a new process through its filesystem path, known as **pathname**. The caller process's memory segments are completely replaced and initialized. Let's call the binary executable for our fork example from the previous section, leaving its command-line arguments set to NULL. This code is similar to the previous example, but a few changes have been made:

```
. . .
void process_creator() {
    if (execv("./test_fork", NULL) == -1) // {1}
        cout << "Process creation failed!" << endl;
    else
        cout << "Process called!" << endl;
}
. . .
```

The result is as follows:

```
Parent with pid: 12191
Child with pid: 12192
```

You can probably see that something's missing from the printed output. Where's the "Process called!" message? If something went wrong, such as the executable not being found, then we will observe "Process creation failed!". But in this case, we know it has been run because of the parent and child outputs. The answer to this can be found in the paragraph before this code example – the memory segments are replaced with the ones from test_fork.

Similarly to exec, clone() is a wrapper function to the real clone() system call. It creates a new process, such as fork(), but allows you to precisely manage the way the new process is instantiated. A few examples are virtual address space sharing, signal handles, file descriptors, and so on. vfork(), as mentioned earlier, is a special variant of clone(). We encourage you to spend some time and take a look at some examples, although we believe that most of the time, fork() and execXX() will be enough.

As you can see, we've chosen the execv() function {1} for the given example. We've used this for simplicity and also because it's related to *Figure 2.5*. But before we look at this figure, there are other functions we can use as well: execl(), execle(), execip(), execve(), and execvp(). Following the execXX() pattern, we need to be compliant with the given requirement:

- e requires the function to use an array of pointers to the environmental variables of the system, which are passed to the newly created process.

- l requires the command-line arguments to be stored in a temporary array and have them passed to the function call. This is just for convenience while handling the array's size.

- p requires the path's environment variable (seen as PATH in Unix) to be passed to the newly loaded process.

- v was used earlier in this book – it requires the command-line arguments to be provided to the function call, but they are passed as an array of pointers. In our example, we are setting it to NULL for simplicity.

Let's see what this looks like now:

```
int execl(const char* path, const char* arg, …)
int execlp(const char* file, const char* arg, …)
int execle(const char* path, const char* arg, …, char*
  const envp[])
int execv(const char* path, const char* argv[])
int execvp(const char* file, const char* argv[])
int execvpe(const char* file, const char* argv[], char
  *const envp[])
```

In a nutshell, their implementation is the same when it comes to how we create a new process. The choice of whether or not to use them strictly depends on your needs and software design. We will revisit the topic of process creation several times in the next few chapters, especially when it goes to shared resources, so this will not be the last time we mention it.

Let's take a look at a trivial example: suppose we have a process-system command that's initiated through the command-line Terminal – **shell**. It is not run in the background – from the previous chapter, we know that in this case, we don't end the line with &. This can be expressed through the following graph:

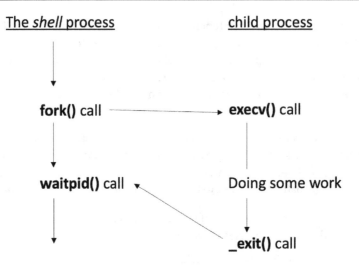

Figure 2.5 – Executing commands from the shell

We have used this figure to emphasize the non-visible system calls for parent-child relationships between processes in Linux. In the background, the **shell** provides the executable's **pathname** to exec(). The kernel takes control and goes to the entry point of the application, where main() is called. The executable does its work and when main() returns, the process is ended. The ending routine is implementation-specific, but you can trigger it yourself in a controlled manner through the exit() and _exit() system calls. In the meantime, the **shell** is put to wait. Now, we'll cover how to terminate a process.

Terminating a process

Usually, exit() is seen as a library function that's implemented on top of _exit(). It does some extra work, such as buffer cleanup and closing streams. Using return in main() could be considered the equivalent of calling exit(). _exit() will handle the process termination by deallocating the data and the stack segments, destroying kernel objects (shared memory, semaphores, and so on), closing the files, and informing the parent about its status change (the SIGCHLD signal will be triggered). Their interfaces are as follows:

- void _exit(int status)
- void exit(int status)

It's a common notion that the `status` value, when set to 0, means a normal process termination, whereas others indicate a termination caused by an internal process issue. Therefore, the EXIT_ SUCCESS and EXIT_FAILURE symbols are defined in `stdlib.h`. To demonstrate this, we could modify our fork example from earlier like so:

```
...
#include <stdlib.h>
...
    if (fork() == 0) {
        cout << "Child process id: " << getpid() << endl;
        exit(EXIT_SUCCESS); // {1}
    }
    else {
        cout << "Parent process id: " << getpid() << endl;
    }
...
```

So, the child will proceed as expected because nothing in particular happens, but we enable it to manage its termination policy better. The output will be the same as in the previous example. We will enrich this even further with a code snippet in the next section.

But before we do that, let's note that both functions are usually related to a controlled manner of process termination. `abort()` will lead a process to termination in a similar fashion, but the SIGABRT signal will be triggered. As discussed in the next chapter, some signals should be handled and not ignored – this one is a good example of gracefully handling the exit routine of a process. In the meantime, what does the parent do and could it be affected by the child's exit code? Let's see.

Blocking a calling process

As you may have noticed in *Figure 2.5*, a process might be set to wait. Using the wait(), waitid(), or waitpid() system calls will cause the calling process to be blocked until it receives a signal or one of its children changes its state: it is terminated, it is stopped by a signal, or it is resumed by a signal. We use wait() to instruct the system to release the resources related to the child; otherwise, it becomes a **zombie**, as discussed in the previous chapter. These three methods are almost the same, but the latter two are compliant with POSIX and provide more precise control over the monitored child process. The three interfaces are as follows:

- `pid_t wait(int *status);`
- `pid_t waitpid(pid_t pid, int *status, int options);`
- `int waitid(idtype_t idtype, id_t id, siginfo_t * infop , int options);`

The status argument has the same role for the first two functions. wait() could be represented as waitpid(-1, &status, 0), meaning the process caller must wait for any child process that terminates and receive its status. Let's take a look at one example directly with waitpid():

```cpp
#include <sys/wait.h>
...
void process_creator() {
    pid_t pids[2] = {0};
    if ((pids[0] = fork()) == 0) {
        cout << "Child process id: " << getpid() << endl;
        exit(EXIT_SUCCESS); // {1}
    }
    if ((pids[1] = fork()) == 0) {
        cout << "Child process id: " << getpid() << endl;
        exit(EXIT_FAILURE); // {2}
    }
    int status = 0;
    waitpid(pids[0], &status, 0); // {3}
    if (WIFEXITED(status)) // {4}
        cout << "Child " << pids[0]
                << " terminated with: "
                << status << endl;

    waitpid(pids[1], &status, 0); // {5}
    if (WIFEXITED(status)) // {6}
        cout << "Child " << pids[1]
                << " terminated with: "
                << status << endl;
...
```

The result from this execution is as follows:

```
Child process id: 33987
Child process id: 33988
Child 33987 terminated with: 0
Child 33988 terminated with: 256
```

As you can see, we are creating two child processes and we set one of them to exit successfully and the other with a failure ([1] and [2]). We set the parent to wait for their exit statuses ([1] and [5]). When the child exits, the parent is notified through a signal accordingly, as described earlier, and the exit statuses are printed out ([4] and [6]).

In addition, `idtype` and the `waitid()` system call allow us to wait not only for a certain process but also for a group of processes. Its status argument provides detailed information about the actual status update. Let's modify the example again:

```
...
void process_creator() {
...
    if ((pids[1] = fork()) == 0) {
        cout << "Child process id: " << getpid() << endl;
        abort(); // {1}
    }
    siginfo_t status = {0}; // {2}
    waitid(P_PID, pids[1], &status, WEXITED); // {3}
    if (WIFSIGNALED(status)) // {4}
        cout << "Child " << pids[1]
            << " aborted: "
            << "\nStatus update with SIGCHLD: "
            << status.si_signo
            << "\nTermination signal - SIGABRT: "
            << status.si_status
            << "\nTermination code - _exit(2): "
            << status.si_code << endl;
}...
```

The output is as follows:

```
Child process id: 48368
Child process id: 48369
Child 48369 aborted:
Status update with SIGCHLD: 20
Termination signal - SIGABRT: 6
Termination code - _exit(2): 2
```

We changed `exit()` to `abort()` ([1]), which caused the child process to receive `SIGABRT` and exit with default handling (not exactly what we advised earlier). We used the `struct status` ([2]) to collect more meaningful status change information. The `waitid()` system call is used to monitor a single process and is set to wait for it to exit ([3]). If the child process signals its exit, then we print out the meaningful information ([4]), which in our case proves that we get `SIGABRT` (with a value of 6), the update comes with `SIGCHLD` (with a value of 20) and the exit code is 2, as per the documentation.

The `waitid()` system call has various options and through it, you can monitor your spawned processes in real time. We will not delve deeper here, but you can find more information on the manual pages should it suit your needs: `https://linux.die.net/man/2/waitid`.

An important remark is that with POSIX and Linux's thread management policy, which we discussed earlier, by default, a thread will wait on children of other threads in the same thread group. That said, we'll get into some thread management in the next section.

Introducing the system calls for thread manipulation in C++

As discussed in *Chapter 1*, we use threads to execute separate procedures in parallel. They exist only in the scope of a process and their creation overhead is bigger than the thread's one, so we consider them lightweight, although they have their own stack and `task_struct`. They are almost self-sufficient, except they rely on the parent process to exist. That process is also known as *the main thread*. All others that are created by it need to join it to be initiated. You could create thousands of threads simultaneously on the system, but they will not run in parallel. You can run only n parallel tasks, where n is the number of the system's concurrent ALUs (occasionally, these are the hardware's concurrent threads). The others will be scheduled according to the OS's task-scheduling mechanism. Let's look at the simplest example of a POSIX thread interface:

```
pthread_t new_thread;
pthread_create(&new_thread, <attributes>,
               <procedure to execute>,
               <procedure arguments>);
pthread_join(new_thread, NULL);
```

Of course, there are other system calls we could use to manage the POSIX threads further, such as exiting a thread, receiving the called procedure's returned value, detaching from the main thread, and so on. Let's take a look at C++'s thread realization:

```
std::thread new_thread(<procedure to execute>);
new.join();
```

This looks simpler, but it provides the same operations as the POSIX thread. To be consistent with the language, we advise you to use the C++ thread object. Now, let's see how these tasks are executed. Since we'll cover the newly added C++20 **jthreads** feature in *Chapter 6*, we will provide a system programming overview in the next few sections.

Joining and detaching threads

Regardless of whether you join threads through POSIX system calls or C++, you require this action to execute a routine through a given thread and wait for its termination. One remark, though – on Linux, the thread object of `pthread_join()` must be joinable, and the C++ thread object is not joinable by default. It is a good practice to join threads separately since joining them simultaneously leads to undefined behavior. It works the same way as the `wait()` system call does, except it relates to threads instead of processes.

And the same way processes could be run as daemons, threads can become daemons as well through detaching – `pthread_detach()` for POSIX or `thread::detach()` in C++. We are going to see this in the following example, but we are also going to analyze the joinable setting of the threads:

```cpp
#include <iostream>
#include <chrono>
#include <thread>
using namespace std;
using namespace std::chrono;
void detached_routine() {
    cout << "Starting detached_routine thread.\n";
    this_thread::sleep_for(seconds(2));
    cout << "Exiting detached_routine thread.\n";
}
void joined_routine() {
    cout << "Starting joined_routine thread.\n";
    this_thread::sleep_for(seconds(2));
    cout << "Exiting joined_routine thread.\n";
}
void thread_creator() {
    cout << "Starting thread_creator.\n";
    thread t1(detached_routine);
    cout << "Before - Is the detached thread joinable: "
        << t1.joinable() << endl;
    t1.detach();
    cout << "After - Is the detached thread joinable: "
        << t1.joinable() << endl;
    thread t2(joined_routine);
    cout << "Before - Is the joined thread joinable: "
        << t2.joinable() << endl;
    t2.join();
    cout << "After - Is the joined thread joinable: "
        << t2.joinable() << endl;
    this_thread::sleep_for(chrono::seconds(1));
    cout << "Exiting thread_creator.\n";
}
int main() {
    thread_creator();
}
```

The respective output is as follows:

```
Starting thread_creator.
Before - Is the detached thread joinable: 1
After - Is the detached thread joinable: 0
Before - Is the joined thread joinable: 1
Starting joined_routine thread.
Starting detached_routine thread.
Exiting joined_routine thread.
Exiting detached_routine thread.
After - Is the joined thread joinable: 0
Exiting thread_creator.
```

The preceding example is fairly simple – we create two thread objects: one is to be detached from the main thread handle (`detached_routine()`), while the other (`joined_thread()`) will join the main thread after exit. We check their joinable status at creation and after setting them to work. As expected, after the threads get to their routines, they are no longer joinable until they are terminated.

Thread termination

Linux (POSIX) provides two ways to end a thread's routine in a controlled manner from the inside of the thread: `pthread_cancel()` and `pthread_exit()`. As you have probably guessed from their names, the second one terminates the caller thread and is expected to always succeed. In contrast with the process `exit()` system call, during this one's execution, no process-shared resources, such as semaphores, file descriptors, mutexes, and so on, will be released, so make sure you manage them before the thread exits. Canceling the thread is a more flexible way to do this, but it ends up with `pthread_exit()`. Since the thread cancelation request is sent to the thread object, it has the opportunity to execute a cancelation cleanup and call thread-specific data destructors.

As C++ is an abstraction on top of the system call interface, it uses the thread object's scope to manage its lifetime and does this well. Of course, whatever happens in the background is implementation-specific and depends on the system and the compiler. We are revisiting this topic later in this book as well, so use this opportunity to familiarize yourself with the interfaces.

Summary

In this chapter, we walked through the low-level events that occur during process or thread creation and manipulation. We discussed the processes' memory layout and its significance. You also learned some important points about the OS's way of task scheduling and what happens in the background during process and thread state updates. We will use these fundamentals later in this book. The next chapter will cover filesystem management and will provide you with some interesting C++ instruments in that domain.

3

Navigating through the Filesystems

In this chapter, we will revisit the concepts of a file, which were discussed briefly in *Chapter 1*. You will learn in detail about the **filesystem** (**FS**) in Linux and its specifics. We will not go to certain filesystem implementations, as you will see there're many, but we will establish the fundamentals of working with them. You will learn more about Linux's FS hierarchy – its partitions, object types, and some frequently used operations.

You will get familiar with the **filesystem library** in C++, allowing you to execute system operations independently from the platform. We will use C++ examples to show you simple applications for file management. You're also going to learn about `string_views`. Some of the operations you learn about here will be revisited again in *Chapter 5*, when we will discuss error handling.

Last but not least, you will learn hands-on about the fundamental **inter-process communication** (**IPC**) mechanism known as **pipes**. We will also discuss signals as system entities and their impact on communication. If you're unfamiliar with data transfers between processes, then this is where you should start. If you are experienced, then you may notice that the code could be much more complicated – implementing server-client applications with pipes, for example. We are aware of that, but we believe that the examples are a good basis to start from – additional scalability of this mechanism has unwanted knock-on effects. We discuss this more in *Chapter 7*.

In this chapter, we will cover the following main topics:

- Going through Linux's filesystem fundamentals
- Executing filesystem operations with C++
- IPC through anonymous pipes and named pipes
- Briefly observing the signal handling

Technical requirements

In order to run the code examples, the reader must prepare the following:

- A Linux-based system capable of compiling and executing C and C++20 (for example, Linux Mint 21):

  - **gcc12.2** compiler: `https://gcc.gnu.org/git/gcc.git gcc-source`

  - **g++** with **-std=c++2a** flags for the C++ code

  - **gcc** without flags for the C code

- For all the examples, you can alternatively use `https://godbolt.org/`.

- Code examples could be found here: `https://github.com/PacktPublishing/C-Programming-for-Linux-Systems/tree/main/Chapter%203`.

Going through Linux's filesystem fundamentals

We went through some of the Unix (and Linux) filesystem definitions in *Chapter 1*. Let's see how they really matter in the bigger picture of system programming. You probably remember what types of files there are in the Linux system – regular files, directories, special files, links, sockets, and named pipes. We are going to deal with most of them in this chapter and learn about what purpose they serve. One way to think about files in Unix, including Linux, is the following simple statement:

"On a UNIX system, everything is a file; if something is not a file, it is a process."

So, everything that's not a process has an API, which includes file operation system calls. Let's agree that a file is the main instrument for the logical organization of data. Then there must be something that is the main instrument for file organization. Well, this is where the file management system, or simply the FS, comes into play. It looks after the files' layout on the physical medium – the **non-volatile memory** (**NVM**), their organization on that medium, the operation abstraction (`open()`, `write()`), and so on.

The FS also allows the user to forget the hardware's specifics for a moment and focus on data operations, as well as using the FS like an ordered catalog. It helps with the files' structure and data visualization on the UI or CLI, access permissions, and the effective usage of resources. While the user has the chance to focus on file creation, deletion, modifications, and sharing, the FS cares more about data accuracy, device driver error handling, multiple user accesses, and so on. This is an important point, as we will observe some error states later in the book – for example, in *Chapter 5*, where the FS is the entity that creates the exception cases. And it also affects task scheduling, as we mentioned earlier. Let's look at the FS structure and its specifics in Linux.

Linux's FS

We have to mention that there are many kinds of FSs. Each of them suits its own purposes, as the user experience implies multiple preferences, and not all of them exist together. Linux has the strength to support over 100 FSes. A combination of them can run simultaneously on a single system. This provides an opportunity for the user to operate with them optimally and benefit from all of them. If the FS is required just to organize the file structure, then an ordinary one could do the trick – for example, `ext2` or `FAT`. If we want file consistency and less error-prone operations, then a **journaling FS** is required, such as `ext4`, `ReiserFS`, or `XFS`. For online data stores, **network FSes**, such as `NFS` and `CIFS`, might come in handy. Large files and a large number of small files require specific management, too, so **volume management FSes**, such as `ZFS` and `btrfs`, are useful. Last, but not least, there are FSes that are not backed by physical storage but represent entities in the **main memory**, which are particularly useful to the system programmers – `proc`, `sys`, `ram`, and `tmp`. However, at an abstract level, the file operations seem to be the same. So, we can have a unified interface. It not only allows system programmers to use the different FSes in the same way but also allows the OS's UI to visualize the file structure – all of the files and directories – under the same FS tree. Linux realizes this through the **virtual filesystem (VFS)**. It is also referred to as **virtual FS switch** – a layer residing in the kernel, providing a generic interface for the programs. Before we go into detail, let's see how it looks from a design standpoint.

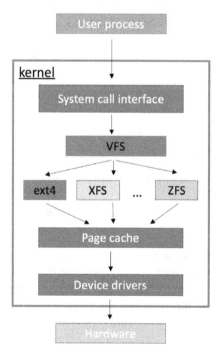

Figure 3.1 – A VFS software layer in Linux kernel

Additionally, the VFS is object-oriented. This will not help us much with C++ code, unfortunately. Still, it is a good example of object-oriented programming in C, as the objects are actually of a `struct` type, containing file data and function pointers to the file operations. We will talk about those objects a bit later in the chapter. Let's look at the directory structure and standardized partitioning now.

Directory structure and partitioning

The directory structure in Linux is well presented in the **Filesystem Hierarchy Standard** (**FHS**). Still, it is important to note that the files, including directories, are arranged in branches of a tree structure. Their character names are case-sensitive, and file suffixes (called *extensions* in Windows) might be useless in some cases – remember that regular files are treated as binary files and their extensions are mostly to help the user about their roles. This can be confusing for newcomers, especially if they use the Terminal and not the OS's UI. The true file type is determined internally through *magic numbers*, or *Magic Bytes*. For example, executable scripts start with `#!`. You can read more about them by executing this command:

```
$ man magic
```

Getting back to the FS structure – it starts with the `root` directory, denoted with `/`. The `root` FS is mounted on that directory in the early stages of the system's boot sequence. Every other FS is mounted during the OS startup or even later during normal operations. You can check your own configuration as follows:

```
$ cat /etc/fstab
# /etc/fstab: static file system information.
...
# <file system> <mount point>   <type> <options>          <dump> <pass>
# / was on /dev/sda5 during installation
UUID=618800a5-57e8-43c1-9856-0a0a14ebf344 /               ext4
errors=remount-ro 0         1
# /boot/efi was on /dev/sda1 during installation
UUID=D388-FA76  /boot/efi       vfat    umask=0077         0      1
/swapfile                               none               swap
sw                      0       0
```

It provides information about the *mount points* and the respective FS types. Outside this file, the FSes will be visible in the system as separate directories with their exact paths. Every one of them can be accessed through the `root` directory. An important point is that `/` and `/root` are different directories, as the first is the `root` directory and the latter is the home directory of the *root user*. Some other important partitions and directories are the following:

- `/bin`: Includes common user executables.
- `/boot`: Includes the Linux system startup files, the static part of the kernel, and the bootloader configuration.

- `/dev`: Includes references to all peripheral hardware, which is represented through files with a special file type, `'c'` or `'b'`, and they provide access to the real devices. We mentioned these special file types in *Chapter 1*.

- `/etc`: Includes the system configuration files.

- `/home`: This is the top-level directory, which is available for user files, and all users have their respective common subdirectory there.

- `/lib`: This includes shared library files that are needed to start the system.

- `/mnt`: The temporary mount point for external FSes. It makes a good combination with `/media`, where media devices such as USB flash drives are mounted.

- `/opt`: This consists of optional files and third-party software applications.

- `/proc`: This contains information about the system resources.

- `/tmp`: This is a temporary directory used by the OS and several programs for temporal storage – it will be cleaned up after reboot.

- `/sbin`: This includes the system binary files, usually utilized by the system administrator.

- `/usr`: This includes read-only files most of the time, but there are exceptions. It is for programs, libraries and binaries, *man* files, and documentation.

- `/var`: This includes variable data files – usually log files, database files, archived e-mails, and so on.

Let's get back to **mount points** and **FS partitions**. As not many people are familiar with those, we will take the opportunity to briefly explain them. A good reason for this is that, as already mentioned, system programmers work with many FSes at a time, and some of them are related to network drives or different devices.

Linux does not assign a letter to a partition as Windows does; therefore, you can easily confuse a separate device for a simple directory. Most of the time, this shouldn't be a big deal, but it might become a problem when you care about resource management, resiliency, and security. For example, vehicles overall have strict requirements for hardware durability, which extends to 10-15 years of serviceability. With this in mind, you must be aware of a device's characteristics, especially if you write on it frequently or fill its entire space meaninglessly. The way an FS manages the data is also crucial to a peripheral's memory exhaustion in time, so this choice is important.

`fstab` shows where FSes are mounted, but it also describes something else. First of all, let's remember that **FS partitions** have the purpose of separating a single device – a hard drive, for example – into multiple partitions. This is used mostly in embedded systems with safety requirements. However, Linux also provides **Logical Volume Manager** (**LVM**), which allows flexible setups. In other words, FSes can easily get shrunk or enlarged, which is preferable on larger-scale systems.

The creation of multiple FSs serves not only as a user data grouping tool but also allows other partitions to remain intact if one goes out due to failure. Another usage is when a device's storage is unavailable – often, it's just full of data. The entire system might stop working because it also relies on storage space. Therefore, it is better to fill only a single FS entirely and raise an error. The other FS will be left intact, and the system will continue working. From that point of view, it is a secure and robust solution. Just keep in mind that it doesn't protect you from overall device failure. For that reason, many network storage devices rely on a **Redundant Array of Inexpensive Disks** (**RAID**). We will not deal with it here, but we encourage you to read more about it.

Now, you probably observed some additional data in the fstab output earlier. Except for the **root partition**, we actually divide the partition types into **data** and **swap** partitions:

- **The data partition**: This includes the root partition, together with all necessary information for system startup and normal run. It also includes standard data on Linux.

- **The swap partition**: This is indicated with swap in fstab, and it provides the system with the option to move data from the main memory to the NVM in cases of memory overflow. It is visible only to the system itself. This doesn't mean you should overflow your RAM, but just keep it for extra flexibility in order to not compromise the system's availability. Just remember, the NVM is much slower than the main memory chips!

> **Important note**
>
> The system administrator generally configures the partitions' layout. Sometimes, one partition is spread across multiple NVM devices. This design is strictly related to the system's purpose. Once the partitions are available to you as a user, you can only add more. We strongly discourage you from changing their properties unless you're well aware of what you're doing and why.

What about the **mount points**? The partitions are attached to the system through the mount points. This is how the FS recognizes a given space for particular data – the best example is the list of directories, as we mentioned earlier. You could display the information for the available mount points on the system, except the **swap partitions**, using the df command. In our case, this is the following:

```
$ df -h
Filesystem     Size  Used Avail Use% Mounted on
udev           5,9G     0  5,9G   0% /dev
tmpfs          1,2G  1,3M  1,2G   1% /run
/dev/sda5       39G   24G   14G  64% /
tmpfs          6,0G     0  6,0G   0% /dev/shm
tmpfs          5,0M  4,0K  5,0M   1% /run/lock
tmpfs          6,0G     0  6,0G   0% /sys/fs/cgroup
/dev/sda1      511M  4,0K  511M   1% /boot/efi
tmpfs          1,2G   16K  1,2G   1% /run/user/29999
```

It is easy to see the relationship between the FS type and the mount point, for example, the `Filesystem` and `Mounted on` columns. We will not go into more detail on this, but we encourage you to read more about the `parted` tool, which is used exactly for the creation and editing of partitions.

Linux FS objects

As we already mentioned in the previous section, the FS is realized through objects, and there are four main types we care about:

- **Superblock**: This represents the mounted FS metadata – the respective device, the modification flags, the corresponding FS type, the FS access permissions, the modified files, and so on.

- **Index node (i-node or inode)**: Each file has its own **inode** that refers to the file itself through a unique number and stores its metadata. This object contains the functions that the VFS can call but not the user-level code, such as `open()`, `create()`, `lookup()`, `mkdir()`. Regular files, special files, directories, and **named pipes** are represented through **inodes**. In other words, all entities in the FS have an **inode** that contains metadata about them. You can visualize this through the `stat` command:

```
$ stat test
  File: test
  Size: 53248          Blocks: 104       IO Block:
4096    regular file
Device: 805h/2053d    Inode: 696116      Links: 1
Access: (0775/-rwxrwxr-x)  Uid: (29999/    oem)   Gid:
(29999/    oem)
. . .
```

Now, look at the permission bits – `0775/-rwxrwxr-x`. Both the numbers and the symbol flags have the same meaning but are different representations. `-` means the flag is not set. `r` means the file is readable by the current user, group, or everyone (reading left to right). `w` means **writable**, and `x` stands for **executable**. The leftmost bit has a specific role – if there is an extra p in front, it marks this file as a **pipe**. You can see this later in the chapter. If not, you can proceed forward and check the permissions bits of the **symbolic link** in the respective example later. Note that its permission bits start with `l`. Other symbols you might see during your operations are `d` for **directories**, `b` for **block devices**, `c` for **character devices**, and `s` for **sockets**.

- **Directory entry (dentry)**: For usability, we will not refer to physical files using numbers as the inode does but, instead, using names and locations. So, we need a translation table, mapping symbolic names (for users) to inode numbers (for the kernel). The easiest way to represent this is through the pathname, such as the following:

```
$ ls -li test
696116 -rwxrwxr-x 1 oem oem 53248 Jul 30 08:29 test
```

As you can see, the inode is the same as the previous example – 696116, and the symbolic name is test.

- **File**: This object type is used to represent the content of an opened file to a process. It is created through open() and destroyed at close(). Some of the members this object contains are the **dentry** pointer, **uid** and **gid**, the file position pointer, and the inode method set, which relates to the methods and which the specific FS can execute for this exact file. The kernel allocates the new file structure and its unique file descriptor. The dentry pointer is initialized as well as the set of methods defined by the inode. The open() method is called for the specific FS realization, and the file is placed into the file descriptor table of the calling process. In user-space, the file descriptor is used for the application's file operations.

The following diagram provides an overview of single-file access through multiple processes:

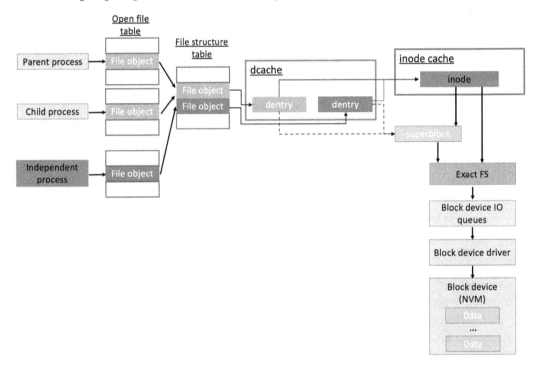

Figure 3.2 – File access organization

We can see a few interesting things here. Although the processes open the same file, they go through different execution paths before reaching the real data. First of all, the processes have their own **open file table**; therefore, they have their own descriptors. Whenever a process calls fork(), the child gets the same **open file table**. The independent process points to a separate one. Then, let's say we have two **dentries** for the same file and our file objects point to it. Such a situation occurs when we reach the same physical file through different pathnames. As we work with the same file, the entries will point to a single inode and **superblock** instances. From then on, the exact FS, where the file resides, will take over with its specific functions.

One disclaimer, though – the OS is not an arbiter of simultaneous file updates by multiple processes. It will schedule those operations by the rules we discussed in the previous chapter. If you want to make a specific policy for such actions, then this must be designed and applied explicitly. Although the FS provides file locking as a **mutual exclusion** technique, which you will learn later in the book, Linux usually doesn't automatically lock open files. If you remove files using sudo rm -rf, you might delete ones that are currently in use. This can lead to irreversible system issues. We use file locking to ensure safe, concurrent access to the file's contents. It allows only one process to access the file at a given time, thus avoiding possible race conditions, which you will learn about in *Chapter 6*. Linux supports two kinds of file locks – advisory locks and mandatory locks, which you can read more about here: https://www.kernel.org/doc/html/next/filesystems/locking.html.

> **Important note**
>
> The unique numbers for physical file identification through the respective inodes are not endless. The VFS might contain so many tiny files that it exhausts its abilities to create new files, while there's still free space on the NVM. This error is observed on high-scale systems more often than you may think.

You've probably also wondered about the ways to reach the same file through different pathnames. Well, do you recall our discussion on link files in *Chapter 1*? We talked about **hard links** and **symbolic links**. The first ones are always available for a given file – for example, when there's at least one hard link, related to a piece of data, then the corresponding file is considered to exist in the FS. Through it, a pathname is directly associated with the point on the NVM where the file resides and can be opened from. Multiple pathnames to the same point on the device lead to multiple hard link constructions. Let's check it out. First, we will list the data for some of our files:

```
$ ls -li some_data
695571 -rw-rw-r-- 1 oem 5 May 28 18:13 some_data
```

Then, we will create a hard link for the same file through the ln command, and list both files:

```
$ ln some_data some_data_hl
$ ls -li some_data some_data_hl
695571 -rw-rw-r-- 2 oem oem 5 May 28 18:13 some_data
695571 -rw-rw-r-- 2 oem oem 5 May 28 18:13 some_data_hl
```

As you can see, they both have the same inode because they have different character names, but they are the same file. The only true representation of the file is the **inode** number – 695571. This means they truly point to the same block of the hard drive. Then, we see that the hard link counter has increased from 1 to 2 (between the access permissions and the uid columns).

Symbolic links are files that point to other files or directories through their respective pathnames, known as targets. The FS creates a new file, which only contains the pathname to the target, and deleting all symbolic links to a file will not cause its deletion from the system. Let's create a symbolic link through the `ln` command again, but this time we will add the `-s` option. We will list all of the files so far:

```
$ ln -s some_data some_data_sl
$ ls -li some_data some_data_hl some_data_sl
695571 -rw-rw-r-- 2 oem oem 5 May 28 18:13 some_data
695571 -rw-rw-r-- 2 oem oem 5 May 28 18:13 some_data_hl
694653 lrwxrwxrwx 1 oem oem 9 May 28 18:16 some_data_sl -> some_data
```

You can easily see that the new file – `some_data_sl` – has a different inode from the original file and its hard link. It points to a new location in the NVM and has its own access permissions. In addition, it shows visually which pathname it truly points to. Even if there's a symbolic link to a symbolic link, `ls -li` will still present the file a symbolic link is set to point to, such as the following:

```
696063 -rw-rw-r--  1 oem oem  4247 Jul  2 13:25 test.dat
696043 lrwxrwxrwx  1 oem oem     8 Aug  6 10:07 testdat_sl -> test.dat
696024 lrwxrwxrwx  1 oem oem    10 Aug  6 10:07 testdat_sl2 ->
testdat_sl
```

And check out the sizes in bytes – the original file is only 4247 bytes in size, while the symbolic link is 8 bytes, and the next is 10. Actually, the original file size doesn't matter for the symbolic link's size, but something else does – you could figure it out by counting the number of characters in the referred file's **pathname**.

All of the preceding filenames will provide you with the ability to access and modify the file. They also provide you with the flexibility to get data from multiple access points without duplication and meaningless usage of extra storage space. Many system programmers use symbolic links to reorder the FS, just for the purposes of easier data management for some specialized user processes. The Linux system itself does that, just to reorder the FS hierarchy for the same reasons. Let's create an overview of this example through the following diagram:

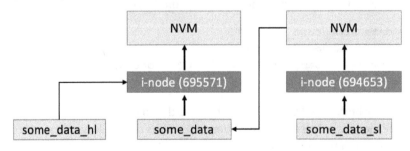

Figure 3.3 – A hard link and symbolic link overview

> **Important note**
>
> Even if the original file is moved or deleted, the symbolic link will continue to point to its pathname as a target, while the hard link must point to an existing file. The symbolic link will work across partitions, but the hard link doesn't link paths on different volumes or FSes.

In the next section, we will continue to manipulate files, but this time through C++ code.

Executing FS operations with C++

With C++17 FS operations that are closer to the system programming are facilitated. The FS library allows the C++ developer to distinguish between the Linux fs types and perform certain operations with them. Let's take a look at an exemplary interface:

```
bool is_directory(const std::filesystem::path& p)
```

This method checks whether a given pathname is a **directory**. In a similar fashion, we can do the other type checks – `is_fifo()`, `is_regular_file()`, `is_socket()`, and `is_symlink()`. Can you tell why we don't have the `is_hardlink()` method? That's right – if two files with different character names point to a single inode, then both of them provide access to the same content. It doesn't matter whether the inode's hard link counter is higher than one, although we could get it through the `hard_link_count()` method.

As the C++ language is compilable on multiple OSes, the FS functions are also dependent on the respective FSes for those exact systems. For example, FAT does not support symbolic links; therefore, the methods related to them will fail, and the error handling is left to the system programmer. You can use the `std::filesystem::filesystem_error` exception object to get details about the current error's FS error state. Such discussions are available in *Chapter 5*.

We mentioned earlier that the concurrent file access has to be managed by the software engineer, or the OS will schedule the operations as it sees fit. The same goes for this library, too. Don't expect it to handle race conditions or modification conflicts itself. Now, let's see how some of the operations can be used. One disclaimer though – as mentioned, error conditions will be discussed later, so we will not focus on them here.

We will create a new directory (marker {1} in the following code segment):

```cpp
#include <iostream>
#include <filesystem>
using namespace std;
using namespace std::filesystem;

int main() {
    auto result = create_directory("test_dir"); // {1}
    if (result)
        cout << "Directory created successfully!\n";
    else
        cout << "Directory creation failed!\n";
    return 0;
}
```

Now, let's see what happened on the FS:

```
$ ./create_dir
Directory created successfully!
```

If you call the program again, it will fail, as the directory already exists:

```
.$ /create_dir
Directory creation failed!
```

We populate the new directory, as described in the example earlier (*see Figure 3.3*), but this time with C++ code (markers {1} and {2} in the following code):

```cpp
...
int main() {
    if (exists("some_data")) {
        create_hard_link("some_data", "some_data_hl");// {1}
        create_symlink("some_data", "some_data_sl"); // {2}
    }
...
```

Of course, it is important to call the program from the directory, where some_data is, or provide its pathname accordingly – through the **absolute** or **relative** path to it. If all is fine, then we proceed. This time, we've added some more characters to some_data, so it's 9 bytes in size. Still, the picture is almost the same – of course, the inodes are different:

```
79105062 rw-rw-r-- 2 oem oem 9 May 29 16:33 some_data
79105062 rw-rw-r-- 2 oem oem 9 May 29 16:33 some_data_hl
79112163 lrwxrwxrwx 1 oem oem 9 May 29 17:04 some_data_sl  -> some_
data
```

We also create by hand a new inner directory, called `inner_test_dir`, with a new file, called `inner_some_data`. Let's iterate through the directory, both non-recursively (marker {1} in the following code) and recursively, and print out the directory contents (marker {2} in the following code):

```
...
int main() {
    const path path_to_iterate{"test_dir"};
    for (auto const& dir_entry :
        directory_iterator{path_to_iterate}) { // {1}
        cout << dir_entry.path() << endl;
    }
    cout << endl;
    for (auto const& dir_entry :
        recursive_directory_iterator{path_to_iterate}) {
        cout << dir_entry.path() << endl; // {2}
    }
    return 0;
}
```

The output is not surprising:

```
"test_dir/inner_test_dir"
"test_dir/some_data"
"test_dir/some_data_sl"
"test_dir/some_data_hl"

"test_dir/inner_test_dir"
"test_dir/inner_test_dir/inner_some_data"
"test_dir/some_data"
"test_dir/some_data_sl"
"test_dir/some_data_hl"
```

Now, we want to check whether some of the files are symbolic links (marker {1} in the following code), and if so, let's print out their targets:

```
...
int main() {
    const path path_to_iterate{"test_dir"};
    for (auto const& dir_entry :
        recursive_directory_iterator{path_to_iterate}) {
        auto result = is_symlink(dir_entry.path()); // {1}
        if (result) cout << read_symlink(dir_entry.path());
    }
}
```

Again, the output is as expected – the target is the initial source file:

```
$ ./sym_link_check
"some_data"
```

Let's try to rename the symbolic link file (marker {1} in the following code segment), before we continue with some other modifications:

```
...
int main() {
    if (exists("some_data_sl")) {
        rename("some_data_sl", "some_data_sl_rndm"); // {1}
    }
...
```

We see that the renaming is successful:

```
79112163 lrwxrwxrwx 1 oem oem 9 May 29 17:04 some_data_sl_rndm ->
some_data
```

Let's remove the initial file – some_data (marker {2} in the following code), and observe the free space on the system changing (markers {1} and {3} in the following code):

```
...
int main() {
    if (exists("some_data")) {
        std::filesystem::space_info space_obj =
            space(current_path());// {1}
        cout << "Capacity: "
            << space_obj.capacity << endl;
        cout << "Free: "
            << space_obj.free << endl;
        cout << "Available: "
            << space_obj.available << endl;

        remove("some_data"); // {2}
        space_obj = space(current_path()); // {3}

        cout << "Capacity: "
            << space_obj.capacity << endl;
        cout << "Free: "
            << space_obj.free << endl;
        cout << "Available: "
            << space_obj.available << endl;
    }
...
```

And here's the output:

```
Capacity: 41678012416
Free: 16555171840
Available: 14689452032
Capacity: 41678012416
Free: 16555175936
Available: 14689456128
```

As you can see 4096 bytes have been freed, although the file was only 9 bytes in size. This is because the minimum value we actually use is the size of one NVM block – the smallest unit of data the OS can write in or read from a file. In this case, it is 4 KB. If the details are not interesting to you, but you only want to check whether the space values have been updated, then with C++ 20, you also have the == operator overload; thus you can directly compare the two space_info objects, which are actually behind the returned values of space() (markers {1} and {3}).

We used these code examples to go quickly through the C++ filesystem library. We hope it is a good overview for you, although we have jumped a bit from function to function. It should be useful in your work. The next section deals with something very important – the fundamentals of multi-process communication. As you already know from the beginning of this chapter, Linux treats everything that's not a process as a file. The same goes for communication resources, and we will delve into them armed with our C++ knowledge. There will be a bit more theory, so stay with us!

IPC through anonymous pipes and named pipes

Before we even start working on this topic, let us ask you this. Have you ever done the following:

```
$ cat some_data | grep data
some data
```

If yes, then you probably call | a **pipe**. Where does this come from? Well, you actually *pipe* the output from one process as an input to another. You can do it with your own code as well – we are not limited to the system's applications. And we can program this **pipe** communication in our own code, too. This is a fundamental instrument for the data transfer between processes. Do you remember reading earlier about **FIFO files** and named pipes? Yes, that's right – they are the same thing, but is the |-symbolled pipe the same as them? No! That's an anonymous pipe. System programmers differentiate between the so-called **anonymous pipes** and the **named pipes**. They have different purposes, so both of them are found on Linux systems nowadays. They are created and managed by pipefs, while the user executes the standard VFS system calls. We are going to use pipes as examples to visualize some observations for the FS as well. Let's get into it then!

Anonymous or unnamed pipes

Anonymous pipes cannot be observed in the FS, as they don't have character names. They are created through a special system call, as you will see in the next example. They reside in the kernel, where a specific file buffer is created. From the example with the | symbol, you can easily conclude that such implementation is related more to short-term communication, and it is not persistent in time. Anonymous pipes have two endpoints – a read one and a write one. Both of these are represented by a file descriptor. As soon as both endpoints are closed, the pipe will be destroyed, as there are no more ways to reference it through an open file descriptor. In addition, this type of communication is known as a simplex FIFO communication – for example, it creates a one-way-only data transfer – most often from a parent process to a child. Let's see one example, which uses the system calls to create an anonymous pipe and a simple data transfer:

```
#include <iostream>
#include <unistd.h>
#include <string.h>
using namespace std;
constexpr auto BUFF_LEN = 64;
constexpr auto pipeIn   = 0;
constexpr auto pipeOut  = 1;
```

We require an integer array to hold the file descriptors, representing the pipe's *in* and *out* endpoints – a_pipe. Then, this array is passed to the pipe () system call, which will return -1 if there is an error, or 0 on success (see marker {1}):

```
int main() {
    int a_pipe[2]{};
    char buff[BUFF_LEN + 1]{};
    if (pipe(a_pipe) == -1) {   // {1}
        perror("Pipe creation failed");
        exit(EXIT_FAILURE);
    }
    else {
        if (int pid = fork(); pid == -1) {
            perror("Process creation failed");
            exit(EXIT_FAILURE);
        }
        else if (pid == 0) {
            // Child: will be the reader!
            sleep(1); // Just to give some extra time!
            close(a_pipe[pipeOut]); // {2}
            read(a_pipe[pipeIn], buff, BUFF_LEN); // {3}
            cout << "Child: " << buff << endl;
        }
```

We create a new process through `fork()`, as we did in *Chapter 2*. Knowing this, can you tell how many pipes are created at the end? That's right – one pipe is created, and the file descriptors are shared between the processes.

As the data transfer is one-way, we need to close the unused endpoint for each process – markers {2} and {4}. If the process writes and reads its own **pipe** in and out file descriptors, it will only get the information that it has written there beforehand:

```
    else {
        // Parent: will be the writer!
        close(a_pipe[pipeIn]); // {4}
        const char *msg = {"Sending message to child!"};
        write(a_pipe[pipeOut], msg, strlen(msg) + 1);
        // {5}
    }
  }
  return 0;
}
```

In other words, we forbid the child from *talking back* to the parent, and the parent can only send data to the child. The data is sent simply by writing it into a file and reading from it (see markers {3} and {5}). This is a very simple piece of code, and usually, the communication through anonymous pipes is that simple. However, be careful – `write()` and `read()` are blocking calls; if there's nothing to be read from the pipe (the pipe buffer is empty), the respective process-reader will be blocked. If the pipe capacity is exhausted (the pipe buffer is full), the process-writer will be blocked. If there's no reader to consume the data, `SIGPIPE` will be triggered. We will provide such an example in the last section of this chapter. There's no risk of race conditions in the way we will present them in *Chapter 6*, but synchronization of data creation and consumption is still in the programmer's hands. The next diagram provides you with some additional information on what happens when we use the anonymous pipe:

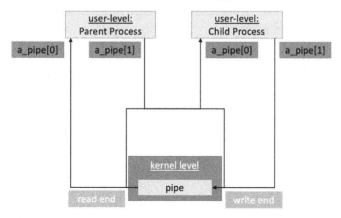

Figure 3.4 – An anonymous pipe communication mechanism

In the background, at the kernel level, there are a few more operations going on:

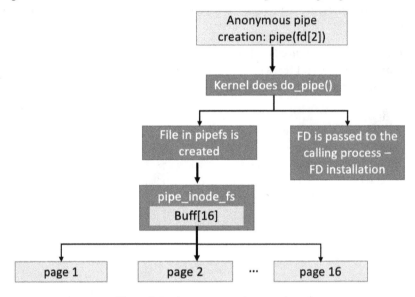

Figure 3.5 – Anonymous pipe creation

The pipe's capacity can be checked and set using the `fcntl(fd, F_GETPIPE_SZ)` and `F_SETPIPE_SZ` operations, respectively. You can see that the pipe has 16 *pages* by default. The *page* is the smallest unit of data the *virtual memory* can manage. If a single page is 4,096 KB, then it could transfer 65,536 bytes of data before it overflows. We will discuss this later in the chapter. However, keep in mind that some systems may vary, and the info from *Figure 3.5* might be wrong for you. In a similar fashion, we can represent what happens at a lower level during `read()` and `write()` operations.

In the following diagram, the question of using an FS as a shared (global) memory arises. Note that although the FS has its own protection mechanisms through mutexes, this will not help us at a user level to synchronize the data correctly. Simply modifying a regular file through multiple processes will cause trouble, as mentioned earlier. Doing so with a pipe will cause less trouble, but we are still not on the safe side. As you can see, the **scheduler** is involved, and we might end up in a **deadlock** of constantly waiting processes. This is easier to avoid with anonymous pipes than with named pipes.

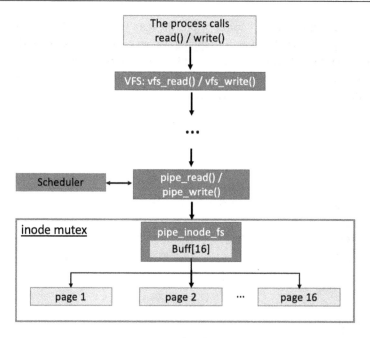

Figure 3.6 – Pipe read and write operations

Now that we have our communication established, why do we need an additional file type such as the named pipe? We will discuss this in the next section.

Named pipes

Named pipes are *a bit more complex* than anonymous pipes, as there's more programable context to them. For example, they have character names and are observable by a user in an FS. They are not destroyed after a process finishes working with them but, instead, when a specific system call for the file removal is executed – unlink(). Therefore, we can say that they provide *persistency*. In a similar fashion to anonymous pipes, we can demonstrate named pipes in the following CLI command, creating fifo_example as a result:

```
$ ./test > fifo_example
$ cat fifo_example
$ Child: Sending message to child!
```

Also, the communication is duplexed – for example, the data transfer could work both ways. Still, your work might push you in the direction of wrapping system calls with C++ code. The next example provides a sample overview, with the disclaimer that it is exemplary, and as C++ context is added to the code, the program becomes larger in size. Let's get an example from the **pipe** from earlier, which we can modify with C++ code, but the behavior remains the same:

```cpp
#include <sys/stat.h>
#include <unistd.h>
#include <array>
#include <iostream>
#include <filesystem>
#include <string_view>
using namespace std;
using namespace std::filesystem;
static string_view fifo_name    = "example_fifo"; // {1}
static constexpr size_t buf_size = 64;
void write(int out_fd,
           string_view message) { // {2}
    write(out_fd,
          message.data(),
          message.size());
}
```

At marker {1}, we introduce the string_view object. It represents a pair of pointers to a string or an array, and its respective size. As it is a view-handle class type, we preferably and cheaply pass it by value (see marker {2}), together with the expected substring operation interface. It is always const, so you don't need to declare it as such. So, it's an object and it's bigger in size, but it has the benefit of being unconditionally safe – taking care of typical C string error cases, such as NULL-termination. Any issue will be handled at compile time. In our case, we can simply use it as a const char* or const string alternative. Let's proceed with the reader:

```cpp
string read(int in_fd) { // {3}
    array <char, buf_size> buffer;
    size_t bytes = read(in_fd,
                        buffer.data(),
                        buffer.size());
    if (bytes > 0) {
        return {buffer.data(), bytes}; // {4}
    }
    return {};
}
```

```
int main() {
    if (!exists(fifo_name))
        mkfifo(fifo_name.data(), 0666); // {5}

    if (pid_t childId = fork(); childId == -1) {
        perror("Process creation failed");
        exit(EXIT_FAILURE);
    }
```

Markers {2} and {3} show the C++ wrappers of `write()` and `read()` respectively. You can see that instead of doing `strlen()` or `sizeof()` acrobatics, we use the `string_view`'s and the `array`'s `data()` and `size()`, respectively, because they are packed together through the respective object. One important point is that we use `array<char, buf_size>` to be specific about the buffer size and type. Similarly, we can use `string` instead of `array`, as it is defined as `basic_string<char>`, and we can limit its size with `reserve(buf_size)`. The choice really depends on your needs later in the function. In our case, we will use `array` as a direct representation of reading a fixed-sized `char` buffer from the pipe. We construct the resultant `string` afterward or leave it empty (see marker {4}).

Now, we will use the already known `exists()` function to discard a second `mkfifo()` call by the process that arrives second. Then, we check whether the file is truly a FIFO (see marker {6}):

```
    else {
        if(is_fifo(fifo_name)) { // {6}
            if (childId == 0) {
                if (int named_pipe_fd =
                        open(fifo_name.data(), O_RDWR);
                    named_pipe_fd >= 0) { // {7}
                    string message;
                    message.reserve(buf_size);
                    sleep(1);
                    message = read(named_pipe_fd); // {8}
                    string_view response_msg
                        = "Child printed the message!";
                    cout << "Child: " << message << endl;
                    write(named_pipe_fd,
                        response_msg); // {9}
                    close(named_pipe_fd);
                }
```

Now, look at markers {7} and {10}. Do you see where we open the pipe, where we keep this result, and where we check its value? Correct – we keep these operations packed together in the `if` statement, thus focusing our scope on the same logical place. Then, we read from the pipe through the newly added function wrapper (markers {8} and {12}). And then we write to the pipe through the `write()` wrapper (markers {9} and {11}). Note that at marker {9}, we pass `string_view` to the function, while at marker {11}, we pass a `string`. It works for both cases, thus additionally proving our point of using `string_views` for such interfaces, instead of `const string`, `const char *`, and so on:

```cpp
            else {
                cout << "Child cannot open the pipe!"
                    << endl;
            }
        }
        else if (childId > 0) {
            if (int named_pipe_fd =
                    open(fifo_name.data(), O_RDWR);
                named_pipe_fd >= 0) { // {10}
                string message
                = "Sending some message to the child!";
                write(named_pipe_fd,
                    message); // {11}
                sleep(1);
                message = read(named_pipe_fd); // {12}
                cout << "Parent: " << message << endl;
                close(named_pipe_fd);
            }
        }
        else {
            cout << "Fork failed!";
    }
```

The pipe is removed at marker {13}, but we will keep it for experiments. For example, we can list the named pipe:

```
$ ls -la example_fifo
prw-r--r-- 1 oem oem 0 May 30 13:45 example_fifo
```

Please observe that its size is 0. This means that everything written in was consumed. On close(), the kernel will flush the file descriptors and will destroy the FIFO object in the main memory, as it did for the anonymous pipe. It is possible sometimes that the *reader* doesn't consume the data fully. As you may remember, it can store data for 16 pages. That's why we encourage you to use the number of bytes, returned by the read() and write() functions, to decide whether the processes have to be terminated or not. Now, look at the permission bits – do you see something interesting there? Yes – there is an extra p in front of them, which marks this file as a pipe. Did you observe this somewhere earlier in the chapter? If not, you can go back and check the permissions bits of the inode.

Let's continue with the last code snippet:

```
            remove(fifo_name); // {13}
        }
    }
    return 0;
}
```

This is a simple one-time ping-pong application with the following output:

```
Child: Sending some message to the child!
Parent: Child printed the message!
```

You can still use an IO operation to send the message, but then string_view wouldn't do. In the next section, we will provide a brief overview of what happens when communication through a pipe is disturbed. To keep the focus on system calls, we will put aside C++ for now.

Let's now return to the C++ filesystem library. We can check whether the current file is truly a FIFO file through the library operations. If so, let's delete it with the remove() function. It will be the same as unlink(), although one level of abstraction over the system call itself. Again, this will give us some platform independency:

```
...
int main() {
    if (exists("example_fifo") && is_fifo("example_fifo")){
        remove("example_fifo");
        cout << "FIFO is removed";
    } ...
```

As you see, we use the already known methods, which were explained earlier in the chapter. Let's see what happens at the VFS and kernel levels now:

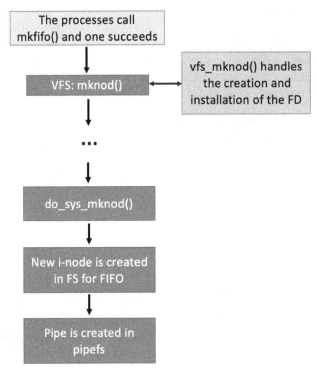

Figure 3.7 – Named pipe creation system operations

This diagram, as well as the next one, gives you an example of why the anonymous pipe is considered a bit more lightweight. See how many functions calls there are between the initial system call from the process caller until the actual FS inode operation is executed. That said, together with the additional effort to close and delete files, it is easy to conclude that even the related code is larger. Still, the named pipe is used for persistency and communication between different processes, including ones that don't have a parent-child relationship. Just think about it – you have the communication resource endpoint in the FS, you know its character name, and then you only have to open it from two independent processes, and start the data transfer. A similar approach is used by other IPC mechanisms, as we will discuss later in *Chapter 7*. Until then, check out the following diagram to see how many operations there are between the simple open() function and the creation of the FIFO buffer in the kernel:

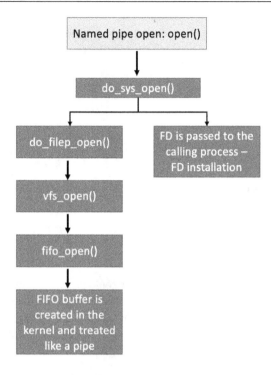

Figure 3.8 – Named pipe opening and transformation to pipe

The filesystem library doesn't allow you to directly work with the file descriptors. At the same time, the system calls expect them. Someday, it might be different in the C++ Standard.

> **Note**
>
> There's an already known non-standard approach to associating a file descriptor with `iostream`. You can refer to it here: `http://www.josuttis.com/cppcode/fdstream.html`.

We will use the next section to provide a brief overview of what happens when communication through a pipe is disturbed.

Briefly observing signal handling

Signals in Linux are a powerful and simple way to synchronize processes through software interrupts sent to them, indicating that an important event has occurred. They have a different nature, depending on their roles. Some of them are ignorable, while others are not and cause a process to be blocked, unblocked, or terminated. We discussed those behaviors in the previous chapter, but is there something we could do to gracefully handle them? We will use the anonymous pipe example to trigger a `SIGPIPE` signal.

Let's see the following example:

```
...
void handle_sigpipe(int sig) { // {1}
    printf("SIGPIPE handled!\n");
}
int main() {
    int an_pipe[2] = {0};
    char buff[BUFF_LEN + 1] = {0};
    if (pipe(an_pipe) == 0) {
        int pid = fork();
        if (pid == 0) {
            close(an_pipe[pipeOut]); // {2}
            close(an_pipe[pipeIn]);
        }
```

We define a SIGPIPE handler (marker {1}), where we could provide additional functionality if this signal is triggered. We intentionally close both the pipe endpoints of the child, so there's no process that would read from it. Then, we declare a signal action, which maps the signal handler to the action itself (markers {3} and {4}). We provide some time for the child to close the file descriptors, and then we try to write in the **pipe**:

```
    else {
        struct sigaction act = {0};
        sigemptyset(&act.sa_mask);
        act.sa_handler = handle_sigpipe; // {3}
        if(sigaction(SIGPIPE, &act, 0) == -1) {// {4}
            perror("sigaction"); return (1);
        }
        close(an_pipe[pipeIn]);
        sleep(1);
        const char *msg = {"Sending message to child!"};
        write(an_pipe[pipeOut], msg, strlen(msg) + 1);
// {5} ...
```

The kernel will trigger `SIGPIPE`, which intends to block the parent until there's someone to read from it. In this case, we print out a message, telling the user that the signal is received and the parent process will be terminated. Actually, this is the default behavior to handle such a signal. We use the handle to inform the user accordingly:

```
$ ./sighandler_test
SIGPIPE handled!
```

However, we can also ignore the signal through the following simple change on marker {3}:

```
act.sa_handler = SIG_IGN; // {3}
```

Calling the program once again will not trigger the handler, which means that the signal is ignored and the process will continue as per its workflow. You can use both approaches in your code, but be careful – some signals cannot be ignored. We will use this knowledge later in the book.

Summary

In this chapter, we didn't show any examples of file data modifications through C++. Our goals were mostly related to explaining the different Linux FS entities. We use the C++ filesystem library to enrich the knowledge in this direction – for example, improving system programming awareness. You learned about the roles of the different FS objects and their specifics. You also have the C++ instruments to manage file resources and level up your abstraction. There were also some hands-on examples of how to communicate between processes through anonymous and named pipes. Their implementation at the OS level was discussed as well, and we briefly explored signal handling in Linux.

In the next chapter, we will finally dive deeper into the C++ language, laying the foundations for its safe and secure usage, according to the latest standard. Later in the book, we will revisit some code segments shown in this chapter. We will continuously improve them through the usage of new C++ features.

4

Diving Deep into the C++ Object

In this chapter, we will pay special attention to the object in the C++ language. But what makes the object in C++ so special that we should pay so much attention to it? Well, considering the fact that C++ supports the object-oriented programming paradigm, it is assumed that the object itself takes a central position in the structure of the language. You will see that there are many specifics around objects in C++.

In this chapter, we will delve into the fundamental aspects of objects in C++. We will start by examining how the C++ standard specifies the definition of an object. Moving on from there, we will take a closer look at the different types of object initializations, such as aggregate, direct, and copy initialization, and their use cases.

We will also explore the concept of storage duration for objects. Additionally, we will take a look at the scope and lifetime of objects in C++. We will also see what references are and how they correlate to objects.

As we progress further, we will learn about temporary objects and why it is important to handle them with care, and the concept of function objects and lambdas in C++. We will explore an example of how to use lambdas with a **Standard Template Library** (**STL**) algorithm, which will help us gain a comprehensive understanding of how to leverage these powerful features to create more efficient and optimized code.

By the end of this chapter, you will have a clear understanding of the fundamental concepts of objects in C++, and you will be familiar with some techniques you can use to create more robust and efficient code.

In this chapter, we will cover the following topics:

- The C++ object model
- Scope, storage duration, and lifetimes
- Functors and lambdas in C++

Alright, it's time to begin!

Technical requirements

All examples in this chapter have been tested in an environment with the following configuration:

- Linux Mint 21 Cinnamon edition

- GCC 12.2 with compiler flags - -std=c++20

- A stable internet connection

- Please make sure your environment uses these versions or later. For all the examples you can alternatively use https://godbolt.org/.

- All code examples in this chapter are available for download from https://github.com/PacktPublishing/C-Programming-for-Linux-Systems/tree/main/Chapter%204.

Understanding the C++ object model

C++ programs involve the creation, manipulation, and destruction of various entities known as *objects*. An object in C++ possesses several attributes such as *type*, *size*, *storage duration*, *lifetime*, *alignment requirements*, and *value*. The *name* of the object is *optional*.

The lifetime of the named object is bounded by its storage duration, and if the object doesn't have a name, it is considered a *temporary* object. However, not all entities in C++ are considered objects. For example, the reference is one such non-object.

First, let's take a brief look at the terminology because it is important to be aware of it, as it will help us in our daily work with the C++ language.

Declaration versus definition

In C++, the terms *declaration* and *definition* are often used to refer to different aspects of a variable, function, or class. Here's what each term means:

- **Declaration**: A declaration introduces a name into a program and specifies the type of the variable, function, or class, such as the following:

    ```
    extern int x;
    void foo(int arg);
    struct Point;
    ```

    In the preceding example, x, foo, and Point are all *declared* but not defined. The extern keyword in the variable declaration indicates that x is defined elsewhere in the program. In declaration, no memory is allocated.

- **Definition**: A definition provides the actual implementation for a name that has been declared. It reserves memory for variables, allocates code space for functions, and defines the layout of classes, such as the following:

```
int x;
void foo(int arg) {
    // function body
}
struct Point {
    // struct members and methods
};
```

In the preceding example, x, foo, and Point are all *defined*.

So, the *declaration* introduces a name and specifies its type, while the *definition* provides the actual implementation and allocates memory for the object.

Now that we are familiar with the terminology, let's dive deep into the specifics of the objects in C++.

Scope, storage duration, and lifetimes

Each object or reference in a C++ program has a specific region in the program where it is visible and accessible, a specific lifetime, and a specific type of memory it occupies. Let's take a closer look at each of them.

Scope

In C++, the scope of a variable, function, or class refers to the region of the program where the name of the entity is visible and can be accessed without qualification. The scope rules determine which identifiers are visible and accessible in different parts of the program. The standard defines several types of scopes in C++. Some of them are as follows:

- **Global**: Variables, functions, and classes declared outside any function or class have global scope. They can be accessed from any part of the program, such as the following:

```
int x = 1; // global variable
void foo() {
    std::cout << x << std::endl; // access global
        variable
}
```

- **Function**: Variables declared inside a function have function scope. They can be accessed only within the function where they are declared, such as the following:

```
void foo() {
    int x = 1; // local variable
    std::cout << x << std::endl; // access local
      variable
}
```

- **Block**: Variables declared inside a block, which is a sequence of statements enclosed in curly braces ({ }), have block scope. They can be accessed only within the block where they are declared, or in inner blocks if there are any, such as the following:

```
void foo() {
    int x = 2; // local variable with function scope
    {
        int y = 4; // local variable with block scope
    }
}
```

These are some of the scopes we use in C++. Now, let's see what storage duration means in C++.

Storage duration

In C++, *storage duration* refers to the lifetime of an object, or how long it exists in memory. There are four types of storage duration:

- **Automatic**: These objects are created when a program enters the block in which they are declared, and they are destroyed when the block is exited. Examples include local variables declared *without* the static keyword and function parameters.

- **Static**: These objects are created either when a program starts or when the program execution reaches this stage for the first time. Also, they are destroyed when the program terminates. They are stored in a global memory area and persist throughout the program's lifetime. Examples include global variables and variables declared *with* the static keyword inside a function.

- **Dynamic**: These objects are created with the new operator and destroyed with the delete operator. They exist on the heap and can be accessed by multiple parts of a program.

- **Thread-local**: These objects are created when a thread is created and destroyed when the thread terminates. They are like objects with static storage duration, but they are specific to a particular thread.

Here is an example that illustrates the different types of storage duration:

```cpp
#include <iostream>
int global_var = 1; // Static storage duration
void foo() {
    int automatic_var = 2;
    static int static_var = 3;
    int* dynamic_var = new int(4);
    std::cout << "Automatic var: " << automatic_var <<
        '\n';
    std::cout << "Static var: " << static_var << '\n';
    std::cout << "Dynamic var: " << *dynamic_var << '\n';
    delete dynamic_var;
}
int main() {
    foo();
    std::cout << "Global var: " << global_var << '\n';
    return 0;
}
```

In this example, `global_var` has static storage duration because it is a global variable. `automatic_var` has automatic storage duration because it is declared inside the `foo` function. `static_var` also has static storage duration, but it retains its value between calls to `foo` because of the `static` keyword. `dynamic_var` itself has an automatic storage duration, but the allocated memory that it points to has dynamic storage duration because it is allocated with the `new` operator. When `foo` returns, `automatic_var` is automatically destroyed, `dynamic_var` is destroyed with the help of the `delete` operator, while `static_var` and `global_var` persist throughout a program's lifetime.

Lifetime

The term *lifetime* refers to the duration of the existence of an object or a reference within a program. Every object and reference in C++ has a specific lifetime. The lifetime of an object begins when memory is allocated for it, and it is initialized. If the object's type has a constructor, then the lifetime begins when the constructor is successfully completed. The lifetime of an object ends either when its destructor is called or, if no destructor exists, when it is destroyed. Thus, an object's lifetime is equivalent to or smaller than the duration of its storage. Similarly, the lifetime of a reference begins when its initialization is completed and ends up like a scalar object.

The object

Each object is created by a definition statement that introduces, creates, and optionally initializes a *variable*. A variable is an *object* or a *reference* that is not a non-static data member, and it is introduced by a declaration (`Object - cppreference.com`).

Let's define a simple variable and create an object from it:

```
void foo() {
    int x;
}
```

We have defined and, at the same time, instantiated an object from an integer type on the stack of the `foo()` function. Each object in C++ occupies a certain amount of memory at a specific memory region. Being on the stack, this object has an automatic storage duration. In our example, it means that the object will be created when the function starts and will be automatically destroyed when the function ends. When it is instantiated, it uses some amount of memory. This amount is a compile-time known value, and it can be acquired with the `sizeof` operator. Keep in mind that the size of some types can vary depending on the underlying hardware where your program runs, so if you need to be sure of the size, always use the operator to calculate it. Such an example is the fundamental `int` type. The standard says that the size of the `int` type can't be less than 16 bits. For Linux Mint 21 with GCC 12.2, in which the examples of this chapter are run, the used underlying data model is LP64. This means that `int` is 4 bytes, and `long` and `pointer` are 8 bytes. In the next example, we demonstrate the size of the types mentioned earlier. In order to compile and run this code, you have to pass it in a function:

```
int i;
long l;
char* p;
std::cout << "sizeof(int) = " << sizeof(int) << "; sizeof(i) = " <<
sizeof(i) << '\n';
std::cout << "sizeof(long) = " << sizeof(long) << "; sizeof(l) = " <<
sizeof(l) << '\n';
std::cout << "sizeof(char*) = " << sizeof(char*) << "; sizeof(p) = "
<< sizeof(p) << '\n';
```

Here is the output of the example:

```
sizeof(int) = 4; sizeof(i) = 4
sizeof(long) = 8; sizeof(l) = 8
sizeof(char*) = 8; sizeof(p) = 8
```

Nothing surprising so far. `int` is 4 bytes, but the pointer, no matter which type it points to, is 8 bytes.

Now, let's define several structures and check their memory footprint:

```
struct Empty {};
struct Padding {
    long test;
    char m;
};
```

```
struct Virt {
    virtual char GetChar() const { return ch; }
    char ch;
};
void foo() {
    std::cout << "Empty: " << sizeof(Empty) << '\n';
    std::cout << "Padding: " << sizeof(Padding) << '\n';
    std::cout << "Virt: " << sizeof(Virt) << '\n';
}
```

We have defined three structures – Empty, Padding, and Virt. The Empty structure, as the name suggests, is just an empty structure without any members in it. The Padding structure contains two members – long and char. As we saw from the previous example, in my testing environment, long is 8 bytes and char is 1 byte. Finally, the Virt structure has only one member of type char and one virtual method. Structure and class methods are not part of the object itself. They reside in the text segment rather than in the memory occupied by the object. Let's execute the earlier code and see the result:

```
Empty: 1
Padding: 16
Virt: 16
```

We can see that all the objects occupy memory. Even the empty one! This is guaranteed by the standard because any object in the system has to have an address on which it resides. If it doesn't occupy any memory, then no address can be assigned to it. Therefore, at least 1 byte is reserved for every object in the program.

The Padding structure occupies more memory than the sum of its members' memory. This is because the compilers are free to place the objects on an address, which requires less instruction arithmetic in order to be accessed faster. Therefore, they add padding bytes to the size of the type if this is required.

Finally, the Virt structure contains only one member, which has type char. However, the structure occupies the same amount of memory as the Padding structure. This is a result of how the mechanics of the polymorphism are implemented in C++. The structure contains a virtual method that notifies the compiler that this user-defined type will be used polymorphically. As a result, the compiler injects in every instantiated object from this type a pointer to a table, with the addresses of all the virtual methods of the class.

As a result of all these examples, we can conclude that each object occupies memory once it is instantiated, and the size of the memory can vary depending on the underlying system and the definition of the type.

Next, we will get familiar with references in C++ and how they differ from objects in the language.

The reference

In the previous section, we found out that we can declare a variable not only from an object but also from a reference. But what is a *reference* in terms of C++? According to the standard, a reference variable is an *alias* to an already-existing object or function. This means that we can use aliases to work with objects without having a difference in the syntax, rather than working with pointers to objects where the syntax is quite different. Let's have a look in the following example. In order to compile and run it, you need to invoke it from a function:

```
char c;
char& r_c{c};
char* p_c;
std::cout << "sizeof(char) = " << sizeof(char) << "; sizeof(c) = " <<
sizeof(c) << '\n';
std::cout << "sizeof(char&) = " << sizeof(char&) << "; sizeof(r_c) = "
<< sizeof(r_c) << '\n';
std::cout << "sizeof(char*) = " << sizeof(char*) << "; sizeof(p_c) = "
<< sizeof(p_c) << '\n';
```

In this example, we declare three variables – a character, a reference to a character, and a pointer to a character. An important detail when working with reference variables is that at the point of its declaration, we must also initialize it with the object it will refer to. From this moment on, every operation invoked on the reference variable is actually invoked on the aliased object. But what indeed is an alias? Does it occupy memory just like the pointer does? Well, this is a gray area. The standard says that the references, unlike objects, do not always occupy storage. However, the compiler may allocate storage if required to implement the intended semantics. As a result of this, you *can't use* the sizeof operator to get the size of a reference:

```
sizeof(char) = 1; sizeof(c) = 1
sizeof(char&) = 1; sizeof(r_c) = 1
sizeof(char*) = 8; sizeof(p_c) = 8
```

You can see that the pointer size matches the expectation rather than the size of the reference type, where it matches the size of the type to which it has an alias.

Understanding why initialization matters

Initialization is the process of setting the initial value of an object during its construction. In C++, there are several types of initializations depending mostly on the following:

- The storage duration which the object belongs to
- The definition of the object

Knowing the different types of initializations and exactly when they happen will certainly make you more confident in writing predictable code.

Let's look at a few examples of various types of initializations that the C++ language supports. This will make it clearer when initialization occurs.

Default initialization

In the next example, you can see a *default initialization*. In order to run and test this code, you have to invoke the `foo()` method:

```
struct Point {
    double x;
    double y;
};
void foo() {
    long a; // {1}
    Point p1; // {2}
    std::cout << "{1}: " << a << '\n';
    std::cout << "{2}: " << p1.x << ", " << p1.y << '\n';
}
```

In marker {1}, we have declared a stack variable from type `long`. The type of initialization that will apply on an object depends mainly on the following:

- **The storage duration it occupies**: This means that different initialization policies may apply, depending on whether the object lives on the stack, in the global space, and so on

- **The type of declaration**: This means that different initialization policies may apply, depending on how syntactically we have declared a variable – whether we have specified an `init` value, how exactly we have passed that `init` value, and so on

The `long a;` variable in our example has automatic storage duration, meaning it lives on the function's stack. In its declaration, we haven't specified any initialization value. For such objects, we will apply *default initialization*. When an object is default-initialized, the C++ compiler will generate code that calls the default constructor of the object's type if one exists. However, since `long` is a fundamental C++ type that lacks a default constructor, the C++ runtime *does not perform any initialization on it*, resulting in an *unpredictable value*. This means that the value that will be used for initialization is not specified and could be literally any. This is also the case with the `Point p1;` object, which is a user-defined type, but we did not specify a default constructor for it. The `Point` structure is a so-called **Plain Old Data (POD)** type because it is fully compatible with the structures from the C language. For such types, the compiler will generate a *trivial default constructor* for you, which effectively does nothing when called.

The output of the earlier example will look like this:

```
{1}: 1
{2}: 4.19164e-318, 4.3211e-320
```

In my environment, the a and p1 objects both have indeterministic values. If you run the example of your own, you will possibly get different values.

Direct initialization

In our next example, we will learn about C++ *direct initialization*. In order to run and test this code, you have to invoke the foo() method again. Bear in mind that the int c_warn{2.2}; // {4.2} statement from this example should be commented out in order to compile successfully:

```
void foo() {
    int b(1);           // {3.1}
    int b_trunc(1.2);  // {3.2}
    int c{2};           // {4.1}
    int c_warn{2.2};    // {4.2}

    std::cout << "{3.1}: " << b << '\n';
    std::cout << "{3.2}: " << b_trunc << '\n';
    std::cout << "{4.1}: " << c << '\n';
}
```

In the first statement from the example, int b(1);, we have defined a variable of type int, and we have explicitly initialized it with a value of 1. This is the *direct initialization* that we have known since the dawn of the C++ language. In order to invoke it, you have to specify the initialization value in parentheses, and that value has to match some of the conversion constructors of the object's type. These conversion constructors can be compiler-generated. In our example, we use int, which is a fundamental C++ type and supports direct initialization with integer values. As a result, the b object will be initialized with a value of 1, so nothing new so far.

With the next statement, we declare an int b_trunc(1.2); variable, but this time, we initialize it with a floating-point value of 1.2. This statement works fine and declares a variable of type int and initializes it with a value of… 1! Yes, according to the C++ standard, which tries to be as compatible as possible with the C language for features that are present in both languages, the value is *truncated down* to its mantissa. In some cases, it could be useful to initialize an integer object with a floating-point value, but in others, this could be an inadvertent error. In such a case, we will expect the compiler to warn us that we are potentially doing something wrong. Therefore, C++11 introduced the so-called *uniform initialization*.

In the next statement from the example, int c{2};, we again declare a variable of type int, but we initialize it using curly braces rather than parentheses. This notifies the compiler to invoke *direct list initialization*, which is a kind of uniform initialization. It is a named list initialization because it can be used as an initialization list of values of different types to initialize complex objects.

One reason to prefer using uniform initialization wherever this is possible is visible in the next statement from the example:

```
int c_warn{2.2};  // {4.2}
```

As we just saw, using direct initialization to initialize an object of a specific type with a value of a wider type leads to a silently truncated initialized value. In some situations, this can lead to bugs. One way to avoid this potential side effect is to use uniform initialization instead. In our example, we defined a variable of type `int` and again initialized it with a floating-point value. However, this time, the compiler will not silently initialize c_warn with a value of 2, but it will generate an error similar to this:

```
error: narrowing conversion of '2.2000000000000002e+0' from 'double'
to 'int' [-Wnarrowing]
```

The error is produced because we try to perform a narrowing conversion in the initialization of an `int` variable with a `double` value. Therefore, it is safer to use uniform initialization over a direct one because it protects you from narrowing conversions during initialization.

Zero and aggregate initialization

Let's see another initialization example. We will initialize an object that holds the personal data for `Person` and a few integer objects:

```
struct Person {
    std::string name;
    int age;
};
void init() {
    int zero1{}; // {1}
    int zero2 = int(); // {2}
    int zero3 = int{}; // {3}
    Person nick{"Nick L.", 42}; // {4}
    Person john{.name{"John M."}, .age{24}}; // {5}
}
```

As we already explained, the objects with automatic storage duration and without explicit initialization get random initialization values. In this example, from markers {1} to {3}, we have initialized the objects using *zero initialization*, which effectively sets their values to zero. Zero initialization happens for non-class, built-in types and for the members of user-defined types that have no constructors. Preferably use curly brace notation and uniform initialization, such as marker {1}, when you need to zero-initialize your objects, rather than copying zero initialization, such as markers {2} and {3}.

Statement {4} demonstrates another method of initialization called *aggregate initialization*. It allows us to initialize an aggregate object using uniform initialization notation. An aggregate is considered any object that is an array or a class type that has no user-declared or inherited constructors; all of its non-static members are publicly visible, and it has no virtual base classes and no virtual methods. Statement {5} performs another way of *aggregate initialization* but using *designators*. The designators explicitly specify the members being initialized, and the order of the designators in the initialization should follow the order of the declaration of the members in the structure.

Copy initialization

Copy initialization occurs when an object of a specific type is initialized by another object of the same type. Let's look at the following examples of syntax that triggers copy initialization. In order to run and test this code, you have to invoke the `foo()` method:

```
void foo() {
    int c{2};

    int d(c);      // {1}
    int e{d};      // {2}
    int f = e;     // {3}
    int f1 = {d};  // {4}
}
```

Markers {1} and {3} from this example demonstrate the well-known copy initialization present in the language even before C++11. An object of type `int` is initialized by another object of the same type. As we already saw, this kind of initialization doesn't give any protection against types narrowing. This means that our `int` objects can be silently initialized by `double` objects, which will lead to narrowing. Fortunately, this is not the case with markers {2} and {4}. They use uniform copy initialization, which forces the compiler to verify that the initialization object is from the same type as the object being initialized.

Now, let's look at several scenarios of copy initialization for user-defined types. We have defined two classes – Person and Employee. The Person class has one user-defined constructor that receives a reference to the `std::string` parameter, used to initialize the name of the person. The constructor is marked as `explicit`. This means that it will be used only as a non-converting constructor. The *converting constructor* is a constructor that makes an implicit conversion from its argument types to its class types.

The other class, Employee, has two constructors, one of which gets a reference to a Person object, while the other is a copy constructor. The copy constructor is also marked as `explicit`:

```
class Person {
public:
    explicit Person(const std::string&  the_name) : name{
        the_name} {}
private:
    std::string name;
};
class Employee {
public:
    Employee(const Person& p) : p{p} {}
    explicit Employee(const Employee& e) : p{e.p} {}
private:
    Person p;
};
```

Let's use these two classes in different initialization scenarios. In order to run and test this code, you have to rework and invoke the `foo()` method again:

```
void foo() {
    Person john{"John M."};

    Employee staff1{john};          // {1}
    // Employee staff2{std::string{"George"}};   // {2}
    Employee staff3{staff1};        // {3}
    // Employee staff4 = staff1;    // {4}
    // Employee staff5 = {staff1};  // {5}
}
```

We first defined a `Person` object named `john`, and in marker {1}, we initialize an `Employee` object using `john`. This is actually valid because the `Employee` class has a constructor that accepts the `Person` objects. The next statement, marker {2}, which is commented out, gets as an argument an object of type `std::string`, but the compiler will generate an error. This is because the `Employee` class doesn't have a constructor that gets a string object. It has a converting constructor from the `Person` object. However, the `Person` constructor is marked as `explicit`, and it is not allowed to be used in implicit type conversions, so the compilation will fail.

The next statement, marker {3}, will compile successfully because `Employee` is copy-constructed and initialized by another `Employee` object without any implicit type conversions.

The final two statements from the example – markers {4} and {5} – are also commented out to avoid compilation errors. The reason for the compiler error is that the copy constructor of the `Employee` class is also marked as `explicit`. This means that copy construction and initialization using equal `"="` sign is not allowed for explicit copy constructors. Only direct copy initialization is permitted.

Now that we are familiar with what the scope, storage duration, and lifetime of the object are, we can have a look at some slightly different kinds of objects, which behave more like functions rather than objects – functors and lambdas.

Functors and lambdas

This section will delve into functional objects – their definition, usefulness, and proper usage. We'll begin by examining an example of a functional object used with an STL algorithm and discuss potential issues, such as the creation of temporary objects and dangling references. After that, we'll move on to exploring lambda expressions – what they are, how to use them, and specific situations where they can be especially advantageous.

Exploring functional objects

In the *Scope, storage duration, and lifetimes* section, we looked at various types of object initialization in C++, but our focus was mostly on objects that represent data, such as integers or coordinates. In this section, we'll shift our attention to another type of object – those designed to be *callable*, such as a function, but with a crucial difference: they can maintain a state between different function calls. These objects are known as *functional objects* or *functors*. We'll start by defining a functor and then use it to compute the mean value of a vector containing floating-point numbers:

```cpp
#include <iostream>
#include <vector>
#include <algorithm>
#include <cmath>
#include <source_location>

struct Mean {
    Mean() = default;
    void operator()(const double& val) {
        std::cout <<  std::source_location::current()
            .function_name() << " of " << this << '\n';
        sum += val;
        ++count;
    }
private:
    double sum{};
    int count{};
    friend std::ostream& operator<<(std::ostream& os, const
      Mean& a);
};
std::ostream& operator<<(std::ostream& os, const Mean& a) {
    double mean{std::nan("")};
    if (a.count > 0) {
        mean = a.sum / a.count;
    }
    os << mean;
    return os;
}
int main() {
    Mean calc_mean;
    std::vector v1{1.0, 2.5, 4.0, 5.5};
    std::for_each(v1.begin(), v1.end(), calc_mean);
    std::cout << "The mean value is: " << calc_mean <<
      '\n';
    return 0;
}
```

The functor is an object like any other. It has a type, storage duration, and scope. In order to define a functor, you have to either define a struct or class of a user-defined type, and this type must have implemented a *function call operator*:

```
operator()
```

In our example, we defined `struct Mean` with two members in it, which are zero-initialized. The first one, `sum`, will be used to accumulate the input data that this object receives during the function call operator invocations, preserving it between different invocations. And the other member, `count`, will be used to count the number of invocations of the function call operator.

The definition of the function call operator gets one parameter of a `double` type, and then the method prints its name and adds the input value to the already accumulated value from the previous invocations. Finally, it increments the invocation counter.

The function call operator doesn't return any type and is not defined as a `const` method because it mutates the state of the `Mean` object. We also overloaded the stream extraction operator, which will be used to report the calculated mean value to the standard output. If there is no accumulated value, then `nan` ("not a number") will be printed:

```
std::ostream& operator<<(std::ostream& os, const Mean& a)
```

Please keep in mind that the operator is overloaded outside of the `Mean` structure, and it is declared as a *friend* method to it. This is because it needs to get `std::ostream` as a left-hand argument and the `Mean` parameter as the right argument, and therefore, it can't be implemented as a member method. It's defined as *friend* because it has to have access to the *private* members of the `Mean` structure.

In order to calculate the mean value, our algorithm iterates over all values in the vector using the `std::for_each` STL algorithm. `std::for_each` expects to receive a container on which to operate and function, which will be invoked with each of the elements from the container; therefore, this function must accept one parameter as an input argument.

In the main method, we define an object of type `Mean calc_mean;`, which will be used to calculate the mean value of `std::vector v1{1.0, 2.5, 4.0, 5.5};`. As you can see, we don't need to explicitly specify the template argument type of the `std::vector` class because it is automatically deduced by the type of the initializer list values it is initialized with. In our case, these are `double` values.

> **Important note**
> Please note that since C++17, the automatic class template argument deduction is already supported, based on the type of its initializer.

We expect that the program will invoke the function operator of the `Mean` object for each element in the vector. The function operator will accumulate all values, and when the result is printed out, it will be 3.25. Let's see the output of the program:

```
void Mean::operator()(const double&) of 0x7ffc571a64e0
void Mean::operator()(const double&) of 0x7ffc571a64e0
void Mean::operator()(const double&) of 0x7ffc571a64e0
void Mean::operator()(const double&) of 0x7ffc571a64e0
The mean value is: nan
```

As we expected, the operator function call is invoked for each of the elements from the vector, but surprisingly, there is no calculated mean value. In order to get a better understanding of what went wrong with the calculation, we need to see what has happened with the `calc_mean` object, which has been used by the `std::for_each` algorithm.

Beware of temporaries

For the sake of investigation, in the Mean structure, we need to define the copy and move constructors, the move operator, and a destructor, whose only goal will be to print whether they are invoked and the address of the object that they belong to. We also need to add markers for when the calculation starts and when it finishes. Let's see the reworked example:

```
struct Mean {
    Mean() noexcept {
        std::cout <<  std::source_location::current()
            .function_name() << " of " << this << '\n';
    }
    Mean(Mean&& a) noexcept : sum{a.sum}, count{a.count} {
        std::cout <<  std::source_location::current()
            .function_name() << " from: " << &a << " to: " <<
                this << '\n';
        a.sum = 0;
        a.count = -1;
    }
    Mean& operator=(Mean&& a) noexcept {
        std::cout <<  std::source_location::current()
            .function_name() << " from: " << &a << " to: " <<
                this << '\n';
        sum = a.sum;
        count = a.count;
        return *this;
    }
    Mean(const Mean& a) noexcept : sum{a.sum},
        count{a.count} {
```

```
        std::cout <<  std::source_location::current()
          .function_name() << " from: " << &a << " to: " <<
            this << '\n';
    }
    ~Mean() noexcept {
        std::cout <<  std::source_location::current()
          .function_name() << " of " << this << '\n';
    }
    void operator()(const double& val) {
        std::cout <<  std::source_location::current()
          .function_name() << " of " << this << '\n';
        sum += val;
        ++count;
    }
private:
    double sum{};
    int count{};
    friend std::ostream& operator<<(std::ostream& os, const
      Mean& a);
};
```

We also need to slightly change the `main()` method implementation:

```
int main() {
    Mean calc_mean;
    std::vector v1{1.0, 2.5, 4.0, 5.5};
    std::cout << "Start calculation\n";
    std::for_each(v1.begin(), v1.end(), calc_mean);
    std::cout << "Finish calculation\n";
    std::cout << "The mean value is: " << calc_mean <<
      '\n';
    return 0;
}
```

When we re-execute the already reworked program, we get the following output:

```
Mean::Mean() of 0x7ffef7956c50
Start calculation
Mean::Mean(const Mean&) from: 0x7ffef7956c50 to: 0x7ffef7956ca0
void Mean::operator()(const double&) of 0x7ffef7956ca0
void Mean::operator()(const double&) of 0x7ffef7956ca0
void Mean::operator()(const double&) of 0x7ffef7956ca0
void Mean::operator()(const double&) of 0x7ffef7956ca0
Mean::Mean(Mean&&) from: 0x7ffef7956ca0 to: 0x7ffef7956c90
```

```
Mean::~Mean() of 0x7ffef7956c90
Mean::~Mean() of 0x7ffef7956ca0
Finish calculation
The mean value is: nan
Mean::~Mean() of 0x7ffef7956c50
```

As we expected, the program starts with the construction of the object with the address 0x7ffef7956c50, then the calculation is started, and we can see that a copy constructor is invoked. This is because std::for_each, like many other algorithms in the standard library, is a template method that gets its functor by value. Here is what the standard says about its prototype:

```
template< class InputIt, class UnaryFunction >
constexpr UnaryFunction for_each( InputIt first, InputIt
  last, UnaryFunction f );
```

This means that no matter what calculation it does, all the accumulated values will be stored in the copied object rather than the original. Actually, the object created by this copy constructor is just a *temporary object*. Temporary objects are unnamed objects that are automatically created and destroyed by the compiler. They often lead to side effects that are not trivially recognizable by the developers. Temporary objects are most frequently created as a result of implicit conversions of arguments and functions' returned values. They frequently have a limited lifetime, till the end of the statement they are created by, if they are not bound to some named reference. So, be careful with them because they can impact the performance of your program, but more importantly, they can lead to unexpected behavior, as in our example.

From the preceding code, we can see that all the accumulations are done in the newly created temporary object. Once the std::for_each method finishes its execution, a move constructor of a new temporary object is invoked. This happens because, according to the definition of std::for_each, the passed-by value input functor is returned back as a result of the operation. So, if we need to get the accumulated value back to the original object, we need to assign the return value of std::for_each back to the original object – calc_mean:

```
calc_mean = std::for_each(v1.begin(), v1.end(), calc_mean);
```

Finally, the result is what we expected but at the price of creating several temporary objects:

```
Finish calculation
The mean value is: 3.25
```

In our example, this is not a problem, but for really complex objects where temporary object creation involves expensive and potentially slow operations, such as resource acquisition, this could be problematic.

Next, let's have a look at how we can improve our example by avoiding unnecessary copy operations.

Passing by reference

One way to improve the earlier example is to pass the functor not by value but by reference. This will avoid the creation of unnecessary temporary objects:

```
using VecCIter = std::vector<double>::const_iterator;
std::for_each<VecCIter, Mean&>(v1.begin(), v1.end(),
  calc_mean);
```

In order to pass by reference the Mean object, you have to explicitly state your intention to the compiler by explicitly specifying that the Mean template parameter is a reference. Otherwise, the automatic template argument deduction will deduce that you are passing by value. As a result, this forces you to avoid using automatic class template argument deduction and makes your code harder to read. Fortunately, the standard provides a solution for this:

```
std::for_each(v1.begin(), v1.end(), std::ref(calc_mean));
```

We need to use the factory method, std::ref, for the creation of the std::reference_wrapper objects. std::reference_wrapper is a class template that wraps a reference inside an assignable, copyable object. It's commonly used to store references within standard containers that can't typically hold them. The usage of std::ref, in our example, eliminates the need to explicitly specify that the functor template parameter of std::for_each is a reference type rather than a value. Here is the result of our refactoring:

```
Mean::Mean() of 0x7ffe7415a180
Start calculation
void Mean::operator()(const double&) of 0x7ffe7415a180
void Mean::operator()(const double&) of 0x7ffe7415a180
void Mean::operator()(const double&) of 0x7ffe7415a180
void Mean::operator()(const double&) of 0x7ffe7415a180
Finish calculation
The mean value is: 3.25
Mean::~Mean() of 0x7ffe7415a180
```

As you can see, there is no additional creation and destruction of temporary objects because the algorithm works directly with the reference of the calc_mean object.

> **Beware of dangling references**
>
> Always make sure that the references you pass across the program will refer to live objects until they are in use!

Functors are just one option that we can use in our example. There is also another approach here that can make our code even more expressive. These are lambda expressions. Let's have a look at them.

Lambda expressions

The *lambda expression,* or just *lambda* in C++, is a concise way to define an *anonymous function* or *functor* inline, which can be used immediately or assigned to a variable for later use. It allows programmers to write small, throwaway functions on the fly without having to define a named function or a `functor` class. Lambdas are commonly used with algorithms and containers from the standard library, allowing for more concise and expressive code.

Let's define a simple lambda that just prints to the standard output:

```cpp
auto min_lambda = [](const auto& name) -> void {
    std::cout << name << " lambda.\n";
};
min_lambda("Simple");
```

Each lambda expression is an *object,* which means that it has a lifetime and occupies memory. Every defined lambda is a de facto functor class definition, and as such, it has a *unique type.* There can't be two or more lambdas with the same *type* in a program. This *type* name is platform-specific, and therefore, if you need to assign a lambda to a variable, you have to define this variable with the `auto` specifier.

The syntax of a lambda consists of the `[ ]` symbol, which is followed by an optional capture list, an optional parameter list, an optional return type, an optional *mutable* specifier, and a function body. Lambdas can capture variables from the outer scope by value or by reference, and they can also have a return type deduction or an explicit return type, which we will see next.

Capturing the outer scope

Lambdas can gain access to other objects in the scope where they're defined by utilizing a *capture list.* If the capture list is empty, then no objects are captured. Global objects are always visible in lambdas without needing to be explicitly captured. When defining the capture list, you can choose to capture objects by *value* or by *reference,* or even a mixture of both.

When capturing variables by value in a lambda expression, the variables are *copied* into the lambda object at the *moment of its definition.* Any modifications made to the original variables after the lambda is defined won't affect the copies stored inside it. All captured objects are, by default, *read-only,* and to modify them, you must explicitly specify the lambda as *mutable.*

Another option to capture variables is by reference, which creates a reference to every captured object inside the lambda. This allows the lambda to communicate with the outer scope, but it's crucial to ensure that the lifetime of all captured objects by reference exceeds the lifetime of the lambda to prevent *dangling references.*

Now, let's refactor the example from the previous section to calculate the mean value of a vector with floating-point numbers, using a lambda instead of a functor. In order to run the following code, you have to invoke the `foo()` method from your program:

```
void foo() {
    double mean{};
    std::vector v1{1.0, 2.5, 4.0, 5.5};
    std::string_view text{"calculating ..."};
    std::for_each(v1.begin(), v1.end(),
                    [&mean, sum{0.0}, count{0}, text](const
                        double& val) mutable {
        std::cout << text << '\n';
        sum += val;
        ++count;
        mean = sum / count;
    });
    std::cout << mean << '\n';
}
```

One of the key advantages of lambdas compared to named functions and functors is that they can be inlined in the place of their invocation. In our example, we have defined the lambda directly inside the `std::for_each` invocation statement. This approach explicitly highlights that this lambda has no other reason to exist except to serve the preceding case.

Let's get a closer look at the lambda prototype:

```
[&mean, sum{0.0}, count{0}, text](const double& val)
    mutable { … }
```

In the capture list, we have captured four objects. The first one, `mean`, is captured by reference. Putting `&` before the variable name specifies that it is captured by reference. We will use `mean` to report outside of the lambda the calculated mean value. The next two variables in the capture list, `sum` and `count`, are captured by value. If `&` doesn't precede the name of the variable, it means that it is captured by value. The only exception to this rule is when capturing the `this` pointer of a class, which will be captured by value, but the access to the class members will be by reference. As you can see, the captures, `sum` and `count`, are not defined in the outer scope; they are defined only in the scope of the lambda for the purpose of our example. Just like the functor example, they are used to store the accumulated sum and the count of the iterations. This is a convenient way to explicitly add state into your lambda for use in further calculations. Of course, you need to initialize them by passing initializers to the captures for two reasons – in order to allow the compiler to deduce their type and to get the expected result in the calculations. The implementation logic will update the values of `sum` and `count` during its execution, but as stated previously, these captures are read-only in the context of the lambda. Therefore, we cannot just mutate them without explicitly stating our intention during the lambda definition. This is done by appending the `mutable` keyword after the argument list and before the body of the lambda.

The last captured object is `text`. It is also captured by value, but this time, it is captured from the outer scope in the `foo()` method.

Once the program is executed, we have the following output:

```
calculating ...
calculating ...
calculating ...
calculating ...
3.25
```

As we expected, our lambda has been called four times, and the calculated mean value is exactly the same as the value calculated by the functor in the previous section.

There are many ways to capture objects in the capture list. The following list shows some rules that apply:

Capture	Effect
[=]	Make a **copy of all used** objects from the outer scope.
[&]	Get access to **all objects** from the outer scope **by reference**.
[a, &b]	Make a **copy** of "a" and a reference to "b".
[&, a]	Get access to all objects from the outer scope **by reference** except "a", which is **copied**.
[this]	Get access to "this" together with its members **by reference**.
[*this]	Make a **copy** of "this" together with a copy of its members.

Figure 4.1 – Ways to capture objects in a capture list

Now that we know how to properly capture the outer scope, let's get familiar with a lambda's parameter list.

Parameter list

The parameter list of a lambda is just like any other function parameter list. This is because the lambda's parameter list is effectively the parameter list of the function call operator in a functor class. You can define your lambda to accept an arbitrary list of parameters, depending on the use case you have.

Using the `auto` specifier as a parameter type of one or more of the parameters in the lambda parameter lists makes it a *generic lambda*. A generic lambda acts as a template function call operator:

```
auto sum = [](auto a, auto b) {
    return a*b;
}
```

This effectively acts as follows:

```
class platform_specific_name {
public:
    template<typename T1, typename T2>
    auto operator()(T1 a, T2 b) const {
        return a*b;
    }
};
```

With the C++20 release, if you wish you can explicitly specify the template parameters that your lambda can get. The preceding example could be rewritten as follows:

```
auto sum = []<typename T1, typename T2>(T1 a, T2 b) {
    return a*b;
}
```

Another important characteristic of lambdas is the return type. Let's see its specifics.

The return type

Specifying the return type of the lambda is *optional*. If you don't explicitly specify it, the compiler will try to deduce it for you. If it doesn't succeed, then a compiler error in type deduction will be generated. Then, you have to either change your code to allow automatic return type deduction or explicitly specify the return type of the lambda.

Here is a compiler error in return type deduction:

```
auto div = [](double x, double y) {
    if (y < 0) { return 0; }
    return x / y;
};
```

This code will not compile because the compiler will fail to automatically deduce the return type of the lambda. It's implementation logic has two execution branches. The first one returns an `integer` literal, 0, but the other one returns the result of a division, the quotient, which is a `double` number.

In order to fix this, we need to explicitly specify that the return type of the lambda is `double`.

Here is an explicitly specified return type:

```
auto div = [](double x, double y) -> double {
    if (y < 0) { return 0; }
    return x / y;
};
```

Now, for the compiler, it is clear that the return result is always converted to `double`.

Summary

In this chapter, we explored various aspects of objects in C++, including storage duration, scope, and lifetimes. We distinguished between objects and references and discussed different ways of initializing objects and when these initializations occur. Additionally, we delved into the world of functors, gaining an understanding of what they are and how to use them effectively. Building on that knowledge, we also learned about lambda expressions and their advantages over functors. We covered how to properly use both lambdas and functors with STL algorithms. Armed with this knowledge of object specifics, we can now move on to discussing error handling in C++ in the next chapter.

5
Handling Errors with C++

This chapter will focus on error handling in C++. As a programmer, you will inevitably encounter situations where you need to determine the best approach to propagate program errors. Whether you use error codes or exceptions, we will delve into them to gain a better understanding of how to use them effectively.

In this chapter, we will examine how to handle errors reported by POSIX APIs using C++. We will begin by covering the `errno` thread-local variable and the `strerror` function. After that, we will introduce `std::error_code` and `std::error_condition` and demonstrate how they help to wrap POSIX errors that come from POSIX APIs. We will also investigate custom error categories, which allow us to compare errors produced by various sources and develop platform-independent error-handling code.

As we progress, we will learn about exceptions in C++ and how to convert `std::error_code` into a `std::system_error` exception. We will also explore some best practices for working with exceptions, such as throwing exceptions by value and catching them by reference. Additionally, we will become acquainted with object slicing, a side effect that can occur when we catch exceptions by value rather than by reference. Finally, we will delve into the RAII technique in C++, which eliminates the need for a `finally` construct in the language.

By the end of this chapter, you will have a thorough understanding of the various ways to handle errors in C++, and you will be familiar with several techniques for creating error-resistant code.

Summing up, we will cover the following topics:

- Handling errors from POSIX APIs with C++
- From error codes to exceptions

Alright, it's time to begin!

Technical requirements

All examples in this chapter have been tested in an environment with the following configuration:

- Linux Mint 21 Cinnamon edition

- GCC 12.2 with compiler flags:

    - `-std=c++20`

- A stable internet connection

- Please make sure your environment is at least that recent. For all the examples, you can alternatively use `https://godbolt.org/`.

- All code examples in this chapter are available for download from `https://github.com/PacktPublishing/C-Programming-for-Linux-Systems/tree/main/Chapter%205`.

Handling errors from POSIX APIs with C++

In POSIX-compliant systems, such as Unix and Linux, error handling is based on the use of error codes and error messages to communicate errors between functions and applications.

In general, when a function encounters an error, it returns a non-zero error code and sets the `errno` global variable to a specific error value that indicates the nature of the error. The application can then use the `errno` variable to determine the cause of the error and take appropriate action.

In addition to error codes, POSIX-compliant functions often provide error messages that describe the nature of the error in more detail. These error messages are typically accessed using the `strerror` function, which takes an error code as input and returns a pointer to a sequence of characters terminated with a null character containing the corresponding error message.

The POSIX error-handling style requires developers to check for errors after each system call or function call that may fail and to handle errors in a consistent and meaningful way. This can include logging error messages, retrying failed operations, or terminating the program in the event of a critical error.

Let's look at the following example where we demonstrate how to use the `errno` variable and the `strerror()` function to handle errors from POSIX functions in C++.

The example uses the open() and close() POSIX functions, which try to open and close a file from the filesystem of our Linux test environment:

```cpp
#include <iostream>
#include <fcntl.h>
#include <unistd.h>
#include <cstring>

int main() {
    const int fd{open("no-such-file.txt", O_RDONLY)}; //
      {1}
    if (fd == -1) {
        std::cerr << "Error opening file: " <<
            strerror(errno) << '\n';
        std::cerr << "Error code: " << errno << '\n';
        return  EXIT_FAILURE;
    }
    // Do something with the file...
    if (close(fd) == -1) {
        std::cerr << "Error closing file: " <<
            strerror(errno) << '\n';
        std::cerr << "Error code: " << errno << '\n';
        return  EXIT_FAILURE;
    }
    return 0;
}
```

In this example, we attempt to open a file for reading called no-such-file.txt using the open() function; see marker {1}. In case of success, open() returns a non-negative integer, which corresponds to the file descriptor ID of the successfully opened file. If open() returns -1, we know an error occurred, so we print the error message using strerror(errno) and return the value of errno where the corresponding error code is written.

If open() succeeds, we do something with the file and then close it using the close() function. If close() returns -1, we print the error message again using strerror(errno) and return the value of errno.

This is a common error-handling technique for POSIX functions. In case of an error, they return -1 and set the errno variable with the corresponding error code. The errno variable is a *thread-local* modifiable variable of the int type. This means that it is safe for you to use it in a multithreaded environment. Each thread will have its own copy, and POSIX methods invoked by this thread will use this instance to report errors.

In order to print a meaningful message in the case of an error, we use the `strerror()` function, which accepts an integer and tries to match its value to a well-known list of descriptions of system-specific error codes. The `open()` function can report several errors and set different values to `errno` depending on the type of the occurred error. Let's see the output of the example:

```
Error opening file: No such file or directory
Error code: 2
```

As we can see, the `open()` method has failed to open the file because it doesn't exist. In this case, it sets `errno` to a value of 2, which corresponds to the ENOENT value specified in the documentation of the function. It is a good practice to explicitly set `errno` to 0 before you do a system call to ensure that after the call, you can read its real response.

Using std::error_code and std::error_condition

The C++ Standard Library provides several classes for handling errors from low-level APIs such as the POSIX interface. These classes are `std::error_code` for handling system-specific errors and `std::error_condition`, which deals with portable error codes. Let us explore both styles in more detail.

std::error_code

Let's rework our previous example in such a way that we provide a function for the creation of a directory with a specific directory path:

```cpp
#include <iostream>
#include <sys/stat.h>

std::error_code CreateDirectory(const std::string& dirPath) {
    std::error_code ecode{};
    if (mkdir(dirPath.c_str(), 0777) != 0) {
        ecode = std::error_code{errno,
            std::generic_category()}; // {1}
    }
    return ecode;
}
int main() {
    auto ecode{CreateDirectory("/tmp/test")};
    if (ecode){ // {2}
        std::cerr << "Error 1: " << ecode.message() <<
            '\n';
    }
    ecode = CreateDirectory("/tmp/test"); // {3}
    if (ecode){
```

```
            std::cerr << "Error 2: " << ecode.message() <<
               '\n';
        }

    if (ecode.value() == EEXIST) {
        std::cout << "This is platform specific and not
            portable.\n";
    }
    return 0;
}
```

Rather than the client of our new function, `CreateDirectory`, using the `errno` variable directly to determine whether the operation was successful, we will make use of a utility class provided by the Standard Library – `std::error_code`. `std::error_code` is used to store and transmit error codes as they were generated by libraries or system calls. It is a kind of wrapper class for which there are predefined categories of errors to work with. The errors returned by the POSIX functions are mostly standard and, as such, are predefined in the Standard Library. Therefore, it is straightforward to create a `std::error_code` instance from the `errno` value and specify that this value corresponds to `std::generic_category()`, as done in marker { 1 } in the preceding example. The `errno` value is de facto casted to a constant of the `std::errc` enumerator.

The created `std::error_code` object has two methods that can give you details about the underlying error. The `std::error_code::message()` method returns a meaningful string that can be used for logging purposes. The `std::error_code::value()` method, in our example, returns the value initially stored in the `errno` variable. But probably the most notable operation that the user can use from the `std::error_code` object is the predefined `operator bool()` of the class. In the case of an error stored in the object, it returns `true`; otherwise, it returns `false`.

As you can see from the preceding example, the caller of the `CreateCategory()` method checks whether an error occurred, and if so, it gets the message stored for this error; see marker { 2 }. Here, you can find the output of the program run on our test environment:

```
Error 2: File exists
This is platform specific and not portable.
```

As is visible from the program's output, the first `CreateDirectory()` invocation succeeds but the second one fails; see marker { 3 }. This is because the implementation of `CreateDirectory()` first checks whether such a directory already exists and if not, it creates it for us. But if the directory exists, the `mkdir()` system call returns −1 and sets `errno` to EEXIST.

Something important about the `std::error_code` class is that it is platform specific. This means that the error values stored in it strongly depend on the underlying OS. In the case of a POSIX-like system, which Linux is, the error value we have is EEXIST. But this is not necessarily true for other OSs.

Therefore, if we design our code to be as platform agnostic as possible, we need to avoid comparisons such as the following:

```
if (ecode.value() == EEXIST)
```

But we also need a way to ensure that a directory that already exists doesn't break our program logic. Yes, from a POSIX standpoint this is an error, but in our specific business logic, this is not a problem for the program execution to continue.

std::error_condition

The right approach to address this problem is with the help of another Standard Library class – std::error_condition. As the name suggests, its main purpose is to provide conditional program logic. Let's slightly rework the CreateDirectory() method from the earlier example:

```
std::error_code CreateDirectory(const std::string& dirPath) {
    std::error_code ecode{};
    if (mkdir(dirPath.c_str(), 0777) != 0) {
        std::errc cond{errno}; // {1}
        ecode = std::make_error_code(cond); // {2}
    }
    return ecode;
}
```

As you can see, the difference from the previous example is how we construct the error_code object. In the reworked code, we first create an object of the std::errc type and initialize it with the value of POSIX errno; see marker {1}. The std::errc class is a scoped enumerator class. It defines *portable error conditions* that correspond to the specific POSIX error codes. This implies that instead of relying on a platform-specific macro that corresponds to a particular POSIX error code, such as EEXIST, we switch to an error that will have the same error condition regardless of the platform it comes from.

> **Important note**
>
> You can find the predefined portable error conditions of the std::errc scoped enumerator, which correspond to their equivalent POSIX error codes, here: https://en.cppreference.com/w/cpp/error/errc.

Once we create an instance of std::errc, we pass it to the factory method for the creation of error codes – std::make_error_code() (see marker {2}) – which generates for us a std::error_code of a generic category.

Now, let's see how the `main()` method is changed in order to be platform independent:

```
int main() {
    auto ecode{CreateDirectory("/tmp/test")};
    if (ecode){
        std::cerr << "Error 1: " << ecode.message() <<
            '\n';
    }
    ecode = CreateDirectory("/tmp/test");
    if (ecode){
        std::cerr << "Error 2: " << ecode.message() <<
            '\n';
    }
    if (ecode == std::errc::file_exists) { // {3}
        std::cout << "This is platform agnostic and is
            portable.\n";
    }
    return 0;
}
```

We still have two invocations of the `CreateDirectory()` method, and the second one still returns an `error_code`. But the main difference comes from how we compare the `ecode` object; see marker {3}. Instead of comparing it with an integer value of the error POSIX code, we compare it against an object that holds a portable error condition – `std::errc::file_exists`. It has the same semantics, saying that the file already exists, but it is platform independent. In the next section, we will see how useful this could be.

Using custom error categories

Every software developer should strive as much as possible to write portable code. Writing portable code provides reusability, which can significantly reduce development costs. Of course, this is not always possible. There are use cases where the code you write is dedicated to a specific system. But for all the rest, abstracting your code from the underlying system allows you to easily migrate it to other systems without carrying out huge refactoring to make it work. This is safer and cheaper.

Let's get back to our previous example, where we tried to abstract the error code received from a POSIX system call. It should be comparable against a portable error condition such as `std::errc::file_exists`. We will extend this with the following use case. Imagine that we have a custom library that also works with files. Let's call it `MyFileLibrary`. But this library doesn't support the POSIX error codes. It provides a different *category* of custom error codes that semantically correspond to some of the POSIX codes but with different error values.

The library supports the following errors with their corresponding error codes:

```
enum class MyFileLibraryError {
    FileNotFound = 1000,
    FileAlreadyExists = 2000,
    FileBusy = 3000,
    FileTooBig = 4000
};
```

As you can see, our library can return the `FileAlreadyExists` enumerated constant, just like the `mkdir()` system call does, but with a different error value – `1000`. So, the main logic that consumes both `MyFileLibrary` and `mkdir()` should be able to handle these errors in the same way, because they are semantically equal. Let's see how this can be done.

In our previous example, we created the error code returned by the POSIX API:

```
ecode = std::error_code{errno, std::generic_category()};
```

We used `std::generic_category`, which is a derived class from the base category class – `std::error_category`. It is predefined for us in the Standard Library in such a way that it *knows* POSIX error codes. This is effectively the place where the translation between the real error code returned by the API and `std::error_condition` is done. So, in order to expose the same capability for `MyFileLibrary`, we need to define a new `std::error_category` derived class. We will name it `MyFileLibraryCategory`:

```
class MyFileLibraryCategory : public std::error_category {
public:
    const char* name() const noexcept override { // {1}
        return "MyFileLibrary";
    }
    std::string message(int ev) const override { // {2}
        switch (static_cast<MyFileLibraryError>(ev)) {
        case MyFileLibraryError::FileAlreadyExists:
            return "The file already exists";
        default:
            return "Unsupported error";
        }
    }
    bool equivalent(int code,
                    const std::error_condition& condition)
                        const noexcept override { // {3}
        switch (static_cast<MyFileLibraryError>(code)) {
        case MyFileLibraryError::FileAlreadyExists:
            return condition == std::errc::file_exists; //
                {4}
```

```
        default:
            return false;
        }
    }
};
```

The `std::error_category` base class has several *virtual* methods that, if overridden in the derived class, allow custom behavior. In our example, we have overridden the following:

- The `name()` method, which is used to report which category this error belongs to; see marker {1}

- The `message()` method, which is used to report a message string that corresponds to a specific error value; see marker {2}

- The `equivalent()` method, which is used to make a comparison between the custom error code generated by our library and the predefined `std::error_condition` values

The `equivalent()` method gets the custom error code, casts it to a value of `MyFileLibraryError`, and, for each specific case, decides what `condition` it matches; see marker {3}.

Now, since we have our new, shiny custom error category – `MyFileLibraryCategory` – let's see how to use it:

```
const MyFileLibraryCategory my_file_lib_category{}; // {1}
int main() {
    std::error_code file_exists{static_cast<int>
      (MyFileLibraryError::FileAlreadyExists),
        my_file_lib_category}; // {2}
    if (file_exists == std::errc::file_exists) { // {3}
        std::cout << "Msg: " << file_exists.message() <<
          '\n'; // {4}
        std::cout << "Category: " << file_exists
          .default_error_condition().category().name() <<
             '\n'; // {5}
    }
    return 0;
}
```

The first step we need to take is to instantiate an object of our custom category; see marker {1}. Then, we create an `error_code` instance, which we initialize with the `FileAlreadyExists` error value and specify that it is from the `MyFileLibraryCategory` category; see marker {2}. Since we have a valid instance of an error code – `file_exists` – we are ready to compare it against the platform-independent `std::errc::file_exists` error condition.

The following is the output of the program:

```
Msg: The file already exists
Category: MyFileLibrary
```

As you can see, the comparison between an error generated from `MyFileLibrary` and the generic `std::errc::file_exists` is now possible with the help of the custom error category we defined – `MyFileLibraryCategory`. The corresponding error message is displayed (see marker {3}) and the category as well (see marker {4}).

> **Important note**
>
> Here, you can find the full description with all virtual methods that the `std::error_category` base class exposes: `https://en.cppreference.com/w/cpp/error/error_category`.

Now that we are familiar with the usage of error codes and error conditions, let's see how we can use the powerful mechanism of C++ exceptions and propagate errors.

From error codes to exceptions

Exception handling is an important aspect of programming, especially when dealing with errors that can disrupt the normal flow of a program. While there are several ways to handle errors in a code base, exceptions provide a powerful mechanism for handling errors in a way that separates error flow from normal program flow.

When working with error codes, it can be challenging to ensure that all error cases are properly handled and that the code remains maintainable. By wrapping error codes in exceptions, we can create a more pragmatic approach to error handling that makes it easier to reason about code and catch errors in a more centralized manner.

It's hard to say which approach is better when dealing with error handling in a code base, and the decision to use exceptions should be based on pragmatic considerations. While exceptions can provide significant benefits in terms of code organization and maintainability, they may come with a performance penalty that may not be acceptable in certain systems.

At their core, exceptions are a way to segregate the normal program flow from the error flow. Unlike error codes, which can be ignored, exceptions cannot be easily overlooked, making them a more reliable way to ensure that errors are handled in a consistent and centralized manner.

While exceptions may not be the right choice for every code base, they offer a powerful way to handle errors that can make code easier to maintain and reason about. By understanding how to correctly use exceptions, programmers can make informed decisions about how to handle errors in their code. Let's get deeper into this.

std::system_error

In the previous section, we created a program that properly handles errors reported by the POSIX system call – mkdir(). Now, let's see how we can improve the error handling in this program using exceptions instead of error codes. Here is the revisited CreateDirectory() method:

```
void CreateDirectory(const std::string& dirPath) { // {1}
    using namespace std;
    if (mkdir(dirPath.c_str(), 0777) != 0) {
        const auto ecode{make_error_code(errc{errno})}; //
            {2}
        cout << "CreateDirectory reports error: " <<
            ecode.message() << '\n';
        system_error exception{ecode}; // {3}
        throw exception; // {4}
    }
}
```

In the CreateDirectory() method, we make a system call using the mkdir() API, which, in the case of failure, returns a non-zero result and stores a POSIX error code in the errno variable. Nothing new so far. Just as in our previous example, we create an std::error_code from the value of errno (see marker {2}) to report it to the caller of our CreateDirectory() method. But instead of returning the error directly as a result of the function, we prefer to use an exception for this and make our function **void**; see marker {1}.

Since we already have an error code object created, we will use it to create an exception from it. In order to do so, we will use a predefined exception class from the Standard Library that is explicitly defined to wrap std::error_code objects – std::system_error.

std::system_error is a derived type from the std::exception interface class from the C++ Standard Library. It is used by various library functions, which typically interface with OS facilities and can report errors either by generating std::error_code or std::error_condition.

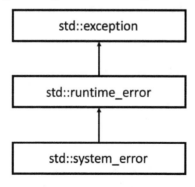

Figure 5.1 – Inheritance diagram of std::system_error exception

In our example, in order to create an std::system_error object, we have to pass to its constructor the instance of std::error_code ecode, which we already created; see marker {3}.

As with any other exception derived from the base exception class from the Standard Library – std::exception – std::system_error has the what() method. It aims to report a meaningful string explaining details about the error behind the exception. More specifically, it calls under the hood the message() method of the std::error_code object it wraps and returns its result.

Since we already have a new, shiny exception object created, we now need to *throw* it back to the caller of our API. This is done with the throw keyword; see marker {4}. An important note is that we throw the exception object by *value*; we don't throw a reference or a pointer to it.

> **Important note**
>
> As a rule of thumb, wherever possible, throw your exceptions by value.

One of the key advantages of exceptions over error codes is that they *can't be omitted* by the caller. When a function returns an error code, it is up to the function's caller to decide whether to check the return value or not. There are some cases where the return value is not checked by mistake, and this leads to bugs in the program. When using exceptions as an error-handling mechanism, there is no such possibility. Once an exception is thrown, it propagates up the call stack until it is either caught by the appropriate program exception-handling logic or reaches the top of the function stack. If the exception is not caught anywhere during its propagation path, known also as *stack unwinding*, then it terminates the program by invoking the std::terminate function.

> **Important note**
>
> Check out the following std::system_error reference page: https://en.cppreference.com/w/cpp/error/system_error.

Now, let's get back to our example and see how the main() method should be reworked in order to handle the exception thrown from the CreateDirectory() method:

```cpp
int main() {
    try {
        CreateDirectory("/tmp/test"); // First try succeeds
        CreateDirectory("/tmp/test"); // Second try throws
    } catch (const std::system_error& se) { // {5}
        const auto econd{se.code()
            .default_error_condition()}; // {6}
        if (econd != std::errc::file_exists) { // {7}
            std::cerr << "Unexpected system error: " <<
                se.what() << '\n';
            throw; // {8}
```

```
        }
        std::cout << "Nothing unexpected, safe to
            continue.\n";
    }
    return 0;
}
```

Unlike error codes, which, once returned by a function, need to be assigned and checked, the exceptions need to be caught and appropriate actions should be taken. Catching exceptions in C++ is done with the help of the try-catch construction in the language. In the preceding example, you can see that we invoke the CreateDirectory() method twice because the second invocation will generate an error, which will be propagated up the stack as an exception. This exception will be caught by the catch clause in marker {5}. As you can see, the catch clause expects a parameter that specifies what should be caught; see marker {5}. Its syntax is similar to the function's parameter list, where you can pass objects either by value or by reference.

In our example, we catch the exception thrown by the CreateDirectory() method by *constant reference*. The reason why we don't catch by value is to avoid unnecessary object copying and – more importantly – to avoid *object slicing*. We will get deeper into the specifics of the exception-catching techniques in C++ soon, but for now, let's focus on our current example. Once we catch the exception, we can extract the error_condition object from it; see marker {6}. This is possible because the system_error class supports error codes and error conditions and enables us to fetch them. When we have error_condition, we can successfully check against the well-known errc codes whether this exception is a real problem for our program or it can be omitted; see marker {7}.

> **Important note**
>
> Wherever possible, catch exceptions by reference (prefer constant) rather than by value to avoid potential object slicing and additional overhead due to object copying.

Our business program logic expects that errors reporting that a file already exists are normal and should not break program execution. Ultimately, it says that we try to create a directory that already exists, and that's fine and we can continue. But if the error is something else that we don't know what to do with, then we have to report that error and rethrow it to the upper methods in the call stack, which could better know what to do with such a kind of error. This is done with the throw clause in the language; see marker {8}. An important detail here is that in order to *rethrow an existing exception* rather than throwing a new one, you have to just use throw; with *no arguments*.

> **Important note**
>
> Use the throw; clause with no arguments to rethrow an existing exception.

Of course, if the error is what we expect, such as `std::errc::file_exists`, then we can safely continue the program execution without the need to rethrow this exception. You can find the output of the program as follows:

```
CreateDirectory reports error: File exists
Nothing unexpected, safe to continue.
```

We can see that the exception is thrown by the `CreateDirectory()` method and it is caught by the `catch` clause in the `main()` method. In this example, we saw that using exceptions instead of error codes clearly segregates the normal program execution path from the error path and makes it easier to rethrow errors that we can't properly deal with.

Throw by value, catch by reference

In C++, we can literally throw every object. You could successfully do this as follows:

```
throw 42;
```

The preceding statement throws an integer object with a value of 42. But just because you can do something, it doesn't mean it's a good idea to do so. The goal of the exception is to bring context to the error that occurred. Throwing the value of 42 doesn't provide much context, right? What does 42 mean for the recipient of your exception? Not much!

This statement is fully confirmed by the C++ Core Guidelines project developed by some of the key members of the C++ Standards Committee. The C++ Core Guidelines are a really useful guide for every C++ developer no matter what level of expertise you have. It gathers recommendations and best practices about different features in C++.

> **Important note**
> Make sure to get familiar with the C++ Core Guidelines, which you can find at `https://isocpp.github.io/CppCoreGuidelines/CppCoreGuidelines#c-core-guidelines`.

The C++ Core Guidelines say that we have to make sure that we throw meaningful exceptions. If you don't have a standard defined exception that works for your case, you can throw a user-defined type that derives from some of the standard exceptions:

`https://isocpp.github.io/CppCoreGuidelines/CppCoreGuidelines#e14-use-purpose-designed-user-defined-types-as-exceptions-not-built-in-types`

The C++ Core Guidelines also suggest throwing our exceptions by value and catching them by reference. Of course, even better if we catch by constant reference. Throwing by value ensures that the lifetime of the thrown object will be managed by the runtime of your system. Otherwise, if you throw a pointer to an object that you have allocated on the heap whose responsibility will be to delete this object when it is no longer needed, it is quite possible you will end up with leaked memory:

https://isocpp.github.io/CppCoreGuidelines/CppCoreGuidelines#e15-throw-by-value-catch-exceptions-from-a-hierarchy-by-reference

Let's go through an example. We will define a method – `Throw()` – which throws by value a `std::system_error` exception with an error code – `bad_file_descriptor`:

```
void Throw() {
    using namespace std;
    throw system_error{make_error_code
        (errc::bad_file_descriptor)};
}
```

This method will be invoked by the `main()` method in which we will catch the thrown exception:

```
int main() {
    using namespace std;
    try {
        try {
            Throw(); // {1}
        } catch (runtime_error e) { // {2}
            throw e; // {3}
        }
    } catch (const exception& e) { // {4}
        const system_error& se{dynamic_cast<const
            system_error&>(e)}; // {5}
        const auto econd{se.code()
            .default_error_condition()};
        std::cerr << econd.message() << '\n';
    }
    return 0;
}
```

As you can see in the preceding example, we have defined two `try-catch` blocks – one inner and one outer. The reason behind this is that exceptions thrown in the `catch` branch can't be caught by another `catch` branch in the same try-catch block. They are propagated out and, therefore, in order to catch them, we need an outer try-catch block.

In marker {1}, we invoke the `Throw()` method, which throws an exception. But in marker {2}, we catch the thrown exception. Actually, we don't catch `std::system_error` directly but we catch its parent class – `std::runtime_error`. Also, you can see that we catch this exception by value with `runtime_error e`.

The only action we take once we catch the `runtime_error` exception is to throw it away from the inner try-catch block with the following statement:

```
throw e;
```

Always be careful when you rethrow an existing exception. The upper statement *doesn't rethrow* the exception caught in the `catch` clause but it throws a new instance of the `runtime_error` exception, which is a copy of the caught exception, instead.

Once the new exception is thrown, it is caught by the outer `catch` clause in marker {4}. As you can see, following the recommendation from the C++ Core Guidelines, we catch a constant reference instead of a value to the Standard Library's base exception class – `std::exception` – which is also a base class for `std::runtime_error`.

In the `catch` clause, we try to downcast it back to its original type – `std::system_error` – and print the message from its `std::error_condition`. Let's see the output from the program:

```
terminate called after throwing an instance of 'std::bad_cast'
  what():  std::bad_cast
```

But surprisingly, we don't get the expected result. The downcast has failed, and when it fails, it generates a standard exception – `std::bad_cast` – which is thrown away from the outer `catch` clause. But this exception is not guarded by another try-catch block, and therefore, it propagates out of the `main()` method, which is de facto the top of the function stack of the program. As we explained earlier, if an exception is not caught during its propagation upwind in the function stack, then the `std::terminate` function will be called.

But why did the cast fail when we tried to downcast to `std::system_error`? The reason is that the `Throw()` method throws `std::system_error` and everything should work fine. Well, it should, but it doesn't really. Let's get deeper into this.

The `Throw()` method really throws an instance of `std::system_error` by *value*. But the inner `catch` clause catches a *base class exception* also *by value* and throws a *copy* of it:

```
catch (runtime_error e) {
    throw e;
}
```

This leads to a problem because the object we rethrow is no longer an instance of `std::system_error`. It has been sliced to its base class – `std::runtime_error`. All the information that has been part of the *original* `std::system_error` object is no longer part of the newly created *copy* of the `std::runtime_error` – e type.

Therefore, the downcast to `std::system_error` doesn't succeed and our program terminates.

To conclude, we can say that these kinds of errors can be successfully prevented by following the rules of throwing exceptions by value, catching them by reference, and rethrowing the existing exceptions rather than their copy wherever this is possible.

try/catch ... finally

You probably noticed that in the C++ language, we have the `try-catch` block, but we don't have the `finally` construct. If you have experience in languages such as C# or Java, you will be used to releasing the resource that you have acquired using the `finally` clause. But this works only for exceptional cases where the `try` clause is preceding the usage of `finally`.

But how do we do it in C++ without `finally`? Let's revisit our initial example for opening and closing a file using the `open()` and `close()` POSIX functions:

```
int main() {
    try {
        const int fd{open("/tmp/cpp-test-file", O_RDONLY)};
            // {1}
        if (fd == -1) { return errno; }
        // Do something with the file and suddenly
            something throws {2}
        if (close(fd) == -1) { return errno; } // {3}
    } catch (...) {
        std::cerr << "Something somewhere went terribly
            wrong!\n";
        return -1;
    }
    return 0;
}
```

As we already discussed earlier in the chapter, opening a file using the `open()` POSIX method returns the ID of the file descriptor if the function successfully opens the file; otherwise, as with many of the POSIX functions, it returns `-1`; see marker {1}.

Once you have your file opened, it is your responsibility to ensure that *finally*, when you finish with it, it will be closed. Therefore, we invoke the `close()` method at the end of the `main()` method to ensure that the file will be closed (see marker {3}) just before we leave `main()`. But how can you be sure that some abnormal situation won't occur, and an exception won't be thrown before you close your file? Actually, the only case in which you can be sure that this won't happen is if exceptions are not supported in your system. But in our test Linux environment, this is not the case. Even worse, when working in real code bases, it's hard to be sure that some of the methods you invoke during your normal business logic execution won't throw.

Imagine what happens if your program throws before you close your file; see marker {2}. Effectively, you will *leak* a resource. As a rule of thumb, we should never leak resources, no matter whether this will lead to a problem or not.

But how can we protect ourselves from leaking resources without having the `finally` clause in the language? Let's have a look into one of the most typical C++ programming techniques:

```cpp
void Throw() {
    cout << "Ops, I need to throw ...\n";
    throw system_error{make_error_code
      (errc::bad_file_descriptor)};
}
int main() {
    const string_view myFileName{"/tmp/cpp-test-file"}; //
       {1}
    ofstream theFile(myFileName.data()); // {2}
    try {
        file_guard guard(myFileName, O_RDONLY); // {3}
        const auto fd = guard.getFileDescriptor();
        Throw(); // {4}
    } catch (const exception& e) {
        cout << e.what();
        return -1;
    }
    return 0;
}
```

We have reworked our `main()` method in such a way that we just create a file (see marker {2}) and pass its filename (see marker {1}) to a new object of the `file_guard` type (see marker {3}), which we will look at it just in a moment. The `file_guard` object is responsible for opening and closing a file with a specific name:

```cpp
using namespace std;
class file_guard final {
public:
    file_guard(string_view file, mode_t mode) : // {5}
        fd{open(file.data(), mode)}
    {
        if (fd == -1) {
            throw system_error
                {make_error_code(errc{errno})};
        }
        cout << "File '" << file <<
        "' with file descriptor '" <<
```

```
        fd << "' is opened.\n";
    }
    explicit file_guard(const file_guard&) = delete; // {6}
    file_guard& operator=(const file_guard&) = delete;
    explicit file_guard(file_guard&& other) noexcept : //
      {7}
        fd{move(other.fd)} { other.fd = -1; }
    file_guard& operator=(file_guard&& other) noexcept
    {
        fd = move(other.fd);
        other.fd = -1;
        return *this;
    }
    int getFileDescriptor() const noexcept { // {8}
        return fd;
    }
    ~file_guard() noexcept { // {9}
        if (fd != -1) {
            close(fd);
            cout << "File with file descriptor '" << fd <<
              "' is closed.\n";
        }
    }
private:
    int fd;
};
```

The class gets in its constructor the file path and the mode in which the file should be opened; see marker {5}. In the initializer list of the constructor, the POSIX open() method is invoked. The result, which is the file descriptor ID, is assigned to the _fd member of the class. If open() fails, an exception is thrown away from the file_guard constructor. We should not care about closing the file in this case because we didn't open it successfully.

In the destructor of the class, we have the reversed operation; see marker {9}. If the file descriptor is different from -1, which means that the file has been successfully opened before that, we close it.

This C++ programming technique is called **Resource Acquisition Is Initialization**, or just **RAII**. It is a resource management technique that acquires the resource during the construction of the RAII object and releases it during the destruction of that object. Unlike in languages such as Java and C# that use automatic garbage collection and whose resource release timing is not entirely clear to the user, C++ objects have a precisely defined storage duration and lifetime. Thus, we can rely on this characteristic and utilize RAII objects to manage our resources.

Going back to our main() method, if the file is opened (see marker {3}) and something goes wrong before it has been explicitly closed (see marker {4}), we will be sure that it will be automatically closed once the file_guard object goes out of scope.

This technique is widely used no matter whether exceptions are available in the system or not. You can wrap your resources using RAII and be assured that they will be automatically released whenever you leave the scope where the RAII object lives.

In our file_guard example, we have removed the copy constructor and the copy assignment operator and left the move constructor and move operator only, claiming that this RAII object is not copyable.

C++ is often questioned about not having the finally construct. However, the inventor of C++, Bjarne Stroustrup, has explained that RAII is a better substitute: https://www.stroustrup. com/bs_faq2.html#finally.

Stroustrup argues that in practical code bases, there are many more resource acquisitions and releases, and using RAII instead of finally results in less code. Additionally, it is less susceptible to errors since the RAII wrapper only needs to be coded once, and there is no need to remember to release the resource manually.

The Standard Library has many examples of RAII objects, such as std::unique_ptr, std::lock_guard, and std::fstreams.

Summary

This chapter has covered various techniques for error handling when working with POSIX APIs in C++. We discussed the use of errno, a thread-local variable, and the strerror function. We also explored how std::error_code and std::error_condition can wrap POSIX errors and how custom error categories enable us to compare errors generated by different sources and develop platform-independent error-handling code. Furthermore, we delved into exceptions in C++ and how to convert std::error_code into an exception of the std::system_error type.

We also examined best practices for working with exceptions, such as throwing them by value and catching them by reference, to avoid issues such as object slicing. Finally, we learned about the RAII technique in C++, which eliminates the need for a finally construct in the language.

In the next chapter, we will explore the topic of concurrency with C++.

Part 2: Advanced Techniques for System Programming

In this part, you will learn about expert-level C++20 features, which will further improve both your OS and C++ development expertise. The examples, though still practical, become more complex and require some preliminary understanding of the subject of system programming.

This part has the following chapters:

- *Chapter 6, Concurrent System Programming with C++*
- *Chapter 7, Proceeding with Inter-Process Communication*
- *Chapter 8, Using Clocks, Timers, and Signals in Linux*
- *Chapter 9, Understanding the C++ Memory Model*
- *Chapter 10, Using Coroutines in C++ for System Programming*

6

Concurrent System Programming with C++

In this chapter, we will look at what concurrency means and how it is different from parallelism. We will go through the fundamentals and the theory behind processes and threads. We will look at the changes in the C++ memory model, which enforce native concurrency support in the language. We will also familiarize ourselves with what a race condition is, how it can lead to a data race, and how to prevent data races. Next, we will get acquainted with the C++20 `std::jthread` primitive, which enables multithreading support. We will learn about the specifics of the `std::jthread` class and how we can stop already running `std::jthread` instances by using the `std::stop_source` primitive. Finally, we will learn how to synchronize the execution of concurrent code and how to report calculation results from executed tasks. We will learn how to use C++ synchronization primitives such as *barriers* and *latches* to synchronize the execution of concurrent tasks, and how to properly report the result of these tasks using *promises* and *futures*.

To sum up, we will be covering the following topics in this chapter:

- What is concurrency?
- Thread versus process
- Concurrency with C++
- Demystifying race conditions and data races
- Practical multithreading
- Sharing data during parallel execution

So, let's get started!

Technical requirements

All examples in this chapter have been tested in an environment with the following configuration:

- Linux Mint 21 Cinnamon Edition

- GCC 12.2 with compiler flags `--std=c++20 -pthread`

- A stable internet connection

- Please make sure your environment is at least this recent. For all the examples, you can alternatively use `https://godbolt.org/`.

- All code examples in this chapter are available to download from `https://github.com/PacktPublishing/C-Programming-for-Linux-Systems/tree/main/Chapter%206`.

What is concurrency?

Modern cars have become highly intricate machines that provide not only transportation but also various other functionalities. These functionalities include infotainment systems, which allow users to play music and videos, and heating and air conditioning systems, which regulate the temperature for passengers. Consider a scenario in which these features did not work simultaneously. In such a case, the driver would have to choose between driving the car, listening to music, or staying in a comfortable climate. This is not what we expect from a car, right? We expect all of these features to be available at the same time, enhancing our driving experience and providing a comfortable trip. To achieve this, these features must operate in parallel.

But do they really run in parallel, or do they just run concurrently? Is there any difference?

In computer systems, **concurrency** and **parallelism** are similar in certain ways, but they are not the same. Imagine you have some work to do, but this work can be done in separate smaller chunks. Concurrency refers to the situation where multiple chunks of the work begin, execute, and finish during overlapping time intervals, without a guaranteed specific order of execution. On the other hand, parallelism is an execution policy where these chunks execute simultaneously on hardware with multiple computing resources, such as a multi-core processor.

Concurrency happens when multiple chunks of work, which we call **tasks**, are executed in an unspecified order for a certain period of time. The operating system could run some of the tasks and force the rest to wait. In concurrent execution, the task continuously strives for an execution slot because the operating system does not guarantee that it will execute all of them at once. Furthermore, it is highly possible that while a task is being executed, it is suddenly suspended, and another task starts executing. This is called **preemption**. It is clear that in concurrent task execution, the order of how the tasks will be executed is not guaranteed.

Let's get back to our car example. In modern cars, the infotainment system is responsible for performing many activities simultaneously. For example, it can run the navigation part while allowing you to listen to music. This is possible because the system runs these tasks concurrently. It runs the tasks related to route calculation while processing the music content. If the hardware system has a single core, then these tasks should run concurrently:

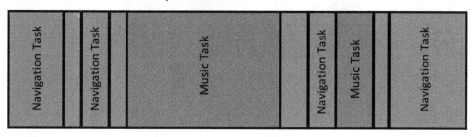

time

Figure 6.1 – Concurrent task execution

From the preceding figure, you can see that each task gets a non-deterministic execution time in an unpredictable order. In addition, there is no guarantee that your task will be finished before the next one is started. This is where the preemption happens. While your task is running, it is suddenly suspended, and another task is scheduled for execution. Keep in mind that task switching is not a cheap process. The system consumes the processor's computation resource to perform this action – to make the context switch. The conclusion should be the following: we have to design our systems to respect these limitations.

On the other hand, parallelism is a form of concurrency that involves executing multiple operations simultaneously on *separate processing units*. For example, a computer with multiple CPUs can execute multiple tasks in parallel, which can lead to significant performance improvements. You don't have to worry about the context switching and the preemption. It has its drawbacks, though, and we will discuss them thoroughly.

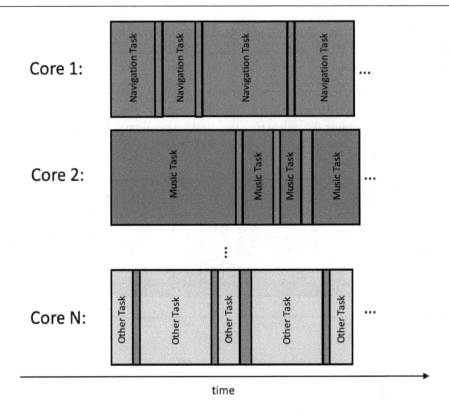

Figure 6.2 – Parallel task execution

Going back to our car example, if the CPU of the infotainment system is multi-core, then the tasks related to the navigation system could be executed on one core, and the tasks for the music processing on some of the other cores. Therefore, you don't have to take any action to design your code to support preemption. Of course, this is only true if you are sure that your code will be executed in such an environment.

The fundamental connection between concurrency and parallelism lies in the fact that parallelism can be applied to concurrent computations without affecting the accuracy of the outcome, but the presence of concurrency alone does not guarantee parallelism.

In summary, concurrency is an important concept in computing that allows multiple tasks to be executed simultaneously, even though that is not guaranteed. This could lead to improved performance and efficient resource utilization but at the cost of more complicated code respecting the pitfalls that concurrency brings. On the other hand, truly parallel execution of code is easier to handle from a software perspective but must be supported by the underlying system.

In the next section, we will get familiar with the difference between execution threads and processes in Linux.

Threads versus processes

In Linux, a **process** is an instance of a program in execution. A process can have one or more threads of execution. A **thread** is a sequence of instructions that can proceed independently of other threads within the same process.

Each process has its own memory space, system resources, and execution context. Processes are isolated from each other and do not share memory by default. They can only communicate through files and **inter-process communication** (**IPC**) mechanisms, such as pipes, queues, sockets, shared memory, and so on.

A thread, on the other hand, is a lightweight unit of execution within a process. The overhead of loading the instructions from non-volatile memory to RAM or even the cache is already paid for by the process creating the thread – the parent process. Each thread has its own stack and register values but shares the memory space and system resources of the parent process. Because threads share memory within the process, they can easily communicate with each other and synchronize their own execution. In general, this makes them more efficient than processes for concurrent execution.

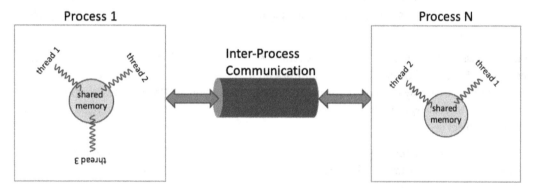

Figure 6.3 – IPC

The main differences between processes and threads are as follows:

- **Resource allocation**: Processes are independent entities that have their own memory space, system resources, and scheduling priority. On the other hand, threads share the same memory space and system resources as the process they belong to.

- **Creation and destruction**: Processes are created and destroyed by the operating system, while threads are created and managed by the process that they belong to.

- **Context switching**: When a context switch occurs, the operating system switches the entire process context, including all its threads. In contrast, a thread context switch only requires switching the state of the current thread, which, in general, is faster and less resource-intensive.

- **Communication and synchronization**: IPC mechanisms such as pipes, queues, sockets, and shared memory are used to enable communication between processes. Threads, on the other hand, can communicate directly by sharing memory within the same process. This also enables efficient synchronization between threads, as they can use locks and other synchronization primitives to coordinate their access to shared resources.

> **Important note**
> Linux schedules tasks in the kernel, which are either threads or single-threaded processes. Each task is represented through a kernel thread; thus, the scheduler does not differentiate between a thread and a process.

Processes and threads have their analogy in real life. Let's say you are working on a project with a group of people, and the project is divided into different tasks. Each task represents a unit of work that needs to be completed. You can think of the project as a process, and each task as a thread.

In this analogy, the process (project) is a collection of related tasks that need to be completed to achieve a common goal. Each task (thread) is a separate unit of work that can be assigned to a specific person to complete.

When you assign a task to someone, you are creating a new thread within the project (process). The person who is assigned the task (thread) can work on it independently, without interfering with the work of others. They may also communicate with other team members (threads) to coordinate their work, just as threads within a process can communicate with each other. They also need to use the common project resource to finish their tasks.

In contrast, if you divide the project into different projects, you create multiple processes. Each process has its own resources, team members, and goals. It is harder to ensure that both processes share a resource needed for the project to finish.

So, processes and threads in computing are like real-life projects and tasks, respectively. A process represents a collection of related tasks that need to be completed to achieve a common goal, while a thread is a separate unit of work that can be assigned to a specific person to complete.

In Linux, processes are separate instances of a program with their own memory and resources, while threads are lightweight execution units within a process that share the same memory and resources. Threads can communicate more efficiently and are more suitable for tasks that require parallel execution, while processes provide better isolation and fault tolerance.

Having all this in mind, let's see how to write concurrent code in C++.

Concurrency with C++

The C++ language has had built-in support for managing and executing concurrent threads since C++11. But it doesn't have any native support for managing concurrent processes. The C++ Standard

Library provides various classes for thread management, synchronization and communication between threads, protection of shared data, atomic operations, and parallel algorithms. The **C++ memory model** is also designed with thread awareness in mind. This makes it a great choice for developing concurrent applications.

Multithreading with C++ is the ability to have multiple threads of execution running concurrently within a single program. This allows a program to take advantage of multiple CPU cores and perform tasks in parallel, leading to faster completion of tasks and improved overall performance.

The C++ Standard Library introduced the `std::thread` thread management class. Once it is instantiated, it is the responsibility of the user to take care of the thread's objective. The users have to choose to either join the thread or detach it from its parent thread. If they don't take care of it, the program terminates.

With the release of C++20, a brand-new thread management class, `std::jthread`, was introduced. It makes it relatively easy to create and manage threads. To create a new thread, you can create an instance of the `std::jthread` class, passing the function or callable object that you want to run as a separate thread. A key advantage of `std::jthread` compared to `std::thread` is that you don't have to explicitly worry about joining it. It will be done automatically during the `std::jthread` destruction. Later in the chapter, we will have a deeper look into `std::jthread` and how to use it.

Bear in mind that multithreading will also make a program more complex, as it requires careful management of shared resources and synchronization of threads. If not properly managed, multithreading can lead to issues such as deadlocks and race conditions, which can cause a program to hang or produce unexpected results.

Additionally, multithreading requires the developers to ensure that the code is thread-safe, which can be a challenging task. Not all tasks are suitable for multithreading; some tasks may actually run slower if attempted to be parallelized.

Overall, multithreading with C++ can provide significant benefits in terms of performance and resource utilization, but it also requires careful consideration of the potential challenges and pitfalls.

Now, let's get familiar with the most common pitfalls of writing concurrent code.

Demystifying race conditions and data races

In C++, multithreading support was first introduced with the C++11 version of the language. One of the key elements provided by the C++11 standard to facilitate multithreading is the memory model. The memory model tackles two problems: the layout of objects in memory and the concurrent access to these objects. In C++, all data is represented by objects, which are blocks of memory that have various properties such as type, size, alignment, lifetime, value, and an optional name. Each object remains in memory for a specific period of time and is stored in one or more memory locations, depending on whether it is a simple scalar object or a more complex type.

In the context of multithreaded programming in C++, it is crucial to consider how to tackle concurrent access by multiple threads to shared objects. If two or more threads try to access different memory locations, there is usually no problem. However, when threads attempt to write in the same memory location simultaneously, it can lead to data races, which can cause unexpected behaviors and errors in the program.

> **Important note**
>
> Data races occur when multiple threads try to access data and at least one of them attempts to modify it, and no precautions are taken to synchronize the memory access. Data races can cause undefined behavior in your program and are a source of trouble.

But how does your program come to a *data race*? This happens when there is a *race condition* that hasn't been properly handled. Let's have a look into the difference between data races and race conditions:

- **Race condition**: A situation where the correctness of a code depends on specific timing or a strict sequence of operation

- **Data race**: When two or more threads access one object and at least one of these threads modifies it

Based on these definitions, we can deduce that every data race that occurs in your program comes as a result of not correctly handling race conditions. But the opposite is not always true: not every race condition leads to a data race.

There is no better way to understand race conditions and data races than by looking at an example. Let's imagine a primitive banking system, really primitive, which we hope doesn't exist anywhere.

Bill and John have accounts in a bank. Bill has $100 in his account and John has $50. Bill owes John a total of $30. To pay off his debt, Bill decides to make two transfers to John's account. The first is worth $10 and the second is $20. So de facto, Bill will repay John. After both transfers are complete, Bill will have $70 left in his account, while John will have accumulated a total of $80.

Let's define an Account structure that contains the name of the owner of the account together with their account balance at a certain moment:

```cpp
struct Account {
    Account(std::string_view the_owner, unsigned
        the_amount) noexcept :
        balance{the_amount}, owner{the_owner} {}
    std::string GetBalance() const {
        return "Current account balance of " + owner +
            " is " + std::to_string(balance) + '\n';
    }
private:
```

```
      unsigned balance;
      std::string owner;
};
```

In the Account structure, we will also add the overloaded operator methods for += and -=. These are responsible for depositing or withdrawing a specific amount of money to the corresponding account, respectively. Before and after each of the operations, the current balance of the account is printed. Here is the definition of these operators, which are part of the Account structure:

```
Account& operator+=(unsigned amount) noexcept {
        Print(" balance before depositing: ", balance,
          owner);
        auto temp{balance}; // {1}
        std::this_thread::sleep_for(1ms);
        balance = temp + amount; // {2}
        Print(" balance after depositing: ", balance,
          owner);
        return *this;
    }
    Account& operator-=(unsigned amount) noexcept {
        Print(" balance before withdrawing: ", balance,
          owner);
        auto temp{balance}; // {1}
        balance = temp - amount; // {2}
        Print(" balance after withdrawing: ", balance,
          owner);
        return *this;
    }
```

Looking into the implementation of the operator functions shows that they first read the current balance of the account, then store it in a local object (marker {1}), and finally, using the value of the local object, they increment or decrement with the specified amount.

As simple as it gets!

The resulting value of the new balance of the account is written back into the balance member of the Account structure (marker {2}).

We also need to define a method that will be responsible for the actual money transfer:

```
void TransferMoney(unsigned amount, Account& from, Account& to) {
    from -= amount; // {1}
    to += amount; // {2}
}
```

The only thing it does is withdraw the desired amount from one account (marker {1}) and deposit it to the other account (marker {2}), which is exactly what we need to successfully transfer money between accounts.

Now, let's have a look at our `main` program method, which will execute our example:

```cpp
int main() {
    Account bill_account{"Bill", 100}; // {1}
    Account john_account{"John", 50}; // {2}

    std::jthread first_transfer{[&]() { TransferMoney(10,
        bill_account, john_account); }}; // {3}
    std::jthread second_transfer{[&]() { TransferMoney(20,
        bill_account, john_account); }}; // {4}

    std::this_thread::sleep_for(100ms); // {5}
    std::cout << bill_account.GetBalance(); // {6}
    std::cout << john_account.GetBalance(); // {7}
    return 0;
}
```

First, we need to create accounts for Bill and John and deposit $100 and $70 into them, respectively (markers {1} and {2}). Then, we have to do the actual money transfers: one transfer for $10 and one for $20 (markers {3} and {4}). I know that this code may look unfamiliar to you but don't worry, we will deep-dive into `std::jthread` shortly in this chapter.

The only important detail you have to know so far is that we try to make both transfers *concurrently* with the help of the C++ multithreading library. At the end of the process, we set some time for both execution threads to finish the money transfers (marker {5}) and print the result (markers {6} and {7}). As we already discussed, after the transfers are finished, Bill should have $70 in his account while John should have $80.

Let's see the program output:

```
140278035490560 Bill balance before withdrawing: 100
140278027097856 Bill balance before withdrawing: 100
140278027097856 Bill balance after withdrawing: 80
140278035490560 Bill balance after withdrawing: 90
140278027097856 John balance before depositing: 50
140278035490560 John balance before depositing: 50
140278027097856 John balance after depositing: 70
140278035490560 John balance after depositing: 60
Current account balance of Bill is 80
Current account balance of John is 60
```

Wait, what? Bill has $80 while John has $60! How is that possible?

It's possible because we created a *race condition* that led to a *data race*! Let's explain. Having a deeper look into the implementation of the `operator+=` method reveals the problem. By the way, the situation is absolutely the same with the other operator method as well:

```
Account& operator+=(unsigned amount) noexcept {
    Print(" balance before withdrawing: ", balance, owner);
    auto temp{balance}; // {1}
    std::this_thread::sleep_for(1ms); // {2}
    balance = temp + amount; // {3}
    Print(" balance after withdrawing: ", balance, owner);
    return *this;
}
```

At marker {1}, we cache the current balance of the account into a local object living on the stack.

> **Important note**
> The C++ memory model guarantees that each thread has its own copy of all objects with automatic storage duration – the stack objects.

Next, we give the current execution thread some rest time of at least 1ms (marker {2}). With this statement, we put our thread to sleep, allowing other threads (if any) to take processor time and start executing. Nothing to worry about so far, right? Once the thread is back on executing, it uses its cached value of the account's balance and increments it with the new amount. Finally, it stores the newly calculated value back to the `balance` member of the `Account` structure.

Having a closer look into the output of the program, we observe the following:

```
140278035490560 Bill balance before withdrawing: 100
140278027097856 Bill balance before withdrawing: 100
140278027097856 Bill balance after withdrawing: 80
140278035490560 Bill balance after withdrawing: 90
```

The first transfer starts executing. It is running as part of a thread with the 140278035490560 identifier. We see that before the withdrawal is finished, the second transfer is started too. Its identifier is 140278027097856. The second transfer finishes the withdrawal first, leaving Bill's bank account with a balance of $80. Then, the first withdrawal is back in action. But what happens then? Instead of taking $10 more from Bill's account, it actually returns $10! This happens because the first thread was suspended when it had already cached the initial account balance of $100. A *race condition* was created. Meanwhile, the second transfer has changed the account balance, and now, when the first transfer is back to execution, it already works with outdated cached values. This results in blindly overriding the newer account balance with the outdated value. A *data race* happened.

How do we avoid them?

Luckily, the C++ programming language provides various concurrency control mechanisms to address these challenges, such as atomic operations, locks, semaphores, condition variables, barriers, and others. These mechanisms help ensure that shared resources are accessed in a predictable and safe manner and that threads are coordinated effectively to avoid a data race. In the next sections, we will get deeper into some of these synchronization primitives.

Practical multithreading

In computer science, a thread of execution is a sequence of code instructions that can be managed independently by a scheduler of the operating system. On a Linux system, the thread is always part of a process. The C++ threads could be executed concurrently with each other via the multithreading capabilities provided by the standard. During execution, threads share common memory space, unlike processes, where each has its own. Specifically, the threads of a process share its executable code, the dynamically and globally allocated objects, which are not defined as `thread_local`.

Hello C++ jthread

Every C++ program contains at least one thread, and this is the thread that runs the `int main()` method. Multithreaded programs have additional threads started at some point in the execution of the main thread. Let's have a look at a simple C++ program that uses multiple threads to print to the standard output:

```
#include <iostream>
#include <thread>
#include <syncstream>
#include <array>
int main() {
    std::array<std::jthread, 5> my_threads; // Just an
        array of 5 jthread objects which do nothing.
    const auto worker{[]{
        const auto thread_id = std::::
            this_thread::get_id();  // 3
        std::osyncstream sync_cout{std::cout};
        sync_cout << "Hello from new jthread with id:"
                    << thread_id << '\n';
    }};
    for (auto& thread : my_threads) {
        thread = std::jthread{worker}; // This moves the
            new jthread on the place of the placeholder
    }
    std::osyncstream{std::cout} << "Hello Main program
```

```
      thread with id:" << std::this_thread::get_id() <<
         '\n';
      return 0; // jthread dtors join them here.
}
```

When the program starts, the `int main()` method is entered. Nothing surprising so far. At the beginning of the execution, we create a variable on the method stack, called `my_threads`. It is a type of `std::array`, which contains five elements in it. The `std::array` type represents a container from the Standard Library, encapsulating C-style, fixed-sized arrays. It has the advantages of a standard container, such as being aware of its own size, supporting assignment, random access iterators, and so on. As with any other array type in C++, we need to specify what kind of elements it contains. In our example, `my_threads` contains five `std::jthread` objects. The `std::jthread` class was introduced in the C++ Standard Library with the C++20 standard release. It represents a single thread of execution, just like `std::thread`, which was introduced with the release of C++11. Some advantages of `std::jthread` compared to `std::thread` are that it automatically rejoins on destruction and it can be canceled or stopped in some specific cases. It is defined in the `<thread>` header; therefore, we must include it in order to compile successfully.

Yes, you are asking the right question! If we already defined an array of `jthread` objects, what job do they really perform? The expectation is that every thread is associated with some job that needs to be done. But here, the simple answer is *nothing*. Our array contains five `jthread` objects, which don't actually represent an execution thread. They are used more like placeholders because, when `std::array` is instantiated, it also creates the objects it contains using their default constructors if no other arguments are passed.

Let's now define some workers that our threads can be associated with. The `std::jthread` class accepts, as a worker, any *callable* type. Such types provide a single operation that can be invoked. Widely known examples of such types are function objects and lambda expressions, which we already covered in detail in *Chapter 4*. In our example, we will use lambda expressions because they provide a way of creating anonymous function objects (functors) that can be utilized in-line or passed as an argument. The introduction of lambda expressions in C++11 simplifies the process of creating anonymous functors, making it more efficient and straightforward. The following code shows our worker method defined as a lambda expression:

```
const auto worker{[]{
    const auto thread_id = std::this_thread::get_id();
    std::osyncstream sync_cout{std::cout};
    sync_cout << "Hello from new jthread with id:" <<
        thread_id << '\n';
}};
```

The defined lambda expression, `const auto worker{...};`, is pretty simple. It is instantiated on the function stack. It has no input parameters, and it doesn't capture any state from outside. The only work it does is to print to the standard output the `jthread` object's ID. Every thread in C++

provided by the standard concurrency support library has a unique identifier associated with it. The `std::this_thread::get_id()` method returns the ID of the specific thread in which it has been invoked. This means that if this lambda expression is passed to several different threads, it should print a different thread ID.

Printing to `std::cout` by many concurrent threads could bring surprising results. The `std::cout` object is defined as a global, thread-safe object, which ensures that each character written to it is done so atomically. However, no guarantees are made about a sequence of characters such as strings, and it is likely that the output when multiple threads are concurrently writing strings to `std::cout` will be a mixture of these strings. Well, this is not what we really want here. We expect that each thread will be able to fully print its messages. Therefore, we need a synchronization mechanism, which ensures that writing a string to `std::cout` is fully atomic. Luckily, C++20 introduces a whole new family of class templates defined in the `<syncstream>` standard library header, which provides mechanisms to synchronize threads writing to one and the same stream. One of them is `std::osyncstream`. You can use it as a regular stream. Just create an instance of it by passing `std::cout` as a parameter. Then, with the help of its `std::basic_ostream& operator<<(...)` class method, you can insert data, just like a regular stream. It is guaranteed that all of the inserted data will be flushed atomically to the output once the `std::osyncstream` object goes out of scope and is destroyed. In our example, the `sync_cout` object will be destroyed when the lambda is about to finish its execution and leave its scope. This is exactly the behavior we want.

Finally, we are ready to give some work to our threads to do. This means that we need to associate worker lambdas with the five threads we have in the `my_threads` array. But the `std::jthread` type supports adding a worker method only as part of its construction. That's why we need to create other `jthread` objects and replace them with the placeholders in the `my_threads` array:

```
for (auto& thread : my_threads) {
    thread = jthread{worker}; // This moves the new jthread
       on the place of the placeholder
}
```

Being a standard container, `std::array` natively supports range-based for loops. Therefore, we can easily iterate through all elements in `my_threads` and replace them with new `jthread` objects that already have associated workers with them. Firstly, we create new `jthread` objects with automatic storage duration and assign them a worker object. In our case, for every newly created thread, we assign one and the same worker object. This is possible because, in the current case, the `jthread` class makes a copy of the worker instance in the `jthread` objects and, therefore, each `jthread` object gets its own copy of the worker lambda. When constructing these objects, the process is carried out within the context of the caller. This means that any exceptions that occur during the evaluation and copying or movement of the arguments are thrown in the current `main` thread.

An important detail is that the newly created jthread objects are not copied to the existing elements of the array, but they are moved. Therefore, the std::jthread class has implicitly deleted its copy constructor and assignment operator because it doesn't make much sense to copy a thread to an already existing thread. In our case, the newly created jthread objects will be created in the storage of the existing array elements.

When a jthread object is constructed, the associated thread starts immediately, although there may be some delays due to Linux scheduling specifics. The thread begins executing at the function specified as an argument to the constructor. In our example, this is the worker lambda associated with each thread. If the worker returns a result, it will be ignored, and if it ends by throwing an exception, the std::terminate function is executed. Therefore, we need to make sure that either our worker code doesn't throw or we catch everything throwable.

When a thread is started, it begins executing its dedicated worker. Each thread has its own function stack space, which guarantees that any local variable defined in the worker will have a separate instance per thread. Therefore, const auto thread_id in the worker is initialized with a different ID depending on the thread it is run by. We do not need to take any precautions to ensure that the data stored in thread_id is consistent. It is guaranteed by the Standard that data with automatic storage duration is not shared between the threads.

Once all the jthread objects have been created, the main thread concurrently prints its ID along with the rest of the threads. There is no guaranteed order of execution for each thread, and it is possible for one thread to be interrupted by another. As a result, it is important to ensure that the code is written in a manner that can handle potential preemption and remains robust in all scenarios:

```
std::osyncstream{std::cout} << "Hello Main program thread
    with id:" << std::this_thread::get_id() << '\n';
```

All threads are now running concurrently with the main thread. We need to make sure that the main thread is also printing to the standard output in a thread-safe manner. We again use an instance of std::osyncstream, but this time, we don't create a named variable – instead, we create a temporary one. This approach is favored due to its ease of use, similar to using the std::cout object. The standard guarantees that the output will be flushed at the end of each statement, as the temporary ones persist until the end of the statement and their destructor is invoked, resulting in the flushing of the output.

Here is a sample output from the program:

```
Hello from new jthread with id:1567180544
Hello from new jthread with id:1476392704
Hello from new jthread with id:1468000000
Hello Main program thread with id:1567184704
Hello from new jthread with id:1558787840
Hello from new jthread with id:1459607296
```

The `std::jthread` name refers to a *joining* thread. Unlike `std::thread`, `std::jthread` also has the ability to *automatically* join the thread that it has been started by. The behavior of `std::thread` can be confusing at times. If `std::thread` has not been joined or detached, and it is still considered *joinable*, the `std::terminate` function will be called upon its destruction. A thread is considered joinable if neither the `join()` nor the `detach()` method has been called. In our example, all the `jthread` objects automatically join during their destruction and do not result in the termination of the program.

Canceling threads – is this really possible?

Before C++ 20 was released, this wasn't quite possible. It was not guaranteed that `std::thread` was stoppable in the sense that there wasn't a standard utility to halt the thread's execution. Different mechanisms were used instead. Stopping `std::thread` required cooperation between the `main` and worker threads, typically using a flag or atomic variable or some kind of messaging system.

With the release of C++20, there is now a standardized utility for requesting `std::jthread` objects to stop their execution. The stop tokens come to help. Looking at the C++ standard reference page about the definition of `std::jthread` (https://en.cppreference.com/w/cpp/thread/jthread), we find the following:

> *"The class jthread represents a single thread of execution. It has the same general behavior as std::thread, except that jthread automatically rejoins on destruction, and can be canceled/stopped in certain situations."*

We already saw that `jthread` objects automatically join on destruction, but what about canceling/stopping and what does "certain situations" mean? Let's dig deeper into this.

First of all, don't expect that `std::jthread` exposes some magical mechanism, some red button that stops the running thread when it is pressed. It is always a matter of implementation, how exactly your worker function is implemented. If you want your thread to be cancelable, you have to make sure that you have implemented it in the right way in order to allow cancellation:

```
#include <iostream>
#include <syncstream>
#include <thread>
#include <array>
using namespace std::literals::chrono_literals;
int main() {
    const auto worker{[](std::stop_token token, int num){
        // {1}
        while (!token.stop_requested()) { // {2}
            std::osyncstream{std::cout} << "Thread with id
            " << num << " is currently working.\n";
            std::this_thread::sleep_for(200ms);
        }
```

```
        std::osyncstream{std::cout} << "Thread with id " <<
            num << " is now stopped!\n";
    }};
    std::array<std::jthread, 3> my_threads{
        std::jthread{worker, 0},
        std::jthread{worker, 1},
        std::jthread{worker, 2}
    };
    // Give some time to the other threads to start
       executing …
    std::this_thread::sleep_for(1s);
    // 'Let's stop them
    for (auto& thread : my_threads) {
        thread.request_stop(); // {3} - this is not a
            blocking call, it is just a request.
    }
    std::osyncstream{std::cout} < "Main thread just
       requested stop!\n";
    return 0; // jthread dtors join them here.
}
```

Looking at the definition of our worker lambda function, we observe that it is now slightly reworked (marker {1}). It accepts two new parameters – std::stop_token token and int num. The stop token reflects the shared stop state that a jthread object has. If the worker method accepts many parameters, then the stop token must always be the first parameter passed.

It is imperative to ensure that the worker method is designed to be able to handle cancellation. This is what the stop token is used for. Our logic should be implemented in such a way that it regularly checks whether a stop request has been received. This is done with a call to the stop_requested() method of the std::stop_token object. Every specific implementation decides where and when these checks are to be done. If the code doesn't respect the stop token state, then the thread can't be canceled gracefully. So, it's up to you to correctly design your code.

Luckily, our worker lambda respects the state of the thread's stop token. It continuously checks whether a stop is requested (marker {2}). If not, it prints the thread's ID and goes to sleep for 200ms. This loop continues until the parent thread decides to send stop requests to its worker threads (marker {3}). This is done by invoking the request_stop() method of the std::jthread object.

Here is the output of the program:

```
Thread with id 0 is currently working.
Thread with id 1 is currently working.
Thread with id 2 is currently working.
Thread with id 1 is currently working.
Thread with id 2 is currently working.
Thread with id 0 is currently working.
Thread with id 1 is currently working.
Thread with id 2 is currently working.
Thread with id 0 is currently working.
Thread with id 2 is currently working.
Thread with id 1 is currently working.
Thread with id 0 is currently working.
Thread with id 1 is currently working.
Thread with id 0 is currently working.
Thread with id 2 is currently working.
Main thread just requested stop!
Thread with id 1 is now stopped!
Thread with id 0 is now stopped!
Thread with id 2 is now stopped!
```

Now that we know how we can stop the execution of a specific `std::jthread` using `std::stop_token`, let's see how we can stop the execution of multiple `std::jthread` objects using a single stop source.

std::stop_source

The `std::stop_source` class enables you to signal a cancellation request for `std::jthread`. When a stop request is issued through a `stop_source` object, it becomes visible to all other `stop_source` and `std::stop_token` objects associated with the same stop state. You just need to signal it, and any thread worker that consumes it will be notified.

By utilizing `std::stop_token` and `std::stop_source`, threads can signal or check for a request to stop their execution asynchronously. The request to stop is made through `std::stop_source`, which affects all related `std::stop_token` objects. These tokens can be passed to the worker functions and used to monitor stop requests. Both `std::stop_source` and `std::stop_token` share ownership of the stop state. The method of the `std::stop_source` class – `request_stop()` – and the methods in `std::stop_token` – `stop_requested()` and `stop_possible()` – are all atomic operations to ensure that no data race will occur.

Let's have a look at how our previous example could be reworked with the help of the stop tokens:

```cpp
#include <iostream>
#include <syncstream>
#include <thread>
#include <array>
using namespace std::literals::chrono_literals;
int main() {
    std::stop_source source;
    const auto worker{[](std::stop_source sr, int num){
        std::stop_token token = sr.get_token();
        while (!token.stop_requested()) {
            std::osyncstream{std::cout} << "Thread with id
              " << num << " is currently working.\n";
            std::this_thread::sleep_for(200ms);
        }
        std::osyncstream{std::cout} << "Thread with id " <<
          num << " is now stopped!\n";
    }};
    std::array<std::jthread, 3> my_threads{
        std::jthread{worker, source, 0},
        std::jthread{worker, source, 1},
        std::jthread{worker, source, 2}
    };
    std::this_thread::sleep_for(1s);
    source.request_stop(); // this is not a blocking call,
      it is just a request. {1}
    Std::osyncstream{std::cout} << "Main thread just
      requested stop!\n";
    return 0; // jthread dtors join them here.
}
```

The `main` method starts with the declaration of the `std::stop_source` source, which will be used by the `main` thread to signal all child worker threads and request them to stop. The worker lambda is slightly reworked in order to accept `std::stop_source sr` as an input. This is in fact the communication channel through which the worker is notified for a stop request. The `std::stop_source` object is copied in all workers associated with the started threads.

Rather than iterating through all the threads and invoking on each of them a stop request, the only operation that we need to invoke is to directly call `request_stop()` on the source instance in the `main` thread (marker {1}). This will broadcast stop requests to all workers that consume it.

As the name suggests, the call to the `request_stop()` method on the stop source object is just a request rather than a blocking call. So, don't expect your threads to stop immediately once the call is finished.

Here is the sample output from the program:

```
Thread with id 0 is currently working.
Thread with id 1 is currently working.
Thread with id 2 is currently working.
Thread with id 1 is currently working.
Thread with id 2 is currently working.
Thread with id 0 is currently working.
Thread with id 1 is currently working.
Thread with id 2 is currently working.
Thread with id 0 is currently working.
Thread with id 1 is currently working.
Thread with id 0 is currently working.
Thread with id 2 is currently working.
Thread with id 1 is currently working.
Thread with id 0 is currently working.
Thread with id 2 is currently working.
Main thread just requested stop!
Thread with id 1 is now stopped!
Thread with id 0 is now stopped!
Thread with id 2 is now stopped!
```

We are now familiar with two mechanisms for halting thread execution in C++. Now, it's time to see how we can share data between multiple threads.

Sharing data during parallel execution

Think in terms of tasks rather than threads (https://isocpp.github.io/CppCoreGuidelines/ CppCoreGuidelines#cp4-think-in-terms-of-tasks-rather-than-threads).

Referring back to the *C++ Core Guidelines*, they advise us that it is better to stick to tasks rather than threads. A thread is a technical implementation idea, a perspective on how the machine works. On the other hand, a task is a practical concept for work that you want to do, ideally alongside other tasks. In general, practical concepts are simpler to understand and provide better abstraction, and we prefer them.

But what is a task in C++? Is it another standard library primitive or what? Let's have a look!

In C++, besides threads, tasks are also available to perform work asynchronously. A task consists of a worker and two associated components: a **promise** and a **future**. These components are connected through a shared state, which is a kind of data channel. The promise does the work and places the result in the shared state, while the future retrieves the result. Both the promise and the future can run in separate threads. One unique aspect of the future is that it can retrieve the result at a later time, making the calculation of the result by the promise independent from the retrieval of the result by the associated future.

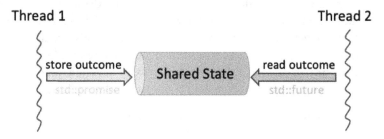

Figure 6.4 – Inter-thread communication

The <future> header, defined in the Standard Library, is necessary for utilizing tasks. It provides the capability to obtain the results of functions executed in separate threads, also referred to as **asynchronous tasks**, and to manage any exceptions they may throw. Using the std::promise class, these results are communicated through a shared state, where the asynchronous task can store its return value or an exception. This shared state can then be accessed using std::future to retrieve the return value or the stored exception.

Let's have a look at a simple example where a thread reports a string as a result to its parent thread:

```
#include <future>
#include <thread>
#include <iostream>
using namespace std::literals::chrono_literals;
int main() {
    std::promise<std::string> promise; // {1}
    std::future<std::string> future{promise.get_future()};
        // {2} - Get the future from the promise.
    std::jthread th1{ [p{std::move(promise)}]() mutable { //
        {3} - Move the promise inside the worker thread.
        std::this_thread::sleep_for(20ms);
        p.set_value_at_thread_exit("I promised to call you
            back once I am ready!\n"); // {4}
    }};
    std::cout << "Main thread is ready.\n";
    std::cout << future.get(); // {5} - This is a blocking
        call!
    return 0;
}
```

As we already discussed, threads communicate with each other using a shared state. In the `int main()` method, we declare `std::promise<std::string> promise`, which is our de facto data source (marker {1}). The `std::promise` class is a template class that needs to be parameterized once it is instantiated. In our example, we want our worker thread, `std::thread th1`, to return a string as a result. Therefore, we instantiate `std::promise` with the `std::string` type. We also need a way for the `main` thread to be able to get the result that will be set by the worker thread. In order to do so, we need to get a `std::future` object from the promise we already instantiated. This is possible because the `std::promise` type has a method that returns its associated future – `std::future<...> get_future()`. In our example, we instantiate a future object, `future`, which is initialized by the `get_future()` method of the promise (marker {2}).

Since we already have a promise and its associated future, we are now ready to move the promise as part of the worker thread. We are moving it in order to be sure that it won't be used by the `main` thread anymore (marker {3}). Our worker thread is quite simple, and it just sleeps for 20ms and sets the result in the promise (marker {4}). The `std::promise` type provides several ways to set a result. The result could be either a value of type by which the promise is parameterized or it could be an exception thrown during worker execution. The value is set by the `set_value()` and `set_value_at_thread_exit()` methods. The main difference between both methods is that `set_value()` immediately notifies the shared state that the value is ready, whereas `set_value_at_thread_exit()` does it when the thread execution is finished.

Meanwhile, the `main` thread execution has been blocked waiting for the result of the worker thread. This is done on the call to the `future.get()` method. This is a blocking call on which the waiting thread is blocked until the shared state is notified that the result of the future is set. In our example, this happens after the completion of the worker thread because the shared state is only notified when the worker is finished (marker {5}).

The expected output from the program is as follows:

```
Main thread is ready.
I promised to call you back once I am ready!
```

Barriers and latches

New thread synchronization primitives were introduced with the C++20 standard. Barriers and latches are straightforward thread synchronization primitives that block threads to wait until a counter reaches zero. These primitives are offered by the standard library in the form of the `std::latch` and `std::barrier` classes.

What distinguishes these two synchronization mechanisms? The key difference is that `std::latch` can only be used once, while `std::barrier` can be used multiple times by multiple threads.

What advantages do barriers and latches offer over other synchronization primitives that the C++ standard provides, such as condition variables and locks? Barriers and latches are easier to use, more intuitive, and, in some circumstances, may provide better performance.

Let's have a look at the following example:

```cpp
#include <thread>
#include <iostream>
#include <array>
#include <latch>
#include <syncstream>
using namespace std::literals::chrono_literals;
int main() {
    std::latch progress{2}; // {1}
    std::array<std::jthread, 2> threads {
        std::jthread{ [&] (int num) {
            std::osyncstream{std::cout} << "Starting thread
              " << num << " and go to sleep.\n";
            std::this_thread::sleep_for(100ms);
            std::osyncstream{std::cout} << "Decrementing
              the latch for thread " << num << '\n';
            progress.count_down(); // {2}
            std::osyncstream{std::cout} << "Thread " << num
              << " finished!\n";
        }, 0},
        std::jthread{ [&] (int num) {
            std::osyncstream{std::cout} << "Starting thread
              " << num << ". Arrive on latch and wait to
                become zero.\n";
            progress.arrive_and_wait(); // {3}
            std::osyncstream{std::cout} << "Thread " << num
              << " finished!\n";
        }, 1}
    };
    std::osyncstream{std::cout} << "Main thread waiting
      workers to finish.\n";
    progress.wait(); // {4} wait for all threads to finish.
    std::cout << "Main thread finished!\n";
    return 0;
}
```

We have an array of two threads that are synchronized on a latch. This means that each thread starts its execution and does its work until it reaches the latch.

The `std::latch` class is a synchronization mechanism that utilizes a downward-counting counter to coordinate threads. The counter is set at initialization and passed as an argument to the constructor. The threads can then wait until the counter reaches zero. It is not possible to increase or reset the counter once it is initialized. Access to the member functions of `std::latch` from multiple threads concurrently is guaranteed to be thread-safe and free from data races.

In our example (marker {1}), we have initialized the latch with a value of 2 because we have two worker threads that need to be synchronized with the main one. Once the worker reaches the latch, it has three options:

- Decrement it and continue (marker {2}). This is done using the member of the `std::latch` class – `void count_down (n = 1)`. This call is non-blocking and automatically decrements the latch's internal counter value by n. It is undefined behavior if you try to decrement with a negative value or with a value greater than the value that the internal counter currently has. In our example, this is a worker thread with an ID of 0, which, once it is ready, decrements the latch counter and finishes.

- Decrement it and wait until the latch becomes zero (marker {3}). In order to do so, you have to use another method of the `std::latch` class – `void arrive_and_wait (n = 1)`. This method, once it is invoked, decrements the latch by n and blocks it until the latch's internal counter hits 0. In our example, this is a worker thread with an ID of 1, which, once it is ready, starts waiting until the other worker is finished.

- Just block and wait until the internal counter of the latch becomes zero (marker {4}). This is possible because `std::latch` provides a method – `void wait() const`. This is a blocking call on which the invoking thread is blocked until the internal counter of the latch hits zero. In our example, the `main` thread blocks and starts waiting for the worker threads to finish their execution.

The result of our program is that the `main` thread execution is suspended until the worker threads finish their jobs. The `std::latch` class provides a convenient way to synchronize the execution of several threads:

```
Main thread waiting workers to finish.
Starting thread 1. Arrive on latch and wait to become zero.
Starting thread 0 and go to sleep.
Decrementing the latch for thread 0
Thread 0 finished!
Main thread finished!
Thread 1 finished!
```

Another very similar synchronization primitive to `std::latch` is `std::barrier`. Barriers are thread synchronization primitives that permit a group of threads to wait until all of them reach a specific synchronization point. Unlike a latch, a barrier can be used multiple times. Once the threads have been released from the synchronization point, they can reuse the barrier. A synchronization point is a specific moment where a thread can pause its execution until a specific condition has been met. This makes barriers ideal for synchronizing repeated tasks or executing different phases from the same bigger task by many threads.

In order to get a better understanding of what barriers are, let's use an example. Imagine that you have a network of temperature sensors installed in your home. In each room, there is a sensor installed. Each sensor takes a temperature measurement at a specific time period and the result is buffered in its memory. When the sensor does 10 measurements, it sends them as a chunk to a server. This server is responsible for collecting all measurements from all sensors in your home and calculating temperature mean values – the mean temperature for each room and the mean temperature for your entire home.

Let's discuss the algorithm now. In order to calculate the mean temperature of your entire home, we first need to process the temperature measurements done by the sensors that are sent to the server at some specific time period. This means that we need to process all the temperature samples received for a specific room to calculate the mean temperature for that room, and we need to do this for all the rooms in your home. Finally, with the calculated mean temperatures for each room, we can calculate the mean temperature for the entire home.

It sounds like we need to process a lot of data. It makes sense to try to parallelize the data processing wherever possible. Yes, you are right: not all of the data processing can be parallelized! There is a strict sequence of actions we need to respect. Firstly, we need to calculate the mean temperature in each room. There are no dependencies between the rooms, so we can execute these calculations in parallel. Once we have all the room temperatures calculated, we can continue to the calculation of the mean temperature of the entire home. This is exactly where `std::barrier` will come to the rescue.

The `std::barrier` synchronization primitive blocks the threads at a specific synchronization point (the barrier) until all of them arrive. Then, it allows a callback to be invoked and a specific action to be performed. In our example, we need to wait for all room calculations to be finished – to wait on the barrier. Then, a callback will be executed where we will calculate the mean temperature for the entire home:

```
using Temperature =
    std::tuple<std::string, // The name of the room
               std::vector<double>, // Temperature
                 measurements
               double>; // Calculated mean temperature
                        // value for a specific room
std::vector<Temperature> room_temperatures {
    {"living_room",{}, 0.0},
    {"bedroom", {}, 0.0},
    {"kitchen", {}, 0.0},
    {"closet", {}, 0.0}
};
```

Let's start with the definition of our data container where we will store the temperature measurements done for each room, together with their calculated mean values by our worker threads. We will use a vector of rooms, `room_temperature`, in which we will store the room name, a vector of measurements, and the mean value.

Now, we need to define the workers that will, in parallel, calculate the mean values for each room:

```
std::stop_source message;
std::barrier measurementBarrier{ // {1}
    static_cast<int>(room_temperatures.size()), // {2}
    [&message]() noexcept { // {3}
        // 1. Compute the mean temperature of the entire
           home.
        // 2. Push new temperature data
        // 3. After 5 measurement cycles request stop.
    }
};

std::vector<std::jthread> measurementSensors;
for (auto& temp : room_temperatures) {
    measurementSensors.emplace_back([&measurementBarrier,
        &message, &temp]() {
        const auto& token = message.get_token();
        while(!token.stop_requested()) {
            ProcessMeasurement(temp);
            measurementBarrier.arrive_and_wait(); // {4}
        }
    });
}
```

We create the same count of `jthread` instances as the count of the rooms. Each `jthread` instance is created and a worker lambda is assigned to it. As you can see, the worker lambda captures a `std::stop_source` object, which will be used to notify it that no other work is pending and the thread execution should be finished. The lambda also captures `std::barrier measurementBarrier`, which will be used to block each thread that is ready with its computation until all other threads are also ready (marker {1}).

The `std::barrier` instance needs to be initialized with the count of the synchronization points (marker {2}). This means that the barrier will be raised when the count of threads reaching the barrier is equal to the initialized value. In our example, we initialize the barrier with the count of the worker threads that will concurrently compute the mean temperatures for each room. An optional initialization parameter that the barrier accepts is a callback function (marker {3}). This function must not throw and, therefore, we mark it as `noexcept`. It will be invoked when all threads in a certain cycle arrive at the barrier and before the barrier is raised. Keep in mind that the standard doesn't specify which thread this callback will be executed on. We will use this callback to do the following:

- Iterate through all already computed mean temperatures for the rooms and compute the mean temperature of the entire home. This is the result we expect our program to deliver.

- Feed the worker threads with new temperature data for the next computation cycle. In contrast to std::latch, std::barrier allows us to use the same barrier as many times as we need.

- Check whether we have already calculated five times the mean temperature of the entire home and, if so, notify the workers that they need to gracefully stop and exit the program.

When a thread starts working and it is ready with its computation, it hits the barrier (marker {4}). This is possible because std::barrier exposes a method: void arrive_and_wait(). This call effectively decrements the internal counter of the barrier, which notifies it that the thread has arrived and blocks the thread until the counter hits zero and the barrier's callback is triggered.

In the following code, you can find the methods responsible for generating example temperature values and calculating the mean temperature value:

```
void GetTemperatures(Temperature& temp) {
    std::mt19937 gen{std::random_device{}()};
    // Add normal distribution with mean = 20
    // and standard deviation of 8
    std::normal_distribution<> d{20, 8};
    auto& input_data{std::get<1>(temp)};
    input_data.clear();
    for (auto n{0}; n < 10; ++n) {
        // Add input data
        input_data.emplace_back(d(gen));
    }
}
void ProcessMeasurement(Temperature& temp){
    const auto& values{std::get<1>(temp)};
    auto& mean{std::get<2>(temp)};
    mean = std::reduce(values.begin(), values.end()) /
        values.size();
}
```

Once we have all the code pieces available, let's see the `main` method implementation of our program:

```cpp
int main() {
    // Init data
    std::ranges::for_each(room_temperatures,
      GetTemperatures);
    std::stop_source message;
    std::barrier measurementBarrier{
        static_cast<int>(room_temperatures.size()),
        [&message]() noexcept {
            // Get all results
            double mean{0.0};
            for (const auto& room_t : room_temperatures) {
                std::cout << "Mean temperature in "
                          << std::get<0>(room_t)
                          << " is " << std::get<2>(room_t)
                          << ".\n";
                mean += std::get<2>(room_t);
            }
            mean /= room_temperatures.size();
            std::cout << "Mean temperature in your home is
              " << mean << " degrees Celsius.\n";
            std::cout << "========================
            ======================\n";
            // Add new input data
            std::ranges::for_each(room_temperatures,
              GetTemperatures);
            // Make 4 measurements and request stop.
            static unsigned timer{0};
            if (timer >= 3) {
                message.request_stop();
            }
            ++timer;
        }
    };
    std::vector<std::jthread> measurementSensors;
    for (auto& temp : room_temperatures) {
        measurementSensors.emplace_back
          ([&measurementBarrier, &message, &temp](){
            const auto& token = message.get_token();
```

```
            while(!token.stop_requested()) {
                ProcessMeasurement(temp);
                measurementBarrier.arrive_and_wait();
            }
        });
    }
    return 0;
}
```

For the input temperature data of our example, we use a random number generator, which produces data with normal distribution. As a result, we get the following output:

```
Mean temperature in living_room is 18.7834.
Mean temperature in bedroom is 16.9559.
Mean temperature in kitchen is 22.6351.
Mean temperature in closet is 20.0296.
Mean temperature in your home is 19.601 degrees Celsius.
================================================
Mean temperature in living_room is 19.8014.
Mean temperature in bedroom is 20.4068.
Mean temperature in kitchen is 19.3223.
Mean temperature in closet is 21.2223.
Mean temperature in your home is 20.1882 degrees Celsius.
================================================
Mean temperature in living_room is 17.9305.
Mean temperature in bedroom is 22.6204.
Mean temperature in kitchen is 17.439.
Mean temperature in closet is 20.3107.
Mean temperature in your home is 19.5752 degrees Celsius.
================================================
Mean temperature in living_room is 19.4584.
Mean temperature in bedroom is 19.0377.
Mean temperature in kitchen is 16.3529.
Mean temperature in closet is 20.1057.
Mean temperature in your home is 18.7387 degrees Celsius.
================================================
```

With the preceding example, we have demonstrated how you can use synchronization primitives with `std::jthread` to provide inter-thread synchronization for your program.

Summary

In this chapter, we explored several topics related to concurrency and parallelism in C++. We began by discussing the terminology and differences between concurrency and parallelism, including preemption. We then delved into how programs execute on single and multiple processing units, distinguishing between processes and execution threads and briefly exploring communication mechanisms such as pipes, sockets, and shared memory.

In the context of C++, we examined how the language supports concurrency, specifically through the `std::thread` class and the new `std::jthread` primitive introduced in C++20. We also discussed the risks associated with race conditions and data races, including an example of a money transfer operation. To avoid these issues, we examined mechanisms such as locks, atomic operations, and memory barriers.

Moving on, we looked closely at the `std::jthread` class, exploring its functionality and proper usage. Additionally, we learned about a new synchronized stream wrapper delivered in C++20 for printing in concurrent environments. We also covered how to cancel running threads using `std::stop_token` and how to request a stop to several threads using `std::stop_source`.

We then shifted our focus to returning results from threads using `std::future` and `std::promise`. Additionally, we discussed the use of `std::latch` and `std::barrier`, using an example of a temperature station to demonstrate how the latter can be used to synchronize threads.

Overall, we explored a range of topics related to concurrency and parallelism in C++, from basic terminology and concepts to more advanced techniques and mechanisms for avoiding data races and synchronizing threads. But please stay tuned because, in the next chapter, you will get familiar with some mechanisms for IPC that are widely used in software programming.

7

Proceeding with Inter-Process Communication

The previous chapter presented many features of C++20 that allow you to execute tasks in parallel. Outside of the global variables, it didn't cover ways to communicate between processes or threads. On a system level, most of the asynchronous calls are born in the continuous communication between processes and different computer systems.

In this chapter, you will learn about the **inter-process communication** (**IPC**) interfaces that Linux provides. Through them, you will get a full picture of possibilities to cover your system and software requirements. You'll start by learning about **message queues** (**MQs**) as a continuation of the discussion about pipes in *Chapter 3*. In addition, we will analyze in detail the work of the **semaphore** and **mutex** synchronization techniques. We will introduce you to some new C++20 features in this area that are easy to use, and you will no longer have to implement such yourself.

This allows us to proceed with the **shared memory** technique, which will give you the option to transfer large amounts of data fast. Finally, if you're interested in communication between computer systems on the network, you'll learn about sockets and network communication protocols. With this, we give you some practical and commands to administer your own system on the network.

We will build on the discussions started in this chapter in *Chapter 9*.

In this chapter, we are going to cover the following main topics:

- Introducing MQs and the pub/sub mechanism
- Guaranteeing atomic operations through semaphores and mutual exclusions
- Using shared memory
- Communicating through the network with sockets

Technical requirements

To run the code examples, you must prepare the following:

- A Linux-based system capable of compiling and executing C++20 (for example, **Linux Mint 21**)

- A GCC 12.2 compiler (`https://gcc.gnu.org/git/gcc.git gcc-source`) with the `-std=c++2a`, `-lpthread`, and `-lrt` flags

- For all the examples, you can alternatively use `https://godbolt.org/`

- All code examples in this chapter are available for download from `https://github.com/PacktPublishing/C-Programming-for-Linux-Systems/tree/main/Chapter%207`

Introducing MQs and the pub/sub mechanism

We're glad to be back on the IPC topic. The last time we discussed it was in *Chapter 3*, where we explained pipes and used some code examples. You learned about the basic mechanism of exchanging data between processes, but as you remember, there are some blocking points. As with any programming instrument, pipes have particular usage – they are fast, and they can help you send and receive data from both related (forked) processes (through **anonymous pipes**) and unrelated processes (through **named pipes**).

In a similar fashion, we could use MQs to transfer data, which are available to related and unrelated processes, too. They provide the ability to send a single message to multiple receiving processes. But as you saw, pipes are primitive in the sense of sending and receiving binary data as is, while MQs bring the notion of a *message* to the table. The policy of the transfer is still configured in the calling process – queue name, size, signal handling, priority, and so on – but its policy and ability to serialize data are now in the hands of the MQ's implementation. This gives the programmer a relatively simple and flexible way to prepare and handle messages of data. Based on our software design, we could easily implement an asynchronous send-receive data transfer or a **publish/subscribe (pub/sub)** mechanism. Linux provides two different interfaces for MQs – one designed for local server applications (coming from System V) and one designed for real-time applications (coming from POSIX). For the purposes of the book, we prefer to use the POSIX interface as it is richer and cleaner in configuration. It is also a file-based mechanism, as discussed in *Chapter 1*, and you can find a mounted queue through the following:

```
$ ls /dev/mqueue
```

This interface is available through the OS real-time functions library, `librt`, so you need to link it during compilation. The MQ itself can be visualized as follows:

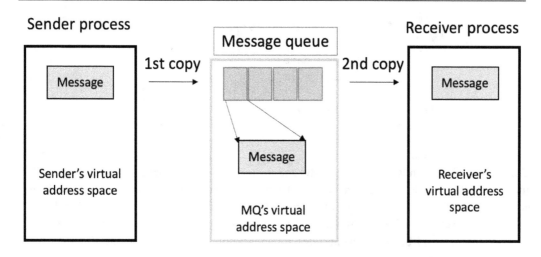

Figure 7.1 – Representation of IPC through the MQ

Let's look at an example where we send data from one process to another. The exemplary data is already stored in a file and loaded to be sent through the MQ. The full example can be found at `https://github.com/PacktPublishing/C-Programming-for-Linux-Systems/tree/main/Chapter%207`:

```
constexpr auto MAX_SIZE = 1024;
string_view QUEUE_NAME  = "/test_queue";
```

We set our initial configuration together with the queue name as the pathname:

```
void readFromQueue() {
...
    mqd_t              mq   = { 0 };
    struct mq_attr attr = { 0 };
    array<char, MAX_SIZE> buffer{};
    attr.mq_flags = 0;
    attr.mq_maxmsg = 10;
    attr.mq_msgsize = MAX_SIZE;
    attr.mq_curmsgs = 0;
    if (mq = mq_open(QUEUE_NAME.data(), O_CREAT | O_RDONLY,
                0700, &attr); mq > -1) { // {1}
        for (;;) {
            if (auto bytes_read = mq_receive(mq,
                                        buffer.data(),
                                        buffer.size(),
                                        NULL);
                            bytes_read > 0) { // {2}
```

```
                buffer[bytes_read] = '\0';
                cout << "Received: "
                        << buffer.data()
                        << endl; // {3}
            }
            else if (bytes_read == -1) {
                cerr << "Receive message failed!";
            }
```

Additional configuration is applied to the MQ and the receiving end is prepared. The mq_open() function is called in order to create the MQ on the filesystem and open its reading end. Through an endless loop, the data is received as it is read from a binary file and printed out (markers {2} and {3} in the preceding code) until the file is fully consumed. Then, the receiving ends and the reading end are closed (marker {4} in the following code). If there's nothing else to be done, the MQ is deleted from the filesystem through mq_unlink():

```
            else {
                cout << "\n\n\n***Receiving ends***"
                        << endl;
                mq_close(mq); // {4}
                break;
            }
        }
    }
    else {
        cerr << "Receiver: Failed to load queue: "
                << strerror(errno);
    }
    mq_unlink(QUEUE_NAME.data());
}
```

This example is implemented with two threads but could be done in the same fashion with two processes. The MQ functionality will remain the same. We call mq_open() again and open the MQ for writing (marker {5} in the following code). The created queue can fit up to 10 messages and each message can be 1,024 bytes in size – this is defined through the MQ attributes in the earlier code snippet. If you don't want the MQ operations to be blocking, you could use the O_NONBLOCK flag in the attributes, or use mq_notify() prior to the mq_receive() call. That way, if the MQ is empty, the reader will be blocked, but mq_notify() will trigger a signal on message arrival and the process will be resumed.

Then, the locally stored file is opened with the test data and we read from it (markers {6} and {7} in the following code). While we read (you could use std::ofstream as well), we send its contents through the MQ (marker {8} in the following code). The message has the lowest priority possible, which means 0. In a system with more messages in a queue, we could set a higher priority and they will be handled in a decreasing order. The maximum value is visible from `sysconf(_SC_MQ_PRIO_MAX)`, where, for Linux, this is `32768`, but POSIX enforces a range from 0 to 31 in order to be compliant with other OSs as well. Let's check the following code snippet:

```
void writeToQueue() {
...
    if (mq = mq_open(QUEUE_NAME.data(), O_WRONLY,
                     0700, NULL); mq > -1) { // {5}
        int fd = open("test.dat", O_RDONLY); // {6}
        if (fd > 0) {
            for (;;) {
                // This could be taken from cin.
                array<char, MAX_SIZE> buffer{};
                if (auto bytes_to_send =
                        read(fd,
                            buffer.data(),
                        buffer.size());
                        bytes_to_send > 0) { // {7}
                    if (auto b_sent =
                        mq_send(mq,
                                buffer.data(),
                                buffer.size(),
                                0);
                                b_sent == -1) {// {8}
                        cerr << "Sent failed!"
                            << strerror(errno);
                }
```

Then, we send a zero-sized message to indicate the end of the communication (marker {9}):

```
...
                else if (bytes_to_send == 0) {
                    cout << "Sending ends...." << endl;
                    if (auto b_sent =
                        mq_send(mq,
                                buffer.data(),
                                0,
                                0); b_sent == -1) {
                                // {9}
                        cerr << "Sent failed!"
                            << strerror(errno);
```

The result is the following (the printed data from the file is reduced for readability):

```
Thread READER starting...
Thread WRITER starting...
Sending ends....
Received: This is a testing file...
Received: ing fileThis is a testing file...
***Receiving ends***
Main: program completed. Exiting.
```

This is a very simple example considering we have only two workers – `readFromQueue()` and `writeToQueue()`. The MQs allow us to scale up and execute a many-to-many communication. This approach could be found on many embedded systems, as it's also real-time compliant and doesn't expect any synchronization primitives to be used. Many microservice architectures and serverless applications rely on it. In the next section, we are going to discuss one of the most popular patterns, based on MQs.

The pub/sub mechanism

You've probably figured out that one MQ could become a bottleneck while scaling up. As you observed in the previous example, there's the message count and size limitation. Another issue is the fact that after a message is consumed, it is removed from the queue – there can be only one consumer of a given message at a time. The data provider (the producer) has to manage the correct message address as well, meaning adding extra data to help the consumers identify to whom the message is sent, and each consumer has to follow that policy.

A preferred approach is to create a separate MQ for each consumer. The producer will be aware of those MQs a priori, either at compile time (all MQs are listed in the data segment by the system programmer) or runtime (each consumer will send its MQ pathname at startup and the producer will handle this information). That way, the consumers are *subscribing* to receive data from a given producer, and the producer *publishes* its data to all MQs it's aware of. Therefore, we call this a **publish-subscribe** mechanism.

Of course, the exact implementations might vary, depending on the software design, but the idea will remain the same. In addition, there could be multiple producers sending data to multiple consumers, and we say this is a **many-to-many** realization. Take a look at the following diagram:

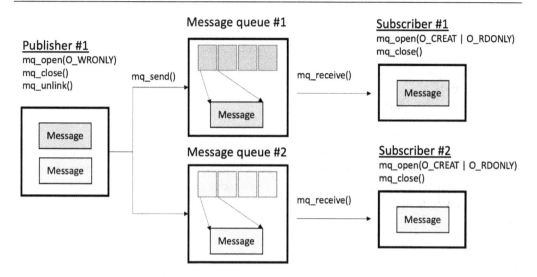

Figure 7.2 – Representation of the MQ realization of the pub/sub mechanism

As we proceed toward the decoupling of processes, we make our system more flexible. It becomes easier to scale as the subscribers don't lose computational time identifying whether the messages are directed to them or not. It is also easy to add a new producer or consumer without disturbing others. The MQ is implemented on an OS level, thus we could take it as a robust IPC mechanism. One possible disadvantage, though, is the fact that producers usually don't receive any health information from the subscribers. This leads to MQs being full of unconsumed data and the producers being blocked. Thus, additional implementation frameworks are implemented on a more abstract level, which takes care of such use cases. We encourage you to additionally research the **Observer** and **Message Broker** design patterns. In-house-developed pub/sub mechanisms are usually built on top of them and not always through MQs. Nonetheless, as you have probably guessed, sending large amounts of data is going to be a slow operation through such mechanisms. So, we need an instrument to get a big portion of data fast. Unfortunately, this requires additional synchronization management to avoid data races, similar to *Chapter 6*. The next section is about the synchronization primitives.

Guaranteeing atomic operations through semaphores and mutual exclusions

Let's try to *zoom in* on a shared resource and see what happens in the CPU. We will provide a simple and effective way to explain where exactly the data races start from. They were already thoroughly discussed in *Chapter 6*. Everything we learn here should be considered as an addition, in a sense, but the analysis methodology of concurrent and parallel processing remains the same as earlier. But now, we focus on concrete low-level problems.

Let's look closely at the following snippet:

```
int shrd_res = 0; //Some shared resource.
void thread_func(){
    shrd_res ++;
    std::cout << shrd_res;
}
```

It is a very simple piece of code in which a variable is incremented and printed out. According to C++ standards, such a modification is an undefined behavior in multithreaded environments. Let's see how – instead of going through the process's memory layout here, we will analyze its pseudo-assembly code side by side:

```
...
int shrd_res = 0;        store 0
shrd_res++;              load value
                         add 1
                         store value
std::cout << shrd_res;   load value
...
```

Suppose this increment procedure is in a thread function and there's more than one thread executing it. The add 1 instruction is done on the loaded value, and not on the actual memory location of shrd_res. The preceding code snippet will be executed multiple times, and most probably in parallel. If we note that the thread is a set of instructions, the intuition would be that the instructions are executed in a monolithic manner. In other words, each thread routine should be run without interruption, which is usually the case. However, there is a small particularity that we should keep in mind – the CPU is engineered to keep a small latency. It is not built for data parallelism. Therefore, figuratively speaking, its main goal is to load itself with a large number of small tasks. Each of our threads is executed in a separate processor; this could be a separate CPU, a CPU thread, or a CPU core – it really depends on the system. If the number of processors (CPUs, cores, or threads) is smaller than N, then the remaining threads are expected to queue themselves and wait until a processor is freed up.

Now, the initial threads' instructions are already loaded there and executed as they are. Even when the CPU cores are architecturally the same, their goal is to be executed as fast as possible. This means that it is not expected for them to be equal in speed because of multiple hardware fluctuations. But shared_resource is a variable that is, well... a shared resource. This means that whoever gets to increment it first will do it and others will follow. Even if we don't care about the std::cout result (for example, the printing order stops being sequential), we still have something to worry about. And you've probably guessed it! We don't know which value we are actually going to increment – is it going to be the last stored value of shared_resource or the newly incremented one? How could this happen?

Let's see:

```
Thread 1: shrd_res++; T1: load value
                      T1: add 1
Thread 2: shrd_res++; T2: load value
                      T2: add 1
                      T2: store value
                      T1: store value
```

Did you follow what just happened? `Thread 1`'s sequence of instructions was disrupted, because of the execution of `Thread 2`. Now, can we predict what's going to be printed? This is known as an **undefined behavior**. In some cases, it will be because `Thread 2` was never executed, as the last value to be stored in `shared_resource` will be the one incremented in:

```
T1: add 1
```

In other words, we lost one increment. There was nothing instructing the CPU that both procedures have to be called separately and continuously executed. It should be clear that a finite number of instruction combinations are possible, all of them leading to unexpected behavior, because it depends on the hardware's state. Such an operation is called **non-atomic**. In order to handle parallelism correctly, we need to rely on **atomic** operations! It is the job of the software developer to consider this and inform the CPU about such sets of instructions. Mechanisms such as mutexes and semaphores are used to manage *atomic* scopes. We are going to analyze their roles thoroughly in the next sections.

Semaphore

If you make a questionnaire asking people in multiple professions what a **semaphore** is, you will get different answers. A person from the airport will tell you that this is a system for signaling someone through the use of flags. A police officer might tell you that this is just a traffic light. Asking a train driver will probably give you a similar response. Interestingly, this is where *our* semaphores come from. Overall, these answers should hint to you that this is a *signaling* mechanism.

> **Important note**
>
> Programming semaphores were invented by Edsger Dijkstra and are mainly used to prevent race conditions. They help us signal when a resource is available or not and count how many shared resource units of a given kind are available.

Like the previously mentioned signaling mechanisms, semaphores don't guarantee error-free code, as they do not prevent processes or threads from acquiring a resource unit – they just inform. In the same way that a train might ignore the signal and proceed to an occupied train track or a car could proceed at a busy crossroad, this might be catastrophic! Again, it is the software engineer's task to figure out how to use semaphores for the system's good health. Therefore, let's get to using them.

Dijkstra provided us with two main functions surrounding a critical section: P(S) and V(S). As you probably know, he was Dutch, so these functions' names come from the Dutch words for *try* and *increase* (*probeer* and *vrhoog*, respectively), where S is the semaphore variable. Just by their names, you already get an idea about what they are going to do. Let's look at them in pseudocode:

```
unsigned int S = 0;
V(S):
    S=S+1;
P(S):
    while(S==0):
        // Do nothing.
    S = S - 1;
```

So, P(S) will endlessly check whether the semaphore has signaled that the resource is available – the semaphore is incremented. As soon as S is incremented, the loop is stopped, and the semaphore value is decreased for some other code to be executed. Based on the increment's value, we recognize two types of semaphores: **binary** and **counting**. The binary semaphore is often mistaken for a **mutual exclusion (mutex)** mechanism. The logic is the same – for example, whether the resource is free to be accessed and modified or not – but the nature of the technique is different, and as we explained earlier, nothing is stopping some bad concurrent design from ignoring a semaphore. We will get to that in a minute, but for now, let's pay attention to what the semaphore does. Before we begin with the code, let's put a disclaimer that there are a few semaphore interfaces on Unix-like OSs. The choice of usage depends on the level of abstraction and the standards. For example, not every system has POSIX, or it is not exposed fully. As we are going to focus on the C++20 usage, we will use the next examples just for reference. The full source code of the next examples can be found at https://github.com/PacktPublishing/C-Programming-for-Linux-Systems/tree/main/Chapter%207.

Let's take a look at two common semaphore interfaces on Linux. The first one is the **unnamed semaphore** – we can present it through the following interface:

```
sem_t sem;
sem_init(sem_t *sem, int pshared, unsigned int value);
int sem_destroy(sem_t *sem);
int sem_post(sem_t *sem);
int sem_wait(sem_t *sem);
```

The sem variable is the semaphore, which is initialized and de-initialized by sem_init() and sem_destroy(), respectively. The P(S) function is represented by sem_wait() and the V(S) function by sem_post(). There are also sem_trywait(), if you want to report an error when the decrement doesn't happen immediately, and sem_timedwait(), which is a blocking call for a time window in which the decrement could happen. This seems pretty clear, except for the initialization part. You've probably noticed the value and pshared arguments. The first one shows the initial value of the semaphore. For example, a binary semaphore could be 0 or 1. The second is more interesting.

As you might recall, in *Chapter 2* we discussed memory segments. Imagine that we create the semaphore on the **data**, the **BSS**, or the **heap**. Then, it would be globally visible only for the threads in a single process but would not be able to be shared between processes. The question is how to use it for process synchronization; pshared is used exactly for this purpose. If it's set to 0, then the semaphore is local for the process, but if it is set to a non-zero value, then it is shared between processes. The catch is to create the semaphore on a globally visible region of memory, such as shmem, including the filesystem as a shared resource pool. Here is an overview of **named semaphores**:

- The **named semaphore** is visible outside the process creator, as it resides in the filesystem, usually under /dev/shm. We treat it as a file. For example, the following code will create a semaphore with the name /sem and 0644 permissions – it will be readable and writable only by its owner, but only readable by others, and it will be visible on the filesystem until it is later removed through code:

```
sem_t *global_sem = sem_open("/sem", O_CREAT, 0644,
    0);
```

- The P(S) and V(S) calls remain the same. After we finish, we must close the file, and remove it, if we don't need it anymore:

```
sem_close(global_sem);
sem_unlink("/sem");
```

As mentioned in *Chapter 1*, you see that the POSIX calls follow the same pattern through the <object>_open, <object>_close, <object>_unlink, and <object>_<specific function> suffixes. This makes their usage common for every POSIX object, as you probably already observed earlier in the chapter.

A quick remark is that there are **lower-level semaphores** where the system calls are strongly related to the OS types or are based on direct OS signal manipulations. Such approaches are complex to implement and maintain because they are specific and considered fine-tuning. Feel free to research more about your own system.

A C++ semaphores primer

With this in mind, we'd like to continue leveling up the abstraction, and so we'll discuss the C++ semaphore objects. This is a new feature in C++20 and it's useful when you want to make the code more system-generic. Let's check it out through the **producer-consumer** problem. We will need a variable that will be visible in the process scope and modified by multiple threads: atomic<uint16_t> shared_resource. As mentioned at the beginning of this section, the semaphores help in task synchronization, but we need a data race guard. The atomic type is making sure we follow the C++ memory model and the compiler will keep the sequence of CPU instructions as per std::memory_oder. You can revisit *Chapter 6* for a data race explanation.

We will continue by creating two global `binary_semaphore` objects in order to synchronize the access appropriately (like a ping-pong). The `binary_semaphore` object is an alias of the `counting_semaphore` object with a maximum value of 1. We will need a program-ending rule so we will define a limit of iterations. We will ask the compiler to make it a constant, if possible, through the `constexpr` keyword. Last, but not least, we will create two threads that will act as a producer (incrementing the shared resource) and a consumer (decrementing it). Let's look at the code example:

```
...
uint32_t shared_resource = 0;
binary_semaphore sem_to_produce(0);
binary_semaphore sem_to_consume(0);
constexpr uint32_t limit = 65536;
```

The semaphores are constructed and initialized. We proceed with the threads. The `release()` function increments an internal counter, which signals the others (marker {2} in the following code, similar to `sem_post()`). We use `osyncstream(cout)` to build a non-interleaved output. Here's the producer thread:

```
void producer() {
    for (auto i = 0; i <= limit; i++) {
        sem_to_produce.acquire(); // {1}
        ++shared_resource;
        osyncstream(cout) << "Before: "
                          << shared_resource << endl;
        sem_to_consume.release(); // {2}
        osyncstream(cout) << "Producer finished!" << endl;
    }
}
```

And here's the consumer thread:

```
void consumer() {
    for (auto i = 0; i <= limit; i++) {
        osyncstream(cout)  << "Waiting for data..."
                           << endl;
        sem_to_consume.acquire();
        --shared_resource;
        osyncstream(cout)  << "After: "
                           << shared_resource << endl;
        sem_to_produce.release();
        osyncstream(cout)  << "Consumer finished!" << endl;
    } }
int main() {
    sem_to_produce.release();
```

```
jthread t1(producer); jthread t2(consumer);
t1.join(); t2.join();}
```

As we do this iteratively, we see this output multiple times, depending on `limit`:

```
Waiting for data...
Before: 1
Producer finished!
After: 0
Consumer finished!
...
```

Going back to the code's logic, we must emphasize that the C++ semaphores are considered lightweight and allow multiple concurrent accesses to the shared resource. But be careful: the provided code uses `acquire()` (marker {1}, similar to `sem_wait()`), which is a blocking call – for example, your task will be blocked until the semaphore is released. You could use `try_acquire()` for non-blocking purposes. We rely on both semaphores to create a predictable sequence of operations. We start the process (for example, the main thread) by releasing the producer semaphore, so the producer would be signaled to start first.

The code could be changed to use POSIX semaphores, just by removing the C++ primitives and adding the aforementioned system calls to the same places in the code. In addition, we encourage you to achieve the same effect with one semaphore. Think about using a helper variable or a condition variable. Keep in mind that such an action makes the synchronization heterogenous and on a large scale, which is hard to manage.

The current code is obviously not able to synchronize multiple processes, unlike the **named semaphore**, so it's not really an alternative there. We also could want to be stricter on the shared resource access – for example, to have a single moment of access in a concurrent environment. Then, we'd need the help of the mutex, as described in the next section.

Mutual exclusion (mutex)

The mutex is a mechanism that comes from the operations of the OS. A shared resource is also known as a **critical section** and it needs to be accessed without the risk of race conditions. A mechanism that allows only a single task to modify the critical section at a given moment, excluding every other task's request to do the same, is called a **mutual exclusion** or a **mutex**. The mutexes are implemented internally by the OS and remain hidden from the user space. They provide a *lock-unlock* access functionality and are considered stricter than the semaphores, although they are controlled as binary semaphores.

> **Important note**
>
> The calling thread locks the resource and is obliged to unlock it. There's no guarantee that a higher entity in the system's hierarchy would be able to override the lock and unblock the parallel functionality. It is advisable for each lock to be released as fast as possible to allow the system threads to scale up and save idle time.

A POSIX mutex is created and used in much the same way as the unnamed semaphore:

```
pthread_mutex_t global_lock;
pthread_mutex_init(&global_lock, NULL);
pthread_mutex_destroy(&global_lock);
pthread_mutex_lock(&global_lock);
pthread_mutex_unlock(&global_lock);
```

The pattern of the function names is followed again, so let's focus on `pthread_mutex_lock()` and `pthread_mutex_unlock()`. We use them to lock and unlock a critical section for manipulation, but they cannot help us in the sequence of events. Locking the resource only guarantees there are no race conditions. The correct sequencing of events, if required, is designed by the system programmer. Bad sequencing might lead to **deadlocks** and **livelocks**:

- **Deadlock**: One or more threads are blocked and cannot change their state because they are waiting for an event that never occurs. A common bug is two (or more) threads being looped together – for example, one is waiting for a shared resource A while holding a lock on shared resource B, and a second thread holds a lock on A but will unlock it when B is unlocked. Both will remain blocked because neither will be the first to *give up on the resource*. Such a behavior could be caused even without mutexes. Another bug is to lock a mutex twice, which, in the case of Linux, is detectable by the OS. There are deadlock resolution algorithms, where locking a number of mutexes will not succeed at first because of the deadlock, but will be successful with a guarantee after a finite number of attempts.

  In the preceding code snippet, we set the mutex attributes to NULL, but we could use them to decide on the mutex kind. The default one, known as a **fast mutex**, is not deadlock-safe. The **recursive mutex** type will not cause a deadlock; it will count the number of lock requests by the same thread. The **error-checking mutex** will detect and mark a double lock. We encourage you to give them a try.

- **Livelock**: The threads are not blocked, but then again, they cannot change their state because they require the shared resource to continue forward. A good real-world example is two people meeting face to face at an entrance. Both will move aside out of politeness, but they will most probably move in the same direction as their counterpart. If that happens and they continue to do that all the time, then nobody will be blocked, but at the same time, they cannot proceed forward.

Both classes of bugs are common and could be reproduced with semaphores, as they are blocking too, and rarely happen on small-scale systems, where they are easy to debug. It is trivial to follow the code's logic with just a few threads, and the processes are manageable. Large-scale systems with thousands of threads execute an enormous number of locks at the same time. The bug reproductions are usually a matter of bad timing and ambiguous task sequences. Therefore, they are hard to catch and debug, and we advise you to be careful when you lock a critical section.

C++ provides a flexible lock interface. It is constantly upgraded and we now have several behaviors to choose from. Let's do a parallel increment of a variable. We use the `increment()` thread procedure for the sake of clarity, similar to the previous code, but we replace the semaphores with one mutex. And you've probably guessed that the code will be guarded against race conditions, but the sequence of the thread executions is undefined. We could arrange this sequence through an additional flag, condition variable, or just a simple sleep, but let's keep it this way for the experiment. The updated code snippet is the following:

```
...
uint32_t shared_resource = 0;
mutex shres_guard;
constexpr uint32_t limit = INT_MAX;
```

We defined our shared resource and the mutex. Let's see how the increment happens:

```
void increment() {
    for (auto i = 0; i < limit; i++) {
        lock_guard<mutex> lock(shres_guard); // {1}
        ++shared_resource;
    }
    cout << "\nIncrement finished!" << endl;
}
...
```

The observed output is as follows:

```
$ time ./test
Increment finished!
Increment finished!
real    3m34,169s
user    4m21,676s
sys     2m43,331s
```

It's obvious that incrementing the variable without multithreading will be much faster than this result. You could even try running it until `UINT_MAX`.

So, the preceding code creates a globally visible mutex and uses a `unique_lock` object (marker {1}) to wrap it. It is similar to `pthread_mutex_init()` – it allows us to defer locking, do a recursive lock, transfer lock ownership, and carry out attempts to unlock it within certain time constraints. The lock is in effect for the scope block it is in – in the current example, it is the thread procedures' scope. The lock takes ownership of the mutex. When it reaches the end of the scope, the lock is destroyed and the mutex is released. You should already know this approach as **Resource Acquisition Is Initialization (RAII)**. You learned about it in detail in *Chapter 4*, and its role is crucial here – we will not be able to leave a resource locked by accident. You could use a `scoped_lock` object to lock multiple mutexes while avoiding a deadlock by its design.

There is something else you should consider when using a mutex. The mutex reaches the kernel level. The task states are affected by it directly and multiple locks will cause multiple **context switches**. As you recall from earlier, we will probably lose time in rescheduling. This means that the OS needs to jump from one memory region in RAM to another just to load another task's instructions. You must consider what's beneficial for you: many locks with small scopes leading to many switches, or a few locks with bigger scope blocks holding resources for longer timespans.

At the end of the day, our goal was just to instruct the CPU about an atomic region. If you remember, we used an `atomic` template in the semaphore example. We could update our code with an `atomic` variable and remove the mutex with the lock:

```
atomic<uint32_t> shared_resource = 0;
```

The result is as follows:

```
$ time ./test
Increment finished!
Increment finished!
real    0m0,003s
user    0m0,002s
sys     0m0,000s
```

As you can see, there is a significant time improvement just by the removal of the mutex. For the sake of argument, you could add the semaphores back and you will still observe a faster execution than the mutex. We advise you to look at the code's disassembly for the three cases – just with the `atomic` variable, with the mutex, and with the semaphore. You will observe that an `atomic` object is very simple instruction-wise and is executed at a user level. As it is truly atomic, the CPU (or its core) will be kept busy during the increment. Bear in mind that any technique for resolving data races will inherently carry a performance cost. The best performance can be achieved by minimizing the places and their scope where synchronization primitives are needed.

> **Important note**
>
> C++20 provides exciting features for concurrent execution, such as **jthread**, **coroutines**, **updated atomic types**, and **cooperative cancelation**. Except for the first one, we will look at the others later in the book. In addition to these, Linux has system calls for using the IPC entities, which are built for the purposes of multiprocessing data exchange. That said, we advise you to think about using an already existing mechanism for asynchronous work before you attempt combinations of mutexes, semaphores, flags, and conditional variables. All those C++ and Linux features are designed to scale up in a stable manner and save you time for solution design.

Everything we did until now is just to make sure we have atomic access to a critical section. Atomics, mutexes, and semaphores will give you this – a way to instruct the CPU about the scope of instructions. But two questions remain: Could we do it faster and lighter? Does being atomic mean we keep the order of the instructions? The answer to the first question is *Probably*. To the second one, the answer is *No*! Now we have the incentive to move and dive into the C++ **memory model** and **memory order**. If this interests you, we invite you to jump to *Chapter 9*, where we discuss more interesting concurrent tasks. Now, we will continue the topic of shared resources through the **shmem IPC** mechanism.

Using shared memory

As with pipes, the MQ data is lost once consumed. Duplex message data copying increases user space-kernel space calls, therefore an overhead is to be expected. The **shmem** mechanism is fast. As you learned in the previous chapter and the previous section, the synchronization of the data access is an issue that must be resolved by the system programmer, especially when it comes to race conditions.

An important remark is that the term *shared memory* is vague in itself. Is it a global variable that two threads could access simultaneously? Or is it a shared region of RAM, which multiple CPU cores use as a common ground to transfer data between each other? Is it a file in the filesystem that many processes modify? Great questions – thanks for asking! In general, all of those are kinds of shared resources, but when we speak about the term *memory*, we should really think about a region in the **main memory** that is visible to many processes and where multiple tasks could use it to exchange and modify data. Not only tasks but also different processor cores and core complexes (such as ARM) if they have access to the same predefined memory region. Such techniques require a specific configuration file – a memory map, which strictly depends on the processor and is implementation-specific. It provides the opportunity to use, for example, **tightly coupled memory** (TCM) to speed up, even more, the frequently used portions of code and data, or to use a portion of the RAM as shmem for data exchange between the cores. As this is too dependent on the processor, we are not going to continue discussing it. Instead, we will move on to discuss Linux's **shmem IPC** mechanism.

> **Important note**
>
> The processes allocate a portion of their **virtual memory** as a shared segment. Traditionally, the OS forbids processes to access each other's memory regions, but the shmem is a mechanism for the processes to ask for the removal of this restriction in the boundaries of the shmem. We use it to ingest and modify large portions of data quickly through simple read and write operations, or the already provided functions in POSIX. Such functionality is not possible through MQs or pipes.

In contrast to MQs, there's no serialization or synchronization here. The system programmer is responsible for managing the IPC's data transfer policy (again). But with the shared region being in the RAM, we have fewer context switches, thus we reduce the overhead. We can visualize it through the following figure:

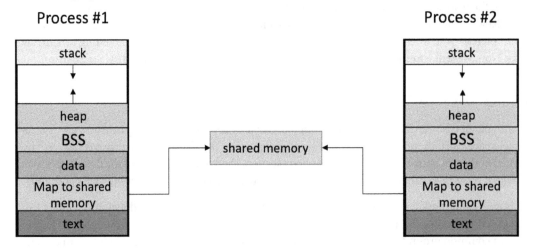

Figure 7.3 – Shmem presentation through the process's memory segments

The shmem region is usually depicted between the two processes' address spaces. The idea is to emphasize how that space is truly shared between the processes. In reality, this is implementation-specific and we leave it to the kernel – what we care about is the map to the shmem segments itself. It allows both processes to observe the same contents simultaneously. Let's get to it then.

Learning about mmap() and shm_open()

The initial system call for the creation of a shmem mapping is shmget(). This is applicable to any Unix-based OS, but for POSIX-compliant systems, there are more comfortable approaches. If we imagine that we do a mapping between a process's address space and a file, then the mmap() function will pretty much get the job done. It is POSIX-compliant and executes the read operation on demand. You can simply use mmap() to point to a regular file, but the data will remain there after the processes have finished their work. Do you remember the pipes from *Chapter 3*? It's a similar case here. There are **anonymous pipes**, which require two processes to have a *family relation*, or you can have **named pipes**, which allow two unrelated processes to share and transfer data. The **shmem** resolves a similar issue, just not through the same technique. Using shmem for IPC will mean that data persistence would probably not be required – all other mechanisms destroy the data after its consumption. But if persistence is what you want, then it's all good – you could freely use the mmap() system call with fork().

If you have independent processes, then the only way for them to know how to address the shared region is through its pathname. The shm_open() function will provide you a file with a name, in the same way that mq_open() did – you could observe it in /dev/shm. It would require librt as well. Knowing this, you intuitively get that we limit the I/O overhead and the context switches because of the filesystem operations, as this file is in the RAM. Last but not least, this kind of shared memory is flexible in size and could be enlarged to gigabytes in size when needed. Its limitations are dependent on the system. The full version of the following example can be found at https://github.com/PacktPublishing/C-Programming-for-Linux-Systems/tree/main/Chapter%207:

```
...
string_view SHM_ID      = "/test_shm";
string_view SEM_PROD_ID = "/test_sem_prod";
string_view SEM_CONS_ID = "/test_sem_cons";
constexpr auto SHM_SIZE = 1024;
sem_t *sem_prod; sem_t *sem_cons;
void process_creator() {
...
    if (int pid = fork(); pid == 0) {
        // Child - used for consuming data.
        if (fd = shm_open(SHM_ID.data(),
                    O_RDONLY,
                    0700); // {1}
            fd == -1) {
....
```

This example is very specific as we intentionally used processes instead of threads. This allows us to demonstrate the usage of shm_open() (marker {1}) as the different processes use the shmem's pathname (which is known at compile time) to access it. Let's continue with reading the data:

```
        shm_addr = mmap(NULL, SHM_SIZE,
                    PROT_READ, MAP_SHARED,
                    fd, 0); // {2}
        if (shm_addr == MAP_FAILED) {
...
        }
        array<char, SHM_SIZE> buffer{};
```

We could use mutexes, but currently, we only need one process to signal to the other that its work is done, so we apply semaphores (markers {3} and {7} in the previous code block) as follows:

```
sem_wait(sem_cons);
memcpy(buffer.data(),
       shm_addr,
       buffer.size()); // {3}
if(strlen(buffer.data()) != 0) {
    cout << "PID : " << getpid()
         << "consumed: " << buffer.data();
}
sem_post(sem_prod); exit(EXIT_SUCCESS);
```

To make the memory region shared, we use the `mmap()` function with the `MAP_SHARED` option, and we mark the reader and the writer credentials accordingly through the following page settings: `PROT_READ` and `PROT_WRITE` (markers {2} and {6}). We also use the `ftruncate()` function to set the region's size (marker {5}). In the given example, the information is written in the shmem, and someone has to read it. It's a kind of a single-shot producer-consumer because after the writing is done, the writer gives the reader time (marker {8}), and then the shmem is set to zero (marker {9}) and deleted (marker {10}). Now, let's proceed with the parent's code - the producer of the data:

```
else if (pid > 0) {
    // Parent - used for producing data.
    fd = shm_open(SHM_ID.data(),
                  O_CREAT | O_RDWR,
                  0700); // {4}
    if (fd == -1) {
...
    res = ftruncate(fd, SHM_SIZE); // {5}
```

Again, the shmem region is mapped:

```
    if (res == -1) {
...
    shm_addr = mmap(NULL, SHM_SIZE,
                    PROT_WRITE, MAP_SHARED,
                    fd, 0); // {6}
    if (shm_addr == MAP_FAILED) {
...
    sem_wait(sem_prod);
    string_view produced_data
        {"Some test data, coming!"};
    memcpy(shm_addr,
           produced_data.data(),
```

```
                produced_data.size());
        sem_post(sem_cons);      // {7}
        waitpid(pid, NULL, 0); // {8}
        res = munmap(shm_addr, SHM_SIZE); // {9}
        if (res == -1) {
...
        fd = shm_unlink(SHM_ID.data()); //{10}
        if (fd == -1) {
```

As done previously, we use the `sem_open()` named semaphore (marker {11}) to allow both processes to synchronize. We wouldn't be able to do so through the semaphores we discussed earlier in the chapter, as they don't have a name and are known only in the context of a single process. At the end, we remove the semaphore from the filesystem as well (marker {12}), as follows:

```
...
}
int main() {
    sem_prod = sem_open(SEM_PROD_ID.data(),
                        O_CREAT, 0644, 0); // {11}
...
    sem_post(sem_prod);
    process_creator();
    sem_close(sem_prod); // {12}
    sem_close(sem_cons);
    sem_unlink(SEM_PROD_ID.data());
    sem_unlink(SEM_CONS_ID.data());
    return 0;
}
```

The program's result is as follows:

```
PID 3530: consumed: "Some test data, coming!"
```

Shmem is an interesting topic, which we will return to in *Chapter 9*. One reason for being so is that C++ allows us to wrap the POSIX code appropriately and make the code safer. Similar to *Chapter 3*, mixing system calls with C++ code should be well thought out. But it's worthwhile to visit the **condition variables** mechanism and discuss the **read/write locks**. We will dive into some `memory_order` use cases as well. If **jthreads** or **coroutines** are not applicable to your use cases, then the currently discussed synchronization mechanisms, together with the **smart pointers**, give you the flexibility to design the best possible solution for your system. But before we get there, we need to talk about something else first. Let's proceed to the communication between computer systems.

Communicating through the network with sockets

If the pipes, MQs, and the shmem could together overcome their problems, then why do we need sockets? This is a great question with a simple answer – we need them to communicate between different systems on the network. With this, we have our full set of instruments to exchange data. Before we understand sockets, we need to get a quick overview of network communication. No matter the network type or its medium, we must follow the design established by the **Open Systems Interconnection (OSI) basic reference model**. Nowadays, almost all OSs support the **Internet Protocol (IP)** family. The easiest way to set up communications with other computer systems is by using these protocols. They follow layering, as described in the **ISO-OSI** model, and now we are going to take a quick look at that.

Overview of the OSI model

The OSI model is typically represented as shown in the next table. System programmers usually require it to analyze where their communication is disturbed. Although sockets are intended to execute the network data transfer, they are also applicable for a local IPC. One reason is that the communication layers, especially on large systems, are separate utilities or abstraction layers over the applications. As we want to make them environmentally agnostic, meaning we don't care whether the data is transferred locally or over the internet, then the sockets fit perfectly. That said, we must be aware of the channel we use and where our data is transported. Let's take a look:

Layers	Entities	Notes	Examples
Application	Data	Interface responsible for communications to and from end user processes and applications	HTTP, FTP, SSH, DNS
Presentation	Data	Ensures the data is reliable and usable	SSL, SSH, IMAP, FTP, XDR, protobufs
Session	Data	Maintains connections, which are a sequence of correlated messages, similar to transactions	Sockets, API's, RPCs
Transport	Segments, Datagrams	Transfers data, following one of the transmission protocols	TCP, UDP
Network	Packets	Routes the physical path of the data	IP, ICMP, IPSec, IGMP
Data Link	Frames	Defines the data format	Ethernet, PPP, Switch, Bridge
Physical	Bits	Transfers a bitstream through a physical environment	Fiber, Wi-Fi, Hub, Repeater

Figure 7.4 – The OSI model represented as a table

Global network communication, especially the internet, is a broad and complex topic, which we cannot grasp in a single section of the book. But it's worthwhile to think about your system – what kind of hardware for network communication it has; maybe you should consider checking out the *Physical* and *Data Link* layers. A simple exercise is to configure your home network – connected devices, routers, and so on – yourself. Could the system be safely and securely addressed by the outside (if needed)? Then check the *Network*, *Presentation*, and *Application* layers. Try out some **port forwarding** and create an application with data exchange encryption. Could the software scale fast enough, with the current bandwidth and speed? Let's see what the *Session* and *Transport* layers have to offer – we will look into them in the next paragraph. Is it robust and does it remain available if attacked? Then revisit all the layers. Of course, these are simple and one-sided observations, but they allow you to double-check your requirements.

So, if we ignore the role of the hardware and just focus on establishing a connection, we could get back to the sockets and the respective *Session* layer. You've probably noticed that some websites log you out automatically after some time. Ever wondered why? Well, the **session** is an established two-way link for information exchange between devices or ends. It's highly recommended to apply time limits and requirements for a session to be destroyed. The opened connection means not only an opened channel for sniffing by attackers but also a used resource on the server side. This requires computational power, which could be redirected elsewhere. The server usually holds the current state and the session history, so we note this kind of communication as *stateful* – at least one of the devices keeps the state. But if we manage to handle requests without the need to know and keep previous data, we could proceed with *stateless* communication. Still, we require the session to build a connection-oriented data exchange. A known protocol for the job is found in the *Transport* layer – the **Transmission Control Protocol** (**TCP**). If we don't want to establish a two-way information transfer channel but just want to implement a broadcast application, then we could proceed with the connectionless communication, provided through the **User Datagram Protocol** (**UDP**). Let's check them out in the following sections.

Getting familiar with networking through UDP

As we said, this protocol could realize connectionless communication, although this doesn't mean there's no connection between the endpoints. It means that they don't need to be constantly in connection to maintain the data transfer and interpret it on their ends. In other words, losing some packets (leading to not hearing someone well on the call while in an online meeting, for example) is probably not going to be crucial for the system's behavior itself. It might be crucial to you, but let's be honest, we bet you require the high speed more, and it comes with a cost. Network applications such as the **Domain Name System** (**DNS**), the **Dynamic Host Configuration Protocol** (**DHCP**), audio-video streaming platforms, and others use UDP. Discrepancies and loss of packets are usually handled by data retransmission, but this is realized on the *Application* layer and depends on the programmer's implementation. Schematically, the system calls for establishing such a connection are as follows:

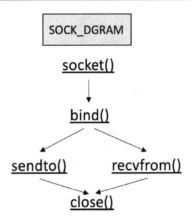

Figure 7.5 – UDP system call realization

As you can see, it is truly simple – applications on both (or more) sides of the communication must only follow that sequence. The protocol doesn't oblige you with the message order or the transfer quality, it's just fast. Let's see the following example, requesting a die roll from a socket *N* number of times. The full version of the code is found at `https://github.com/PacktPublishing/C-Programming-for-Linux-Systems/tree/main/Chapter%207`:

```
...
constexpr auto PORT     = 8080;
constexpr auto BUF_SIZE = 16;
auto die_roll() {
...
void process_creator() {
    auto sockfd = 0;
    array<char, BUF_SIZE> buffer{};
    string_view stop{ "No more requests!" };
    string_view request{ "Throw dice!" };
    struct sockaddr_in servaddr {};
    struct sockaddr_in cliaddr {};
```

As you can see, the communication configuration is fairly easy – one side has to bind to an address in order to be aware of where to receive data from (marker {3}), whereas the other only writes data directly to the socket. The socket configuration is described at marker {1}:

```
servaddr.sin_family = AF_INET; // {1}
servaddr.sin_addr.s_addr = INADDR_ANY;
servaddr.sin_port = htons(PORT);
if (int pid = fork(); pid == 0) {
    // Child
    if ((sockfd = socket(AF_INET, SOCK_DGRAM, 0))
            < 0) {
```

```
        const auto ecode
            { make_error_code(errc{errno}) };
        cerr << "Error opening socket!";
        system_error exception{ ecode };
        throw exception;
    } // {2}
    if (bind(sockfd,
        (const struct sockaddr*)&servaddr,
        sizeof(servaddr)) < 0) {
        const auto ecode
            { make_error_code(errc{errno}) };
        cerr << "Bind failed!";
        system_error exception{ ecode };
        throw exception;
    } // {3}
```

The address family is defined as AF_INET, meaning we will rely on IPv4-compliant addresses. We could use AF_INET6 for IPv6, or AF_BLUETOOTH for Bluetooth. We are using the UDP through the SOCK_DGRAM setting of the socket (markers {2} and {10}). Through this, we are transferring a number from one process to another. You could imagine them as a server and a client:

```
        socklen_t len = sizeof(cliaddr);
        for (;;) {
            if (auto bytes_received =
                recvfrom(sockfd, buffer.data(),
                    buffer.size(),
                    MSG_WAITALL,
                    (struct sockaddr*)&cliaddr,
                    &len);
                bytes_received >= 0) { // {4}
                buffer.data()[bytes_received] = '\0';
                cout << "Request received: "
                    << buffer.data() << endl;
                if (request.compare(0,
                                bytes_received,
                                buffer.data()) == 0) {
                                        // {5}
                    string_view res_data
                        { to_string(die_roll()) };
```

A request for a new die roll is received (marker {4}) and the request data is printed out. Then, the request string is compared to an immutable one, so we know that this request is just for a die roll (marker {5}). As you can see, we use the MSG_WAITALL setting, which means that the socket operation will block the calling process – usually when there is no incoming data. In addition, this is a UDP communication, therefore the packet order might not be followed, and receiving 0 bytes through `recvfrom()` is a valid use case. That said, we use additional messages to mark the ending of the communication (markers {6} and {14}). For simplicity, if the `request.compare()` result is not 0, the communication is ended. Additional checks for multiple options could be added, though. We could use a similar handshake to start the communication in the first place – this is depending on the system programmer's decision and the application requirements. Proceeding with the client's functionality:

```
            sendto(sockfd, res_data.data(),
                   res_data.size(),
                   MSG_WAITALL,
                   (struct sockaddr*)&cliaddr,
                   len);
        }
        else break; // {6}
...

    }
    if (auto res = close(sockfd); res == -1) { // {8}
        const auto ecode
            { make_error_code(errc{errno}) };
        cerr << "Error closing socket!";
        system_error exception{ ecode };
        throw exception;
    }
    exit(EXIT_SUCCESS);
```

The `die_roll()` function is called for `dice_rolls` a number of times (markers {10} and {11}) and the result is sent through the socket (marker {12}). After the results are received back (marker {13}), an ending message is sent (marker {14}). We have mostly used `MSG_CONFIRM` for this example, but you must be careful with this flag. It should be used when you expect a response from the same peer you send to. It is telling the Data Link layer of the OSI model that there's a successful reply. We could change the `recvfrom()` setting to `MSG_DONTWAIT`, as in marker {12}, but it would be a good idea to implement our own retry mechanism, or switch to TCP:

```
    for (auto i = 1; i <= dice_rolls; i++) { // {11}
        if (auto b_sent = sendto(sockfd,
                                 request.data(),
                                 request.size(),
                                 MSG_DONTWAIT,
                                 (const struct
                                  sockaddr*)&servaddr,
                                 sizeof(servaddr));
            b_sent >= 0) { // {12}
...
```

```
            if (auto b_recv =
                    recvfrom(sockfd,
                            buffer.data(),
                            buffer.size(),
                            MSG_WAITALL,
...                             { // {13}
                buffer.data()[b_recv] = '\0';
                cout << "Dice roll result for throw number"
                    << i << " is "
                    << buffer.data() << endl;
            }
```

We close the communication after the closing statement (markers {8} and {15}):

```
        sendto(sockfd,
                stop.data(),
                stop.size(),
                MSG_CONFIRM,
                (const struct sockaddr*)&servaddr,
                sizeof(servaddr)); // {14}
    if (auto res = close(sockfd); res == -1) {
            const auto ecode
                { make_error_code(errc{errno}) };
            cerr << "Error closing socket!";
            system_error exception{ ecode };
            throw exception; // {15}
        }
...
```

The shortened version of the output is as follows:

```
Choose a number of dice throws between 1 and 256.
5
Request received: Throw dice!
Dice roll result for throw number 1 is 2
....
Dice roll result for throw number 5 is 6
Request received: No more requests
```

We have to set the address and port where our server could be accessed from. Usually, server computers have many applications constantly running, some of which execute services for customers. These services bind with the ports of the server and users can call them to do some work – get an online store's contents, check the weather, get some banking details, visualize a graphical website, and so on. Only one application (service) can work with a given port at a time. If you try to use it with another while the first one is active, you will get an `Address already in use` error (or similar). Currently, we're using port `8080`, which is commonly opened for TCP/UDP (and HTTP). You could also try `80`, but on Linux, non-root users don't have this capability – you will need higher user permissions to use ports less than `1000`. Last but not least, the IP address is set as `INADDR_ANY`. This is often used when we do the communication on a single system and we don't care about its address. Still, we could use it, if we want, after we take it from the result of the following command:

```
$ ip addr show
1: lo: <LOOPBACK,UP,LOWER_UP> mtu 65536 qdisc noqueue state UNKNOWN
group default qlen 1000
    link/loopback 00:00:00:00:00:00 brd 00:00:00:00:00:00
    inet 127.0.0.1/8 scope host lo
        valid_lft forever preferred_lft forever
    inet6 ::1/128 scope host
        valid_lft forever preferred_lft forever
2: ens32: <BROADCAST,MULTICAST,UP,LOWER_UP> mtu 1500 qdisc fq_codel
state UP group default qlen 1000
    link/ether 00:0c:29:94:a5:25 brd ff:ff:ff:ff:ff:ff
    inet 192.168.136.128/24 brd 192.168.136.255 scope global dynamic
noprefixroute ens32
        valid_lft 1345sec preferred_lft 1345sec
    inet6 fe80::b11f:c011:ba44:35e5/64 scope link noprefixroute
        valid_lft forever preferred_lft forever...
```

In our case, this is `192.168.136.128`. We could update the code at marker {1} as follows:

```
servaddr.sin_addr.s_addr = inet_addr("192.168.136.128");
```

Another option is that the localhost address – `127.0.0.1` – could be used with the loopback device address: `INADDR_LOOPBACK`. We use it to run local servers, usually for testing purposes. But if we use an exact IP address, then this is done when we need to be very specific about the application's endpoint, and if the IP address is a static one, we expect others on the local network to be able to call it. If we want to expose it to the outside world so we make our service available to others (let's say we own an online shop and we want to provide our shopping service to the world), then we must think about **port forwarding**.

> **Important note**
> Nowadays, just exposing the port is considered unsafe because the device can be accessed by anybody. Instead, services are not only guarded by firewalls, encryption mechanisms, and so on but are also deployed on virtual machines. This creates an extra layer of security as the attacker will never have access to the real device, just to a very limited version of it. Such a decision also provides higher availability as the attacked surface could be immediately removed and the system administrator could bring up a new virtual machine from a healthy snapshot, making the service available again. Depending on the implementation, this could be automated as well.

One last thing – the file's contents might be misplaced if we are transferring larger amounts of data. This is again expected from UDP, as expressed earlier, because of the packets' ordering. If it does not suit your purpose and you require a more robust implementation, then you should check the TCP description in the next section.

Thinking about robustness through TCP

The alternative to UDP is TCP. It is considered reliable – the messages are ordered, it is connection-oriented, and it has a lengthened latency. Applications such as the **World Wide Web** (**WWW**), email, remote administration applications, and so on are based on this protocol. What you've probably noticed already (and you're going to observe in *Figure 7.6*) is that the respective system calls are in the same sequence and have similar names as in other programming languages. This helps people with different areas of expertise to have a common ground for designing network applications and easily understand the sequence of events. This is a very simple way to help them follow the protocols in the OSI model, using those names as hints for where the communication is currently at. As we already mentioned in the previous section, sockets are used for environment-agnostic solutions, where systems have different OSs and the communicating applications are in different programming languages. For example, they are implemented in C, C++, Java, or Python, and their clients could be in PHP, JavaScript, and so on.

The system calls for TCP communication are represented in the following diagram:

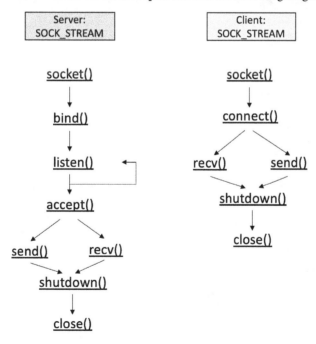

Figure 7.6 – TCP system call realization

As you can see, it is more complicated than UDP, as was expected. How so? Well, we need to keep an established connection and the kernel acknowledges the packet transfer. If you remember, in *Chapter 1* and *Chapter 2*, we discussed that sockets are files as well, and we could treat them as such. Instead of doing the `send()` and `recv()` calls, you could simply do `write()` and `read()` calls. The first ones are specialized in the role of network communication, while the latter are generally for all files. Using the `read()` and `write()` calls will be like communicating through a pipe but between computer systems, therefore it again depends on your needs.

Let's look at the following example – a simple request-response exchange, which we will execute on different machines on the local network, as the IP address from earlier is valid only for our internal network. First, let's see whether we can ping the server:

```
$ ping 192.168.136.128
Pinging 192.168.136.128 with 32 bytes of data:
Reply from 192.168.136.128: bytes=32 time<1ms TTL=64
Reply from 192.168.136.128: bytes=32 time<1ms TTL=64
Reply from 192.168.136.128: bytes=32 time<1ms TTL=64
```

So, we have access to the machine. Now, let's run the server as a separate application (the full code can be found at `https://github.com/PacktPublishing/C-Programming-for-Linux-Systems/tree/main/Chapter%207`). The configuration is almost the same, so we skip those parts from the snippet:

```
...
constexpr auto PORT     = 8080;
constexpr auto BUF_SIZE = 256;
constexpr auto BACKLOG  = 5;
constexpr auto SIG_MAX  = 128;
void exitHandler(int sig) {
    cerr << "Exit command called - terminating server!"
         << endl;
    exit(SIG_MAX + sig);
}
int main() {
    signal(SIGINT, exitHandler);
    constexpr auto ip = "192.168.136.128";
...
```

We open the socket:

```
if (auto server_sock =
        socket(AF_INET, SOCK_STREAM, 0);
        server_sock < 0) {
```

We use `SOCK_STREAM` to indicate this ias a TCP connection. We also use the hardcoded IP. After we bind to the address, we need to listen for a `BACKLOG` number of active connections. Each new connection could be accepted in general if the number of connections is smaller than the `BACKLOG` value:

```
...
        server_addr.sin_addr.s_addr = inet_addr(ip);
        result = bind(server_sock,
            (struct sockaddr*)&server_addr,
            sizeof(server_addr));
...
        result = listen(server_sock, BACKLOG);
        if (result != 0) {
            cerr << "Cannot accept connection";
        }
        cout << "Listening..." << endl;
        for (;;) {
            addr_size = sizeof(client_addr);
            client_sock =
                accept(server_sock,
                        (struct sockaddr*)&client_addr,
                        &addr_size);
```

Until this point, we just have the following:

```
$ ./server
Listening...
```

Now, let's prepare to accept a client and handle its requests. We use the `MSG_PEEK` flag to check for incoming messages, and we send messages with `MSG_DONTWAIT`. We leave `sendto()` without a result check for simplicity and readability:

```cpp
if (client_sock > 0) {
    cout << "Client connected." << endl;
    array<char, BUF_SIZE> buffer{};
    if (auto b_recv = recv(client_sock,
                            buffer.data(),
                            buffer.size(),
                            MSG_PEEK);
                    b_recv > 0) {
        buffer.data()[b_recv] = '\0';
        cout << "Client request: "
            << buffer.data() << endl;
        string_view response =
            { to_string(getpid()) };
        cout << "Server response: "
            << response << endl;
        send(client_sock,
            response.data(),
            response.size(),
            MSG_DONTWAIT);
    }
```

And the socket is closed at the end:

```cpp
...
if (auto res =
        close(client_sock); res == -1) {
...
```

Now, let's connect a client from another system. Its implementation is similar to the UDP one, except `connect()` must be called and must be successful:

```cpp
...
if (auto res =
        connect(serv_sock,
            (struct sockaddr*)&addr,
            sizeof(addr)); res == -1) {
    const auto ecode
        { make_error_code(errc{errno}) };
    cerr << "Error connecting to socket!";
```

```
                    system_error exception{ ecode };
                    throw exception;
            }
        string_view req = { to_string(getpid()) };
        cout << "Client request: " << req << endl;
```

The server's output changes as follows:

```
$ ./server
Listening...
Client connected.
Client request: 12502
Server response: 12501
```

Let's continue the communication, sending information back:

```
        if (auto res =
                send(serv_sock,
                    req.data(),
                    req.size(),
                    MSG_DONTWAIT);
            res >= 0) {
        array<char, BUF_SIZE> buffer{};
        if (auto b_recv =
                recv(serv_sock,
                    buffer.data(),
                    buffer.size(),
                    MSG_PEEK);
            res > 0) {
            buffer.data()[b_recv] = '\0';
            cout << "Server response: "
                << buffer.data();
...
        if (auto res = close(serv_sock); res == -1) {
...
        cout << "\nJob done! Disconnecting." << endl;
```

We are closing the communication on the client side, including the socket. The client's output is as follows:

```
$ ./client
Client request: 12502
Server response: 12501
Job done! Disconnecting.
```

As the client's job is done, the process terminates and its socket is closed, but the server remains active for other clients, so if we call the client multiple times from different shells, we will have the following output for the server:

```
Listening...
Client connected.
Client request: 12502
Server response: 12501
Client connected.
Client request: 12503
Server response: 12501
```

The server will handle up to five client sessions in its backlog. If the clients don't close their sockets or the server doesn't forcefully terminate their connections after some timeout, it will not be able to accept new clients, and the `Client connection failed` message will be observed. In the next chapter, we will discuss different time-based techniques, so think about combining them with your implementation to provide a meaningful session timeout.

If we want to gracefully handle the server termination, we could simply implement a signal handler, as we did in *Chapter 3*. This time, we will handle the *Ctrl + C* key combination, leading to the following output:

```
...
Client request: 12503
Server response: 12501
^CExit command called - terminating server!
```

As mentioned earlier, ungraceful termination of servers and clients could lead to hanging sockets and opened ports. This will become problematic for a system, as simple application restarts will fail with `Address already in use`. If this happens, double-check for remaining processes through the `ps` command. You can terminate the running process through the `kill` command, as you learned in *Chapter 1* and *Chapter 2*. Sometimes, this is not enough either, and servers should not be terminated that easily. Therefore, you could just change a port after checking which ports are opened. You could do that through the following command:

```
$ ss -tnlp
State Recv-Q Send-Q Local Address:Port Peer Address:Port  Process
LISTEN 0        5            192.168.136.128:8080
0.0.0.0:*       users:(("server",pid=9965,fd=3))
LISTEN   0      4096         127.0.0.53%lo:53             0.0.0.0:*
LISTEN   0      5            127.0.0.1:631                0.0.0.0:*
LISTEN   0      5            [::1]:631                    [::]:*
```

You can see the server is up and running on the respective address and port: `192.168.136.128:8080`. We can also check the connections to a certain port by using the following:

```
$ lsof -P -i:8080
COMMAND    PID USER    FD    TYPE DEVICE SIZE/OFF NODE NAME
server   10116  oem    3u    IPv4  94617      0t0  TCP oem-virtual-
machine:8080 (LISTEN)
```

With multiple online services nowadays, we cannot escape network programming. We encourage you to use these examples as simple applications to start from. It's also important to spend some time learning more about the multiple socket settings as they will help you cover your specific requirements.

Summary

In this chapter, you've learned about various ways to execute IPC. You got familiar with MQs as simple, real-time, and reliable instruments for sending small chunks of data. We also got into the details of fundamental synchronization mechanisms such as semaphores and mutexes, along with their C++20 interfaces. In combination with shmem, you observed how we could exchange large amounts of data fast. At the end, the network communication through sockets was introduced to you through the main protocols, UDP and TCP.

Complex applications usually rely on multiple IPC techniques to achieve their goals. It's important to be aware of them – both their strengths and their disadvantages. This will help you decide on your particular implementation. Most of the time, we build layers on top of IPC solutions in order to guarantee the robustness of an application – for example, through retry mechanisms, polling, event-driven designs, and so on. We will revisit these topics in *Chapter 9*. The next chapter will give you the instruments to self-monitor your availability and performance through different timers.

8

Using Clocks, Timers, and Signals in Linux

In this chapter, we will commence by exploring the various timers available in the Linux environment. Subsequently, we will delve into the significance of the clock epoch and delve into the concept of UNIX time. Following this, we will unveil the methodology for employing POSIX in Linux to precisely measure time intervals. Transitioning further, we will uncover the realm of `std::chrono` and examine the capabilities that C++ offers for effective time-related operations. Our journey then progresses to a comprehensive examination of duration, timepoints, and clocks as delineated within the `std::chrono` framework. Venturing onward, we will acquaint ourselves with the diverse array of clocks at our disposal within `std::chrono`. As we navigate our path, we will take our initial steps into harnessing the calendar functionalities provided by `std::chrono`. In the final leg of our exploration, we will become familiar with time zones and refine our expertise in executing seamless time conversions using the powerful tools of `std::chrono`.

In this chapter, we are going to cover the following main topics:

- Exploring timers in Linux
- Handling time in C++
- Using clocks, timers, and ratios
- Using calendar and time zone capabilities

So, let's get started!

Technical requirements

All examples in this chapter have been tested in an environment with the following configuration:

- Linux Mint 21 Cinnamon edition.

- GCC 13.2 with compiler flags: `-std=c++20`.

- A stable internet connection.

- Please make sure your environment is at least this recent. For all the examples, you can alternatively use `https://godbolt.org/`.

- All code examples in this chapter are available for download from `https://github.com/PacktPublishing/C-Programming-for-Linux-Systems/tree/main/Chapter%208`.

Handling time in Linux

Timing is an essential aspect of any computer system, and Linux is no exception. In Linux, there are different types of timers available, each designed to handle specific tasks and requirements.

These timers can be used to measure the execution time of programs, schedule tasks, trigger events, and more. In this section, we'll explore the different types of timers available in Linux and how to use them effectively.

Here are the different kinds of timers used in the Linux system:

- **System timers**: The Linux kernel uses system timers to keep track of the time and schedule various tasks. System timers are used to measure the system uptime, delay, and timeouts. The most important system timer in Linux is the *Jiffies* timer, which increments by 1 with every tick of the system clock. The Jiffies timer is used to track the time elapsed since the system booted up, and it is frequently used by various kernel modules and drivers.

- **Real-Time Clock (RTC)**: The RTC is a hardware clock that keeps track of the date and time, even when the system is powered off. The Linux kernel can read and set the RTC through the `/dev/rtc` device file or the `hwclock` command-line tool. The RTC is used to synchronize the system time during startup and to maintain an accurate timestamp for system events.

- **High-Resolution Timers (HRTs)**: HRTs provide nanosecond-level resolution, which makes them suitable for real-time applications that require precise timing. HRTs can be used to measure the execution time of a code segment, schedule events with high accuracy, or drive high-speed hardware.

- **POSIX timers**: POSIX timers are a set of timers defined by the POSIX standard that provide a uniform interface for timer management in Linux. POSIX timers can be used to set up one-shot or periodic timers, which can be triggered by a signal or a thread. POSIX timers are implemented using the `timer_create()`, `timer_settime()`, and `timer_delete()` system calls.

- **Timer queues**: Timer queues are a mechanism provided by the Linux kernel to schedule events and timeouts. Timer queues are implemented as a priority queue of events, where each event is associated with a timer. Timer queues can be used to schedule periodic tasks, implement timeouts, or trigger events at specific intervals. Timer queues are used extensively in various kernel modules and device drivers.

But speaking about timers, we first need to understand what time means in computer systems. Let's have a look.

Linux epoch

In computing, an *epoch* refers to a specific point in time used as a reference for measuring time in a particular system or context. It serves as a starting point from which other time values are calculated or represented. In other words, this is the time from when the computer measures the system time.

The epoch is often defined as a specific point in time, typically represented as the number of seconds or milliseconds, or other time intervals even smaller than a millisecond elapsed since a particular epoch time. The choice of epoch varies depending on the system and context. For example, in UNIX-like systems, which Linux is, the epoch is defined as *January 1, 1970, at 00:00:00 UTC* (Coordinated Universal Time). This epoch time is often referred to as the *UNIX epoch* or *UNIX time*. The time values in UNIX-based systems are typically represented as the number of seconds elapsed since the UNIX epoch.

Now, having a better understanding of the UNIX epoch, let's have a look at some examples of how to use these timers in practice.

Using timers in Linux

Since we already know about the different types of timers available in Linux, let's explore how to use them in our applications. We will look at an example that starts a POSIX timer and waits until it is signaled:

```cpp
#include <iostream>
#include <csignal>
#include <unistd.h>
#include <sys/time.h>
#include <atomic>
static std::atomic_bool continue_execution{true};
int main() {
    struct sigaction sa{};
    sa.sa_handler = [](int signum) {
        // Timer triggered, stop the loop.
        std::cout << "Timer expired. Stopping the
          task...\n";
        continue_execution = false;
    };
    sigemptyset(&sa.sa_mask);
    sa.sa_flags = 0;
    sigaction(SIGALRM, &sa, nullptr);

    // Configure the timer to trigger every 1 seconds
    struct itimerval timer{
        .it_interval{.tv_sec{1}, .tv_usec{0}},
        .it_value{.tv_sec{1}, .tv_usec{0}}
    };
    // Start the timer
    setitimer(ITIMER_REAL, &timer, nullptr);
    std::cout << "Timer started. Waiting for timer
      expiration...\n";
    // Keep the program running to allow the timer to
      trigger
    while (continue_execution) {
        sleep(1);
    }
    return 0;
}
```

In this example, we define a lambda handler that will be called whenever the timer expires. Inside the handler, we print a message indicating that the timer has expired and set the exit condition of the busy loop.

We set up the signal handler using the `sigaction` function. Then, we configure the timer using the `it_interval` and `it_value` members of the `itimerval` structure. After configuring the timer, we start it by calling the `setitimer` POSIX function with the `ITIMER_REAL` option, which sets a real-time timer that sends `SIGALRM` signals when it expires. We enter a loop to keep the program running indefinitely. The `sleep(1)` call inside the loop ensures that the program does not exit immediately and allows the timer to trigger.

The output of the program is as follows:

```
Program returned: 0
Timer started. Waiting for timer expiration...
Timer expired. Stopping the task...
```

Another common task in software development is measuring the execution time of a code segment. It can also be achieved by using the POSIX time capabilities. To measure the execution time of a code segment, we can use an HRT in POSIX.

To use an HRT in POSIX, we will use the `clock_gettime()` function along with the CLOCK_MONOTONIC clock ID. Here's an example demonstrating the usage of HRTs in POSIX:

```cpp
#include <iostream>
#include <ctime>
static const auto LIMIT{10000};
void just_busy_wait_f() {
    for (auto i{0}; i < LIMIT; ++i) {
        for (auto j{0}; j < LIMIT; ++j);
    }
}
int main() {
    timespec start, end;
    // Start the timer
    clock_gettime(CLOCK_MONOTONIC, &start);
    // Measured code segment
    just_busy_wait_f();
    // Stop the timer
    clock_gettime(CLOCK_MONOTONIC, &end);
    // Calculate the elapsed time
    const auto elapsed{(end.tv_sec - start.tv_sec) +
      (end.tv_nsec - start.tv_nsec) / 1e9};
    std::cout << "Elapsed time: " << elapsed << "
      seconds\n";
    return 0;
}
```

In this example, we declare two `timespec` structures, `start` and `end`, to hold the start and end timestamps of the timer. We use the `clock_gettime()` function to obtain the current time with a high-resolution clock.

We call `clock_gettime()` twice: once at the beginning of the task (to record the start time) and once at the end (to record the end time). The `CLOCK_MONOTONIC` clock ID is used, which represents a monotonic clock unaffected by system time adjustments.

After capturing the start and end timestamps, we calculate the elapsed time by subtracting the respective second and nanosecond components of the timestamps. The result is then printed as the elapsed time in seconds.

The example output in our test lab is as follows:

```
Program returned: 0
Elapsed time: 0.169825 seconds
```

Keep in mind that in your environment, the result could be different.

Note that this example demonstrates one way to measure execution time using a timer. Depending on your requirements, you can choose different timer mechanisms.

POSIX timer characteristics

Let's look at some of the characteristics that POSIX timers have:

- **Powerful and flexible**: POSIX timers provide a rich set of features, including different timer types (for example, interval timers and one-shot timers), various clock sources, and precise control over timer behavior

- **Low-level control**: POSIX timers offer fine-grained control over timer settings, such as signal handling and timer expiration behavior

- **Legacy support**: POSIX timers are part of the POSIX API and have been available on UNIX-like systems for a long time, making them suitable if you need to maintain compatibility with legacy code or specific POSIX requirements

- **Platform-specific**: POSIX timers are not available on all platforms, so if portability is a concern, it is better to switch to a more suitable choice

But what better alternative do we have in C++? We will see in the next section.

Handling time in C++

While POSIX timers have their own merits, in C++ there are libraries that provide higher-level and more portable solutions for timing and time-related operations.

One good example of such a library is `std::chrono`. This is a C++ library that provides a set of utilities for working with time-related operations and measurements. It is part of the Standard Library and is included in the `<chrono>` header. The `std::chrono` library provides a flexible and type-safe mechanism for representing and manipulating time durations, time points, clocks, and time-related operations. By using `std::chrono`, you will benefit from the standardization, type safety, flexibility, and integration that comes with the C++ Standard Library. Some of the advantages of `std::chrono` compared to the traditional POSIX approach are as follows:

- **Standardization**: `std::chrono` is part of the C++ Standard Library, making it a cross-platform solution that works consistently across different operating systems and compilers. POSIX, on the other hand, is specific to UNIX-like systems and may not be available or behave consistently on all platforms.

- **Type safety**: `std::chrono` provides type-safe representations of time durations and points in time. It offers a rich set of duration and clock types that can be used together seamlessly, enabling safer and more expressive code. POSIX timers, while powerful, often rely on low-level types, such as the `timespec` struct, which can be error-prone and require manual conversions.

- **Flexibility and expressiveness**: `std::chrono` offers a flexible and expressive interface for time-related operations. It provides convenient ways to perform arithmetic operations on durations, convert between different time units, and format time values. POSIX timers, while suitable for specific timing requirements, lack the high-level abstractions and utilities provided by `std::chrono`.

- **Integration with the Standard Library**: `std::chrono` seamlessly integrates with other parts of the C++ Standard Library. It can be used in conjunction with algorithms, containers, and concurrency facilities, allowing for more cohesive and efficient code. POSIX timers, being a lower-level interface, may require additional work to integrate with other C++ Standard Library components.

- **Compatibility with modern C++ features**: `std::chrono` benefits from the advancements and features introduced in modern C++. It supports features such as user-defined literals, lambda functions, and type deduction, making it easier to write concise and expressive code. POSIX timers, being part of the POSIX API, may not fully leverage the modern C++ language features.

The `<chrono>` library provides a comprehensive set of features for working with time-related operations, such as measuring time durations, representing points in time, and performing various time calculations and conversions. Here are some key components and features of `std::chrono`:

- **Clocks**: `<chrono>` defines several clock types that represent different sources of time and different epochs. `std::chrono::system_clock` represents the system-wide RTC, which is adjustable. `std::chrono::steady_clock` represents a steady monotonic clock unaffected by system time adjustments, and `std::chrono::high_resolution_clock` represents a clock with the highest available resolution (if supported by the system).

- **Duration**: The `std::chrono::duration` template class represents a time interval, that is, a specified period of time The duration is the tick count using a specific unit of time; for example, a duration of five hours is five ticks of the unit *hour*. Different types of durations can be defined, from years to nanoseconds. Example durations include `std::chrono::seconds`, `std::chrono::milliseconds`, and `std::chrono::months`.

- **Time point**: A time point represents a specific point in time compared to the epoch of a specific clock. The `std::chrono::time_point` template class is parameterized by a clock and duration type.

- **Time conversions**: `std::chrono` allows for conversions between durations and time points, as well as arithmetic operations involving durations. It provides functions such as `std::chrono::duration_cast` to convert between different durations and `std::chrono::time_point_cast` to convert between different time points.

- **Clock utilities**: `std::chrono` provides utilities for querying the current time, such as `std::chrono::system_clock::now()`, which returns the current system time point.

- **Chrono literals**: `std::chrono` provides user-defined, time-related literals in the `std::literals::chrono_literals` namespace. They allow you to create `std::chrono::duration` objects using literals with time units. This makes the code more readable and convenient when dealing with time-related computations.

- **Calendar**: `std::chrono` provides calendar capabilities, such as working with days, months, and years. It also provides notation for leap years and leap seconds.

- **Time zones**: `std::chrono` provides information about different time zones across the globe depending on the geographical location.

By using `std::chrono`, you can perform accurate and portable time measurements, handle timeouts, calculate time differences, and work with time-related operations in a type-safe manner.

> **Important note**
>
> The following is a link to the `<chrono>` header in the C++ reference documentation: `https://en.cppreference.com/w/cpp/header/chrono`.

Here's an example of how to use `std::chrono` to measure the execution time of a code snippet:

```cpp
#include <iostream>
#include <chrono>
using namespace std::chrono;
int main() {
    const auto start{steady_clock::now()}; // {1}
    just_busy_wait_f(); // {2}
    const auto end{steady_clock::now()}; // {3}
    const auto dur{duration_cast<milliseconds>(end -
      start)}; // {4}
    std::cout << "Execution time: " << dur.count() << "
      milliseconds\n"; // {5}
    return 0;
}
```

In the preceding example, `std::chrono::steady_clock` is used to measure the execution time of the same function as from the previous example (see marker {2}). The `start` and `end` variables represent the *timepoints* taken before and after the code execution using the `now()` static function of `steady_clock` (see markers {1} and {3}). `std::chrono::duration_cast` is used to convert the calculated duration between the time points in milliseconds (see marker {4}).

The output of the program should be similar to this:

```
Program returned: 0
Execution time: 179 milliseconds
```

As you can see, the `std::chrono::duration` class has a `count()` method, which returns the number of units in a specific duration; see marker {5}.

But let's get deeper into how this really works.

Using clocks, timers, and ratios

Before getting into more examples with clocks and timers, we first have to get a better understanding of how the chrono library defines a *duration*.

As we saw in the previous example, a duration is the distance between two points of time, called *timepoints*. In our previous example, these were the `start` and `end` timepoints.

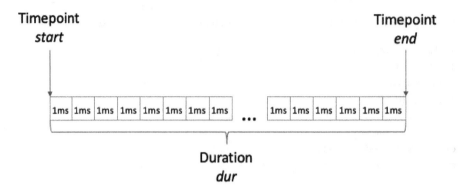

Figure 8.1 – Timepoint and duration

The duration itself is a combination of the count of ticks and a fraction that represents the time in seconds from one tick to the next. The fraction is represented by the std::ratio class. Here are some examples:

```
using namespace std::chrono;
constexpr std::chrono::duration<int, std::ratio<1>>
  six_minutes_1{360};
constexpr std::chrono::duration<double, std::ratio<3600>>
  six_minutes_2{0.1};
constexpr std::chrono::minutes six_minutes_3{6};
constexpr auto six_minutes_4{6min};
std::cout << six_minutes_1 << '\n';
std::cout << six_minutes_2 << '\n';
std::cout << six_minutes_3 << '\n';
std::cout << six_minutes_4 << '\n';
static_assert(six_minutes_1 == six_minutes_2);
static_assert(six_minutes_2 == six_minutes_3);
static_assert(six_minutes_3 == six_minutes_4);
```

In the preceding example, we have defined the duration of six minutes in several ways. In the six_minutes_1 variable, we have specified this duration as a value of 360 seconds. The same duration can also be represented as 1/10 of an hour – the six_minutes_2 variable. The last two durations – six_minutes_3 and six_minutes_4 – represent the same duration of six minutes but using the std::chrono predefined duration types and literals. Here is the output of the preceding code block:

```
360s
0.1h
6min
6min
```

As you can see, `std::duration` also provides pretty formatting capabilities so that once the duration is passed to a string or stream operator, it will add the corresponding suffix so we can see the duration type.

In order to ensure that the preceding durations really correspond to six minutes, we have tested them against `static_assert`, which would fail the program if they don't match.

> **Important note**
>
> The following is a link to the `std::duration` class in the C++ reference documentation: `https://en.cppreference.com/w/cpp/chrono/duration`.

Let's go back to our previous example, slightly change it, and have a closer look at a `timepoint` object:

```
using namespace std::chrono;
const time_point start{steady_clock::now()}; // {1}
const duration epoch_to_start{start.time_since_epoch()}; //
    {2}
std::cout << "Time since clock epoch: " << epoch_to_start
    << '\n'; // {3}
```

As you can see, we again construct a `timepoint` object, `start`, in which we get the time at the moment of its instantiation from the `steady_clock` instance of the Linux system; see marker {1}. The `std::chrono::time_point` class stores a `std::chrono::duration` value, which actually indicates the time interval from the start of the clock's epoch. In order to allow getting that value, the `std::chrono::duration` class exposes a method that returns the duration, `time_since_epoch()`, in nanoseconds; see marker {2}.

Here is the result of the preceding code executed in our test environment. Please keep in mind that if you execute this code, the result could be different:

```
Time since clock epoch: 2080809926594ns
```

Having a time duration in nanoseconds could be inconvenient in some use cases, such as our example of calculating the time it takes for a code block to execute. However converting a duration from a higher-precision type into a lower-precision type results in a loss of precision. Therefore, if we need to see the duration in minutes then in nanoseconds, we can't just do this:

```
using namespace std::chrono;
const minutes
   dur_minutes{steady_clock::now().time_since_epoch()};
```

This is because the preceding code won't compile. The reason behind this is that the `time_since_epoch()` method returns the duration with a precision of nanoseconds. If we store that data in minutes, we will certainly lose precision. In order to be sure that this won't be done by mistake, the compiler stops us.

But how can we intentionally convert duration values from one precision into another? As we saw in the first example, we can use the `std::chrono::duration_cast` function provided by the library. It enables us to make conversions from a duration type with higher precision to a duration type with lower precision. Let's rework the preceding example and see how this works:

```
using namespace std::chrono;
auto dur_from_epoch{steady_clock::now()
  .time_since_epoch()}; // {1}
minutes dur_minutes{duration_cast<minutes>
  (dur_from_epoch)}; // {2}
std::cout << "Duration in nanoseconds: " << dur_from_epoch
  << '\n'; //{3}
std::cout << "Duration in minutes: " << dur_minutes <<
  '\n'; //{4}
```

As you can see in marker {1}, we again get the duration in nanoseconds from the clock's epoch. In marker {2}, we initialize another duration variable but this time in minutes. In order to do so, we use `std::chrono::duration_cast<minutes>`, which converts the value from the source resolution into the destination one and truncates it down to the closest integer value. In our test environment, the result of the preceding code block is as follows:

```
Duration in nanoseconds: 35206835643934ns
Duration in minutes: 586min
```

We can see that the measured duration in nanoseconds is equivalent to about 586.78 minutes but it is truncated down to 586 minutes.

Of course, we could also need to round up rather than just truncate down values. Fortunately, the `chrono` library gives us this capability with the `std::chrono::round` method, which does exactly this. Here is an example:

```
using namespace std::chrono;
seconds dur_sec_1{55s}; //{1}
seconds dur_sec_2{65s}; //{2}
minutes dur_min_1{round<minutes>(dur_sec_1)}; //{3}
minutes dur_min_2{round<minutes>(dur_sec_2)}; //{4}
std::cout << "Rounding up to " << dur_min_1 << '\n';
std::cout << "Rounding down to " << dur_min_2 << '\n';
```

In this example, we define two duration variables, dur_sec_1 and dur_sec_2. dur_sec_1 is initialized to 55 seconds (see marker {1}) and dur_sec_2 is initialized to 65 seconds (see marker {2}). Then, using the std::chrono::round function, we initialize another two duration variables but this time with a resolution of minutes (see markers {3} and {4}). Both duration variables are rounded to one minute:

```
Rounding up to 1min
Rounding down to 1min
```

The chrono library also supplies methods for ceil and floor durations. All of them can be found in the official documentation.

> **Important note**
> The documentation for round, floor, and ceil methods for duration values can be found at these links: https://en.cppreference.com/w/cpp/chrono/duration/round, https://en.cppreference.com/w/cpp/chrono/duration/floor, and https://en.cppreference.com/w/cpp/chrono/duration/ceil.

Since we have a better understanding of time operations, let's have a closer look at the different types of clocks that std::chrono provides for us.

More about clocks in C++20

We already used std::chrono::steady_clock in our previous examples. This is just one of the predefined clocks in the C++ chrono library that you can use. std::chrono::steady_clock, as its name suggests, is a clock that is steady. This means that it is a monotonic clock in which time only moves forward, and its timepoint values are always increasing. It is suitable for use when we want to measure intervals of time. Its epoch can vary.

Another frequently used clock is std::chrono::system_clock. In Linux, it represents the time measured by the system. This means that it is not guaranteed to be monotonic, and it can be adjusted at any moment. In Linux, its epoch matches the UNIX epoch. Let's see an example:

```
using namespace std::chrono;
time_point<system_clock> systemClockEpoch;
std::cout << std::format("system_clock epoch:
  {0:%F}T{0:%R%z}.", systemClockEpoch) << '\n';
```

The preceding example prints the Linux system clock epoch, which corresponds to the UNIX epoch – 00:00:00: UTC on 1 January 1970:

```
system_clock epoch: 1970-01-01T00:00+0000.
```

Keep in mind that `std::chrono::system_clock` doesn't take into account *leap seconds*, which can be added or subtracted from the measured time. In general, a leap second is a one-second adjustment of UTC, which can occur twice per year to reflect the accuracy of the Earth's rotation around the Sun.

> **Important note**
>
> More information about leap seconds can be found at `https://en.wikipedia.org/wiki/Leap_second`.

C++20 introduces several more predefined clocks. Some of them are `std::chrono::utc_clock`, which measures UTC, and `std::chrono::tai_clock`, which measures **International Atomic Time (TAI)**.

> **Important note**
>
> More information about UTC and TAI can be found here: `https://en.wikipedia.org/wiki/Coordinated_Universal_Time` and `https://en.wikipedia.org/wiki/International_Atomic_Time`.

A key difference between the TAI and UTC clocks is that the UTC clock is guaranteed to take into account the leap-second corrections made since the clock epoch, but the TAI clock doesn't take them into account. Let's see an example:

```
using namespace std::chrono;
tai_time tai{tai_clock::now()};
utc_time utc{utc_clock::now()};
std::cout << "International atomic time (TAI): " << tai <<
    '\n';
std::cout << "Coordinated universal time (UTC): " << utc <<
    '\n';
```

In the preceding example, we get the current time from both clocks – `utc` and `tai`. Here is the result:

```
International atomic time (TAI): 2023-08-04 14:02:57.95506
Coordinated universal time (UTC): 2023-08-04 14:02:20.95506
```

As you can see, regardless of whether both clocks are invoked at the same time, they show different times. And their difference is *exactly 37 seconds*. This difference comes from the leap-second adjustments made since they were introduced back in 1972.

`std::chrono::utc_clock` applies leap-second adjustments. By using chrono's UTC clock, these leap-second adjustments will be done automatically for you, and you don't need to take any special action. Therefore, the chrono library provides a method to convert between clock types – `std::chrono::clock_cast`, which converts `std::chrono::time_point` values from one clock into another. Let's see another example:

```
using namespace std::chrono;
tai_time tai{tai_clock::now()};
std::cout << "International atomic time (TAI): " << tai <<
    '\n';
utc_time utc{clock_cast<utc_clock>(tai)};
std::cout << "Coordinated universal time (UTC): " << utc <<
    '\n';
```

As you can see, the `time_point tai` object generated by chrono's TAI clock is converted into a time point from the UTC clock. The result is as follows:

```
International atomic time (TAI): 2023-08-04 14:16:22.72521
Coordinated universal time (UTC): 2023-08-04 14:15:45.72521
```

As we expected, the TAI clock is 37 seconds ahead of the UTC one. Therefore, UTC cannot be used to properly measure time differences as a leap second might be added or removed.

> **Important note**
> You can find all the predefined clocks in the C++ chrono library here: `https://en.cppreference.com/w/cpp/chrono#Clocks`.

Now, since we have a good understanding of timing and clocks, let's see what capabilities the C++ chrono library provides for calendars and time zones.

Using calendar and time zone capabilities

C++20 introduces brand-new support for calendar and time zone operations to the standard. When we talk about calendar operations, this means operations in days, months, and years. They, together with the time zone notion, allow conversions of time between different time zones taking into account time zone adjustments such as daylight saving time.

Let's define a date and print it with the help of the `chrono` library:

```
using namespace std::chrono;
year theYear{2023};
month theMonth{8};
day theDay{4};
std::cout << "Year: " << theYear;
std::cout << ", Month: " << theMonth;
std::cout << ", Day: " << theDay << '\n';
```

As you can see, the `std::chrono` namespace provides `year`, `month`, and `day` classes, which make it easy to work with dates. The benefit of these classes is that they provide strict type and boundary checks, some operators for summation and subtraction, and formatting capabilities. The result of the preceding code is as follows:

```
Year: 2023, Month: Aug, Day: 04
```

As you can see, passing the `Month` variable to `operator<<` applies formatting so that the value of the month is printed as Aug. Also, these classes provide validation and boundary checks on the applied values:

```
using namespace std::chrono;
std::cout << "Year: " << year{2023} ;
std::cout << ", Month: " << month{13};
std::cout << ", Day: " << day{32} << '\n';
```

In the preceding example, we have applied an invalid month and day of the month. The result is as follows:

```
Year: 2023, Month: 13 is not a valid month, Day: 32 is not a valid day
```

As you can see, `month` and `day` values are validated, and when they are passed to `operator<<`, it prints that these values are not valid.

The `year` class represents a year in the proleptic Gregorian calendar, which enables us to ask whether the year is a leap year or not:

```
using namespace std::chrono;
sys_time now{system_clock::now()};
year_month_day today{floor<days>(now)};
std::cout << "Today is: " << today << '\n';
year thisYear{today.year()};
std::cout << "Year " << thisYear;
if (thisYear.is_leap()) {
    std::cout << " is a leap year\n";
} else {
    std::cout << " is not a leap year\n";
}
```

In this example, we first get the current system time – now – and then we convert it into an object of the `year_month_day` type. This object represents a convenient field-based timepoint. It holds `year`, `month`, and `day` objects and allows direct access to them. It also supports instantiation from `std::chrono::sys_days`, which effectively is a timepoint of the system clock in days. Therefore, we pass the now timepoint and create the `today` object. Then, we get the `year` object – `thisYear` – and it checks whether this is a leap year or not using the `is_leap()` method of the `year` class:

```
Today is: 2023-08-05
Year 2023 is not a leap year
```

As expected, 2023 is not a leap year.

The `chrono` library heavily utilizes `operator/` for date creation. C++20 provides about 40 overloads of the parameters of this operator. Let's see an example:

```
using namespace std::chrono;
year_month_day date1{July/5d/2023y};
year_month_day date2{1d/October/2023y};
year_month_day date3{2023y/January/27d};
std::cout << date1 << '\n';
std::cout << date2 << '\n';
std::cout << date3 << '\n';
```

As you can see, we create a `year_month_day` object by passing the newly introduced *chrono literals* for months, days, and years together with `operator/`. chrono provides convenient literals for the creation of days; you just have to append `d` to the day value. The same is the case for years, you have to append `y` and you construct a `year` object. For months, the chrono library defines named constants for all months of the year.

> **Important note**
>
> The following is a link to a list of the month constants in the chrono library: `https://en.cppreference.com/w/cpp/chrono/month`.

During the instantiation of the `year_month_day` object, we pass date values using `operator/`. As is visible from the preceding example, chrono supports many combinations of day, month, and year values. All of them can be found in the standard documentation.

> **Important note**
>
> The following is a link to the documentation on all overloads of `operator/` for date management: `https://en.cppreference.com/w/cpp/chrono/operator_slash`.

All the used overloads in our example are supposed to create valid `year_month_date` objects. Let's see the output:

```
2023-07-05
2023-10-01
2023-01-27
```

As we can see, we have successfully created three separate valid dates with the help of chrono literals and `operator/`.

Working with time zones in C++

The C++20 `chrono` library provides capabilities for working with time zones. It integrates the IANA time zone database, which contains information about the local time in many geographical locations around the globe.

> **Important note**
>
> Find more information about the IANA time zone database here: `https://www.iana.org/time-zones`.

Using `chrono`, you can get a copy of the IANA database and browse it for a specific geographical location:

```
using namespace std::chrono;
const tzdb& tzdb{get_tzdb()};
const std::vector<time_zone>& tzs{tzdb.zones};
for (const time_zone& tz : tzs) {
    std::cout << tz.name() << '\n';
}
```

As we can see from the example, in the `std::chrono` namespace, there is a method – `get_tzdb()` – that returns a reference to the IANA database. In the database, you can find information about its version and also get a sorted list of all available `std::chrono::time_zone` objects.

The `std::chrono::time_zone` class stores information about transitions between time zones for its specific geographic area and name. The output from the preceding example is as follows:

```
Africa/Abidjan
Africa/Accra
Africa/Addis_Ababa
Africa/Algiers
Africa/Asmara
Africa/Bamako
...
```

Now, once we have all available time zones, let's try to find a specific one based on a geographical location and see what the time is there:

```cpp
using namespace std::chrono;
const tzdb& tzdb{get_tzdb()};
const std::vector<time_zone>& tzs{tzdb.zones};
const auto& res{std::find_if(tzs.begin(), tzs.end(), []
    (const time_zone& tz){
      std::string name{tz.name()};
      return name.ends_with("Sofia");
})};
if (res != tzs.end()) {
    try {
        const std::string_view myLocation{res->name()};
        const std::string_view london{"Europe/London"};
        const time_point now{system_clock::now()};
        const zoned_time zt_1{myLocation, now};
        const zoned_time zt_2{london, now};
        std::cout << myLocation << ": " << zt_1 << '\n';
        std::cout << london << ": " << zt_2 << '\n';
    } catch (const std::runtime_error& e) {
        std::cout << e.what() << '\n';
    }
}
```

In this example, we again get the list of the available time zones and try to find the time zone for the city of Sofia. Then, we use the full name of the found time zone to create another object that uses a specific geographical location and the value of the system time – std::chrono::zoned_time. This class represents a logical pair between a time zone and a point in time. We also create another zoned_time zt_2 object but for the city of London, which represents the same time point as zt_1 but in another geographical location. The result of the preceding code is as follows:

```
Europe/Sofia: 2023-08-05 13:43:53.503184619 EEST
Europe/London: 2023-08-05 11:43:53.503184619 BST
```

As you can see, both objects display a valid time but with respect to their geographical locations. This is how we can safely get the current time in a specific geographical location where daylight saving time is also considered.

Summary

In this chapter, we explored the different timers available within the Linux environment. Subsequently, we gained an understanding of the significance behind the clock epoch and the concept of UNIX time. Following this, we delved into the practical implementation of POSIX in Linux for accurate time measurement. Additionally, we investigated the realm of `std::chrono` and examined the array of capabilities that C++ affords for effective time-related operations. Our exploration then took us on a detailed journey through duration, timepoints, and clocks as they are defined within the `std::chrono` framework. Moving forward, we acquainted ourselves with the various clock types at our disposal within `std::chrono`. As our journey continued, we initiated our exploration into the calendar capabilities presented by `std::chrono`. Finally, we developed familiarity with time zones and honed our proficiency in executing seamless time conversions utilizing the tools offered by `std::chrono`. Now, we are ready for the next chapter, where we will go deeper into the specifics of the C++ memory model.

9

Understanding the C++ Memory Model

This chapter is a continuation of the discussion from *Chapter 7*, where we discussed a few multiprocess and multi-threaded techniques; this chapter will enhance their usage. We will guide you through various techniques while narrowing down to the main focus of the chapter – the C++ memory model. But in order to discuss this, you will start first with a brief examination of memory robustness through the smart pointer and the optional objects. We will use them later to implement *lazy initialization* and handle *shared memory* regions safely. An improved memory access analysis of *cache-friendly* code follows. You will learn when and why using multi-threaded execution could be a trap, even though you did everything right in the software design.

This chapter gives you the opportunity to broaden your understanding of the synchronization primitives. While learning about the *condition variables*, you will also understand the benefits of the *read-write locks*. We will use the *ranges* from C++20 to visualize the same shared data differently. Combining these mechanisms one by one, we will finalize our analysis with the biggest topic – instruction ordering. Through the C++ *memory order*, you will learn more about the significance of the correct atomic routine setup. The *spinlock* implementation will be used to summarize all techniques at the end.

In this chapter, we are going to cover the following main topics:

- Getting to know smart pointers and optionals in C++

- Learning about condition variables, read-write locks, and ranges in C++

- Discussing multiprocessor systems – cache locality and cache friendliness in C++

- Revisiting shared resources through the C++ memory model via the spinlock implementation

Technical requirements

In order to run the code examples, the reader must prepare the following:

- A Linux-based system capable of compiling and executing C++20 (for example, **Linux Mint 21**)

- The GCC12.2 compiler: `https://gcc.gnu.org/git/gcc.git gcc-source`

  - With the `-std=c++2a`, `-lpthread`, and `-lrt` flags

- For all the examples, you can alternatively use `https://godbolt.org/`.

- All code examples in this chapter are available for download from `https://github.com/PacktPublishing/C-Programming-for-Linux-Systems/tree/main/Chapter%209`.

Getting to know smart pointers and optionals in C++

In *Chapter 4*, we revisited the C++ fundamentals in order to be on the same page when it comes to the language. One instrument that is also considered a *must* is smart pointers. Through these, we are able to improve the safety of the program and also manage our resources more effectively. And as discussed in the earlier chapters, this is one of our main goals as system programmers. Remember the **RAII** principle? Smart pointers are based on this, helping the C++ developer reduce and even eliminate *memory leaks*. They could also help with shared memory management as you will see later in the chapter.

Memory leaks appear when we allocate memory but fail to free it. This could happen not only because we forgot to call the object's destructor, but also when we lose the pointer to that memory address. In addition to these, there are also the *wild* and *dangling pointers* to consider as well. The first one happens when the pointer is there on the *stack*, but it's never associated with the real object (or address). The second one happens when we free the memory, used by the object, but the value of the pointer remains *dangling* around, and we reference an already-deleted object. Altogether, these errors can lead not only to **memory fragmentation**, but also to **buffer overflow** vulnerabilities.

These issues are hard to catch and reproduce, especially on large systems. System programmers and software integration engineers use tools such as address sanitizers, static and dynamic code analyzers, and profilers, among others, relying on them to predict future defects. But such tools are expensive and consume a lot of computational power, so we cannot rely on them constantly for higher code quality. That said, what can we do, then? The answer is simple – use smart pointers.

> **Note**
>
> You can read more on the subject of smart pointers in the standard, or refer to `https://en.cppreference.com/w/cpp/memory`.

Retracing RAII via smart pointers

Even experienced C++ developers make mistakes when it comes to the right time for memory deallocation. Other languages use garbage collection techniques to handle memory management, but it's important to mention that memory leaks happen there as well. Multiple algorithms are implemented for detecting such cases in the code but are not always successful. For example, the cycle dependency between objects is sometimes difficult to resolve – should two objects pointing to each other be deleted, or should they remain allocated? If they remain allocated, does this constitute a leak or not? So, it's our job to be cautious about memory usage. In addition, garbage collectors work to free up memory, but do not manage opened files, network connections, locks, and so on. To this end, C++ implements its own instrument for control – wrapper classes over the pointers, helping us free the memory at the right time, usually when the object goes out of scope (the object life cycle was discussed already in *Chapter 4*). Smart pointers are efficient in terms of memory and performance, meaning they don't cost (much) more than raw pointers. At the same time, they give us robustness in memory management. There are three types of smart pointers in the C++ standard:

- `unique_ptr`: This is a pointer that is allowed one owner only. It cannot be copied or shared, but the ownership can be transferred. It has the size of a single raw pointer. It is destroyed and the object deallocated when it goes out of the scope.

- `shared_ptr`: This can have multiple owners and is destroyed when all owners have given up ownership on it or all go out of scope. It uses a reference counter to the pointer of an object. Its size is two raw pointers – one for the allocated object, and one for the shared control block containing the reference count.

- `weak_ptr`: This provides access to an object owned by one or more shared pointers, but doesn't count references. It is used for observing an object, but not for managing its life cycle. It consists of two pointers – one for the control block, and one for pointing to the shared pointer it was constructed from. Through `weak_ptr` you can learn whether the underlying `shared_ptr` is still valid – just call the `expired()` method.

Let's demonstrate their initial roles through the following example:

```cpp
struct Book {
    string_view title;
    Book(string_view p_title) : title(p_title) {
        cout << "Constructor for: " << title << endl; }
    ~Book() {cout << "Destructor for: " << title << endl;}};
int main() {
    unique_ptr<Book> book1 =
        make_unique<Book>("Jaws");
    unique_ptr<Book> book1_new;
    book1_new = move(book1); // {1}
    cout << book1_new->title << endl;
    shared_ptr<Book> book2 =
        make_unique<Book>("Dune");
    shared_ptr<Book> book2_new;
    book2_new = book2; // {2}
    cout << book2->title <<" "<< book2_new->title << endl;
    cout << book2.use_count() << endl;
```

As you can see, we use the heap as we call new for the creation of the Book objects. But as the smart pointer handles memory management, we don't need to call the destructor explicitly:

```
Constructor for: Jaws
Jaws
Constructor for: Dune
Dune Dune
2
Destructor for: Dune
Destructor for: Jaws
```

First, we move the ownership of book1's object to another unique_ptr – book1_new (marker {1}). We print out its title through the second unique_ptr as the first one is already invalid. We do the same operation for another Book object, but through a shared_ptr object (marker {2}). This time the title variable can be accessed from both pointers. We also print the reference count, and we see there are two references to that object.

weak_ptr has useful strengths in system programming, too. You can use weak_ptr to check for pointer validity. weak_ptr could also resolve the issue of cyclic dependency between objects. Let's consider an example of a list node of a doubly linked list. The next example illustrates the benefits of weak_ptr. This is a good time to advise you not to implement such data structures yourself, especially when they are already a part of the C++ standard.

Now, let's use the Book object as content of the ListNode struct:

```cpp
struct ListNode {
    Book data;
    ListNode(string_view p_title) {
        data.title = p_title;
        cout << "Node created: " << data.title << endl;
    }
```

We also add two member variables for the previous and following nodes, but one of them will be weak_ptr. One remark is that the weak_ptr reference is not counted as such in the shared_ptr control block. Now, we have both access to the objects and the opportunity to count the references to zero with each deallocation:

```cpp
    ~ListNode() {
        cout << "Node destroyed: " << data.title
            << endl;
    }
    shared_ptr<ListNode> next;
    weak_ptr<ListNode> prev;
};

int main() {
    shared_ptr<ListNode> head =
        make_shared<ListNode>("Dune");
    head->next = make_shared<ListNode>("Jaws");
    if (!head->next->prev.expired())
        head->next->prev = head;
```

From the output, it's clear that all objects were removed successfully:

```
Node created: Dune
Node created: Jaws
Node destroyed: Dune
Node destroyed: Jaws
```

weak_ptr is also useful for cache implementation. Think about it – if you lose all references to an object, you will lose the object itsel; but with smart pointers, it will certainly be destroyed. So, imagine that recently accessed objects or objects with higher importance are kept through shared_ptr in the current code scope. But weak_ptr allows us to keep a reference to an object in the same scope if we need to reference the object later in that same scope. We would create a weak_ptr object to it in this case. But imagine that meanwhile, some other code scope holds a reference to the object through shared_ptr, thus keeping it allocated. In other words, we know about the object, but we don't need to be concerned about its management. Thus, that object is accessible if it's still required later, but removed when nothing else needs it. The following diagram shows how `shared_ptr` could be incorrectly used on the left-hand side, along with the implementation just described on the right-hand side:

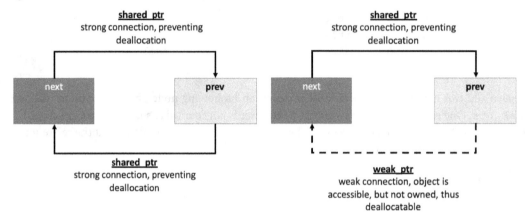

Figure 9.1 – Cyclic dependency through shared_ptr and resolving through weak_ptr

We are not going to dive further into other design solutions where smart pointers could come in handy in this section, but we will return to them in the realm of system programming later in the chapter. In the next section, we discuss a technique that's the opposite to `weak_ptr`, where we retain the awareness of an object that hasn't been created in memory yet.

Doing a lazy initialization in C++

Do you play video games? Have you ever seen a missing texture somewhere in the graphics while playing? Has a graphical resource appeared suddenly when you moved close to it with your character? Have you observed such behavior in other UIs as well? If your answers are mostly in the positive, then you have probably encountered **lazy initialization** already. It's easy to figure out that its purpose is to postpone the construction of an object until it's really needed. By doing so, we allow the system to allocate the required resources only. We also use it to speed up our code, especially if it's run during high CPU loads, such as at system startup. Instead of wasting CPU cycles to create large objects that won't be needed until (much) later, we free up the CPU to handle other requests. On the negative side, we might end up failing to load the object on time, as you have likely observed in video games. As we discussed in *Chapter 2*, this is also used when a program is loaded, and the kernel allocates virtual memory in a lazy fashion – a page of executable code is not loaded until referenced.

As with every other pattern, **lazy initialization** cannot solve all of the problems. So, the system programmer has to choose whether it should be applied for the given application's functions or not. Usually, it is preferred that parts of the graphical and network storage resources remain lazily initialized as they are loaded on demand either way. In other words, the user doesn't see the UI in its entirety all the time. Therefore, it's not required to store it in memory a priori. C++ has features that allow us to easily implement this approach. We present **lazy initialization** in the following example:

```cpp
#include <iostream>
#include <chrono>
#include <optional>
#include <string_view>
#include <thread>
using namespace std;
using namespace std::literals::chrono_literals;
struct Settings {
    Settings(string_view fileName) {
        cout << "Loading settings: " << fileName << endl;
    }
    ~Settings() {
        cout << "Removing settings" << endl;
    }
```

We propose a `Settings` class that will help us simulate the loading and updating of a list of settings from the disk. Note that we pass it by value and not by reference:

```cpp
    void setSetting(string_view setting,
                    string_view value) {
        cout << "Set setting: " << setting
             << " to: " << value << endl;
    }
};
```

This technique saves time due to reduced loading from memory. In C++, pass-by-value (or pass-by-copy) is the default argument passing technique, except for in the case of arrays. It is cheap and optimal for small types, such as `int`. Pass-by-reference is an alternative to pass-by-value and the `string_view` object is handled in the same manner as `int`, using a cheaper copy constructor than other standard objects such as `string`. Getting back to our example, we're creating a configuration object, `Config`, which will consist of the settings file (which could be more than one file in real-world scenarios) and will allow settings to be changed in that configuration. Our `main()` method simulates an application's startup. The `Config` object will be constructed, but the settings file will be loaded only when the startup is finished, and the process resources are available:

```cpp
struct Config {
    optional<Settings> settings{};
    Config() {
        cout << "Config loaded..." << endl;
    }
    void changeSetting(string_view setting,
                       string_view value) {
        if (!settings)
            settings.emplace("settings.cfg");
        settings->setSetting(setting, value);
    }
};
int main() {
    Config cfg;
    cout << "Application startup..." << endl;
    this_thread::sleep_for(10s);
    cfg.changeSetting("Drive mode", "Sport");
    cfg.changeSetting("Gear label", "PRNDL");
```

We observe that the file is loaded after the startup has finished, as we expected:

```
Config loaded...
Application startup...
Loading settings: settings.cfg
Set setting: Drive mode to: Sport
Set setting: Gear label to: PRNDL
Removing settings
```

The `optional` class template is designed so that functions can return *nothing* when they fail, or a valid result when they succeed. We could also use it to handle objects whose construction is expensive. It also manages a value that may or may not be present at a given time. It is also readable, and its intent is clear. If an `optional` object contains a value, the value is guaranteed to be allocated as part of the `optional` object, and no dynamic memory allocation happens. Thus, an `optional` object models a *reservation* to an object, not a pointer. This is a key difference between `optional` and the smart pointer. Although using a smart pointer to handle large and complex objects might be a better idea, `optional` gives you the opportunity to construct an object at a later point in time when all parameters are known, if they weren't known earlier in the execution. Both of them will work well in implementing **lazy initialization** – it's a matter of your preference.

Later in the chapter, we will return to smart pointers and their usability for managing shared memory. First, though, we will use the next section to present some useful mechanisms for synchronization.

Learning about condition variables, read-write locks, and ranges in C++

Let's now start our discussion of synchronization primitives, a fundamental one of which is the **condition variable**. Its purpose is to allow multiple threads to remain blocked until an event occurs (i.e., a condition is satisfied). The implementation of **condition variables** requires an additional Boolean variable to indicate whether the condition is met or not, a *mutex* to serialize the access to the Boolean variable, and the condition variable itself.

POSIX provides an interface for multiple use cases. Do you remember the producer-consumer example in *Chapter 7, Using Shared Memory*? So, `pthread_cond_timedwait()` is used to block a thread for a given period of time. Or simply wait for a condition through `pthread_cond_wait ()` and signal with `pthread_cond_signal()` to one thread, or `pthread_cond_broadcast()` to all threads. Typically, the condition is checked periodically in the scope of a mutex lock:

```
...
pthread_cond_t  condition_variable;
pthread_mutex_t condition_lock;
...
pthread_cond_init(&condition_variable, NULL);
...
void consume() {
    pthread_mutex_lock(&condition_lock);
    while (shared_res == 0)
        pthread_cond_wait(&condition_variable,
                          &condition_lock);
    // Consume from shared_res;
    pthread_mutex_unlock(&condition_lock);
}
void produce() {
    pthread_mutex_lock(&condition_lock);
    if (shared_res == 0)
        pthread_cond_signal(&condition_variable);
    // Produce for shared_res;
    pthread_mutex_unlock(&condition_lock);
}
pthread_mutex_unlock(&condition_lock);
...
pthread_cond_destroy(&condition_variable);
...
```

If we level up the abstraction, as we did in *Chapter 7*, C++ gives us access to the same technique, but a bit simpler and safer to use – we are guarded by the RAII principle. Let's check the following snippet in C++:

```cpp
...
#include <condition_variable>
mutex cv_mutex;
condition_variable cond_var;
...
void waiting() {
    cout << "Waiting for work..." << endl;
    unique_lock<mutex> lock(cv_mutex);
    cond_var.wait(lock);
    processing();
    cout << "Work done." << endl;
}
void done() {
    cout << "Shared resource ready."  << endl;
    cond_var.notify_one();
}
int main () {
    jthread t1(waiting); jthread t2(done);
    t1.join(); t2.join();
    return 0;
}
```

The output is as follows:

```
Waiting for work...
Shared resource ready.
Processing shared resource.
Work done.
```

In this form, the code is not correct. There is no condition to be checked, and the shared resource itself is missing. We are simply setting the stage for the following examples, which are a continuation of what we covered in *Chapter 7*. But observe the use of a **conditional variable** by one thread to notify another that a resource is ready to be consumed (marker {4}), while the first one was waiting (marker {2}). As you see, we rely on a *mutex* to lock the shared resource in the scope (marker {1}) and the condition variable is triggered through it in order to continue to work (markers {2} and {3}). Thus, the CPU is not busy waiting, as there's no endless loop to wait for a condition, freeing up access to the CPU for other processes and threads. But the thread remains blocked, because the wait() method of the **condition variable** unlocks the **mutex** and the thread is put to sleep atomically. When the thread is signaled, it will be resumed and will re-acquire the **mutex**. This is not always useful as you will see in the next section.

Cooperative cancellation through condition variables

An important remark is that the condition variable should wait only with a condition and through a predicate. If not, the thread waiting on it will remain blocked. Do you remember the thread cancellation example from *Chapter 6*? We used jthread and sent *stop notifications* between threads through the stop_token class and the stop_requested method. This mechanism is known as **cooperative cancellation**. The jthread technique is considered safe and easy to apply, but it might not be an option for your software design, or it might not be enough. Canceling threads could be directly related to waiting for an event. In that case, **condition variables** could come in handy as no endless loops or polling will be required. Revisiting the thread cancellation example from *Chapter 6, Canceling Threads, Is This Really Possible?*, we have the following:

```
while (!token.stop_requested())
```

We are doing polling as the thread worker checks periodically whether the cancellation has been sent while doing something else in the meantime. But if the cancellation is the only thing we care about, then instead of polling, we could simply *subscribe* to the cancellation event using the stop_requested function. C++20 allows us to define a stop_callback function, so together with the condition variable and get_stop_token(), we can do the cooperative cancellation without endless loops:

```cpp
#include <condition_variable>
#include <iostream>
#include <mutex>
#include <thread>
#include <syncstream>
using namespace std;
int main() {
    osyncstream{cout} << "Main thread id: "
                      << this_thread::get_id()
                      << endl;
```

So, let's finish the work from the example in the previous section and add a predicate to the **condition variable** in a worker thread:

```cpp
jthread worker{[](stop_token token) {
    mutex mutex;
    unique_lock lock(mutex);
    condition_variable_any().wait(lock, token,
        [&token] { return token.stop_requested(); });
    osyncstream{cout} << "Thread with id "
                      << this_thread::get_id()
                      << " is currently working."
                      << endl;
}};
```

```
stop_callback callback(worker.get_stop_token(), [] {
osyncstream{cout} <<"Stop callback executed by thread:"
                << this_thread::get_id()
                << endl;
});
auto stopper_func = [&worker] {
    if (worker.request_stop())
        osyncstream{cout} << "Stop request executed by
        thread: "
                            << this_thread::get_id()
                            << endl;
};
jthread stopper(stopper_func);
stopper.join(); }
```

The output is as follows:

```
Main thread id: 140323902175040
Stop callback executed by thread: 140323893778176
Stop request executed by thread: 140323893778176
Thread with id 140323902170880 is currently working.
```

So, the worker thread remains in execution, but the stopper thread gets the stop token in the stop_callback function. When the stop is requested through the stopper function, the **condition variable** is signaled through the token.

Now that we have another mechanism besides the **semaphore** to signal between threads, we can get the **shared memory** back in the game. Let's see how this can work together with the condition variables and smart pointers.

Combining smart pointers, condition variables, and shared memory

We already explored the concept of **shared memory** in *Chapter 7, Using Shared Memory*. Let's use the knowledge from the earlier sections in this chapter to enhance the code safety through some C++ techniques. We're simplifying the scenario a little bit. The full example can be found at https://github.com/PacktPublishing/C-Programming-for-Linux-Systems/tree/main/Chapter%209.

We use the `unique_ptr` argument to provide a specific deallocator:

```
template<typename T>
struct mmap_deallocator {
    size_t m_size;
    mmap_deallocator(size_t size) : m_size{size} {}
    void operator()(T *ptr) const {
        munmap(ptr, m_size);
    }
};
```

We rely on the following:

```
unique_ptr<T, mmap_deallocator<T>>(obj, del);
```

As you see, we are also using templates in order to provide the possibility of storing any type of objects in the **shared memory**. It is easy to keep complex objects with large hierarchies and members in the heap, but storing and accessing their data is not trivial. Multiple processes will have access to those objects in the **shared memory**, but are the processes able to reference the memory behind the pointers? If the referenced memory is not in there or the shared virtual address space, then a memory access violation exception will be thrown. So, approach this with caution.

We proceed with the next example. The already-known condition variable technique is used, but this time we add a real predicate to wait for:

```
mutex cv_mutex;
condition_variable cond_var;
bool work_done = false;
```

Our `producer()` method creates and maps the **shared memory** in the familiar fashion. But this time, instead of doing system calls to write, the shared resource is created directly in the *shared memory* (marker {1}). This technique is known as **placement new**. The memory is allocated a priori, and we construct an object into that memory. The standard `new` operator does these two operations together. Additionally, the object itself is wrapped by a `unique_ptr` object with the respective deallocator. As soon as the scope is left, that portion of the memory will be reset through the `munmap()` method. A **condition variable** is used to signal to the consumer that the data has been prepared:

```
template<typename T, typename N>
auto producer(T buffer, N size) {
    unique_lock<mutex> lock(cv_mutex);
    cond_var.wait(lock, [] { return work_done == false; });
    if (int fd =
            shm_open(SHM_ID, O_CREAT | O_RDWR, 0644);
                    fd != -1) {
        ftruncate(fd, size);
```

The shm region is created and sized. Now, let us use it to store the data:

```
        if (auto ptr =
                mmap(0, size,
                        PROT_RW, MAP_SHARED,
                        fd, 0); ptr != MAP_FAILED) {
            auto obj = new (ptr) T(buffer);
            auto del = mmap_deallocator<T>(size);
            work_done = true;
            lock.unlock();
            cond_var.notify_one();
            return unique_ptr<T,
                mmap_deallocator<T>>(obj, del);
        }
        else {
            const auto ecode{ make_error_code(errc{errno}) };
...

        }
    }
    else {
        const auto ecode{ make_error_code(errc{errno}) };
...

        throw exception;
    }
    // Some shm function failed.
    throw bad_alloc();
}
```

The consumer is implemented similarly, just waiting for the following:

```
cond_var.wait(lock, []{ return work_done == true; });
```

Finally, two threads are started and joined as a producer and consumer to provide the following output:

```
Sending: This is a testing message!
Receiving: This is a testing message!
```

Of course, the example could be much more complex, adding periodic production and consumption. We encourage you to try it out, just using another type of buffer – as you may remember, the string_view object is a constant. Be sure that the deallocator is correctly implemented and called. It is used to make the code safer and discard the possibility of memory leaks.

As you may have observed, throughout our work in this book, we often want to access an object just to read it, without modifying its data. In that case, we don't need full-scale locking, but something to make a difference between just reading data or modifying it. This technique is the *read-write lock* and we present it in the following section.

Implementing read-write locks and ranges with C++

POSIX provides the read-write locks mechanism directly, while C++ hides it under different names – `shared_mutex` and `shared_timed_mutex`. Let's see how it works traditionally in POSIX. We have the *read-write lock* object (`rwlock`) with the expected POSIX interface, where a thread could hold multiple concurrent read locks on it. The goal is to allow multiple readers to access the data until a thread decides to modify it. That thread locks the resource through a write lock. Most implementations favor the write lock over the read lock in order to avoid write starvation. Such behavior is not necessary when it comes to data races, but it definitely causes a minimal application execution bottleneck.

This is especially true when dealing with large-scale systems' data readers – for example, multiple read-only UIs. The C++ features again give us a simple and robust instrument for this task. Therefore, we will not devote time to studying examples of POSIX. We advise you to take a look yourself if interested, starting with `https://linux.die.net/man/3/pthread_rwlock_rdlock`.

Proceeding with the C++ example, let's consider the following scenario – a small number of threads want to modify a shared resource – a vector of numbers – and a larger number of threads wants to visualize the data. What we want to use here is `shared_timed_mutex`. It allows two levels of access: *exclusive*, where only one thread can own the mutex; and *shared*, where multiple threads share ownership of the mutex.

> **Important note**
> Keep in mind that both the `shared_timed_mutex` and `shared_mutex` types are heavier than a simple `mutex`, although `shared_mutex` is considered more efficient on some platforms than `shared_timed_mutex`. You're expected to use them when your read operations are really resource-hungry, slow, and frequent. For short operation bursts it would be preferable to stick with just the mutex. You'll need to measure your resource usage specifically for your system in order to work out which to choose.

The following example illustrates the usage of `shared_mutex`. We'll also use the opportunity to present the `ranges` library in C++. This feature comes with C++20 and together with `string_views` provides an agile way to visualize, filter, transform, and slice C++ containers, among other things. Through this example, you'll learn about some useful techniques with the `ranges` library, which will be explained along with the code. The full example can be found at `https://github.com/PacktPublishing/C-Programming-for-Linux-Systems/tree/main/Chapter%209`.

Let's have a Book struct with a shared resource – vector of books. We are going to use shared_
mutex to handle read-write locking:

```
struct Book {
    string_view title;
    string_view author;
    uint32_t    year;
};
shared_mutex shresMutex;
vector<Book> shared_data =  {{"Harry Potter", ...
```

We implement the method for adding a book to the shared resource with the wr_ prefix in order to
distinguish its role from the other methods. We also execute a write lock on the resource (marker {1}):

```
void wr_addNewBook(string_view title,
                   string_view author,
                   uint32_t year) {
    lock_guard<shared_mutex> writerLock(shresMutex); // {1}
    osyncstream{cout} << "Add new book: " << title << endl;
    shared_data.emplace_back(Book {title, author, year});
    this_thread::sleep_for(500ms);
}
```

Now, we start with the implementation of multiple reader routines. They are marked with the
rd_ prefix, and each of them executes a read lock, meaning that the resource will be available for
multiple readers at a time:

```
void rd_applyYearFilter(uint32_t yearKey) {
    auto year_filter =
        [yearKey](const auto& book)
        { return book.year < yearKey; };
    shared_lock<shared_mutex> readerLock(shresMutex);
    osyncstream{cout}
  << "Apply year filter: " << endl; // {2}
    for (const auto &book : shared_data |
                            views::filter(year_filter))
        osyncstream{cout} << book.title << endl;
}
```

Observe the for loop after marker {2}. It not only iterates through the shared resource, but with
the pipe (|) character we filter out portions of it, which is similar to piping and grep as covered in
Chapter 3, except here, it's not a pipe. We are creating a *range view* through the pipe operator, thus
providing additional logic to the iteration. In other words, we manipulate the view to the container.
This approach can be used not only for vectors, but for the other C++ iterable objects as well.

Why? *Ranges* are used to extend and generalize the algorithms with iterators so the code becomes tighter and less error prone.

It's easy to see the intention of the *range* here, too. Additionally, the *range view* is a lightweight object, similar to `string_view`. It represents an iterable sequence – the *range* itself, created on top of the containers' iterators. It is based on the *Curiously Recurring Template Pattern*. Through the *range* interface, we can change the presentation of a container, present its values as transformed in a given manner, filter out values, split and combine sequences, present unique elements, shuffle elements, slide a window through the values, and so on. All of this is done via the simple syntax of already-implemented *range adapters*. In our example, `rd_applyYearFilter` has a `for` loop wherein books older than `yearKey` are filtered out. We could also print out the shared resource's elements in reverse order:

```
void rd_Reversed() {
    for (const auto &book : views::reverse(shared_data))
        osyncstream{cout} << book.title << endl; ...
```

We could even combine views, as follows:

```
for (const auto &book :
        views::reverse(shared_data) |
        views::filter([nameSizeKey](Book book)
            {return book.author.size() < nameSizeKey;}))}
```

The previous snippet iterates through the elements in reverse order, but it also filters out those books where the length of the author's name is longer than a given value. With the next snippet, we demonstrate how to simply drop a portion of the container during iteration:

```
for (const auto &book :
    ranges::drop_view(shared_data, dropKey))
        osyncstream{cout} << book.title << endl;
```

If this is too generic, you could instead use a specific subrange, which will create a `range` object. The `range` object can be used like any other, as follows:

```
auto const sub_res =
    ranges::subrange(shared_data.begin(),
                     shared_data.begin()+5);
    for (const auto& book: sub_res){
        osyncstream{cout}
        << book.title << " " << book.author
            << " " << book.year << endl;
```

With all of this complete, we create threads to execute all of these actions in a concurrent manner and see how the *read-write lock* manages them. Running the example will produce different output orders depending on the thread's scheduling:

```
thread yearFilter1(
    []{ rd_applyYearFilter(1990); });
thread reversed(
    []{ rd_Reversed(); });
thread reversed_and_filtered(
    []{ rd_ReversedFilteredByAuthorNameSize(8); });
thread addBook1(
    []{ wr_addNewBook("Dune", "Herbert", 1965); });
thread dropFirstElements(
    []{ rd_dropFirstN(1); });
thread addBook2(
    []{ wr_addNewBook("Jaws", "Benchley", 1974); });
thread yearFilter2(
    []{ rd_applyYearFilter(1970); });
```

The output is per the described *range views* (the following has been rearranged slightly for easier reading):

```
Apply reversed order:
It
East of Eden
Harry Potter
Drop first N elements:
East of Eden
It
Apply reversed order and filter by author name size:
It
Harry Potter
Apply year filter:
East of Eden
It
Add new book: Dune
Apply year filter:
East of Eden
Dune
Add new book: Jaws
Print subranged books in main thread:
East of Eden Steinbeck 1952
It King 1986
```

You have now learned about another combination of techniques with which you can scale up a system with multiple threads that handle presentation tasks. Let's now take a step back and discuss the possible traps arising from concurrent execution that are not directly related to data races. We continue with cache-friendly code.

Discussing multiprocessor systems – cache locality and cache friendliness in C++

You probably recall *Chapter 2* at this point, where we discussed multi-thread and multi-core processors. The respective computational units were presented as processors. We also visualized the transport of instructions from the **NVM** (the disk) to the processors, through which we explained the creation of processes and *software* threads.

We want our code to be as performant as required. The most important aspect of getting the code to perform well is the choice of appropriate algorithms and data structures. With a bit of thought, you can try to squeeze the most out of every last CPU cycle. One of the most common examples of misusing algorithms is sorting a large, unordered array with bubble sort. So, make sure to learn your algorithms and data structures – together with the knowledge from this section and beyond, it will make you a really powerful developer.

As you already know, the further we get from the RAM and the closer we get to the processor registers, the faster the operations and the smaller the memory capacity becomes. Each time the processor loads data from the RAM to the cache, it will either just sit and wait for that data to show up, or execute other non-related tasks. Thus, from the perspective of the current task, the CPU cycles are wasted. Of course, reaching 100% CPU utilization might be impossible, but we should at least be aware when it's doing needless work. All of this might sound meaningless to you at this point, but concurrent systems will suffer if we act carelessly.

The C++ language provides access to multiple tools for even better performance improvements, including **prefetching mechanisms** through hardware instructions and **branch prediction optimization**. Even without doing anything in particular, modern compilers and CPUs do a great job with these techniques. Still, we could improve this performance further by providing the right hints, options, and instructions. It's also a good idea to be aware of the data in the cache to help reduce the time taken when accessing it. Remember that the cache is just a type of fast, temporary storage for data and instructions. So, we can use the features of C++ to our advantage when we treat the cache in a good manner, known as **cache-friendly code**. An important remark to note is the inverse of this statement – misusing C++ features will lead to poor cache performance, or at least not the best performance possible. You've probably already guessed that this is related to the system's scale and the requirement for fast data access. Let's discuss this further in the next section.

Considering cache locality through cache-friendly code

We mentioned the concept of cache-friendly code already, but what does it truly mean? First of all, you need to be aware of the **cache locality**. This means that our first goal is to make frequently used data easily accessible, thus the process will run faster. The second goal is to store in memory only what we need to store. Let's keep the allocations small. For example, if you need to store a number of dice values (1-6), you don't need unsigned long longs. Those values will fit in an unsigned `int` or even an unsigned `char`.

As a result, caching has become a major aspect of almost every system. Earlier in the book we mentioned that slower hardware, such as disks, sometimes has its own cache memory to reduce the time taken to access frequently opened files. OSs can cache frequently used data, for example, files, as chunks of virtual address space, thus improving performance even more. This is also known as **temporal locality**.

Consider the following scenario: a piece of data is not found in the cache on the first try – this is known as a **cache miss**. Then it is looked up in the RAM, is found, and is loaded into the cache as one or multiple **cache blocks** or **cache lines**. Afterwards, if this data is requested a number of subsequent times and is still found in the cache, known as a **cache hit**, it will remain in the cache and guarantee faster access, or at least faster than the first **cache miss**. You can observe this in the following diagram:

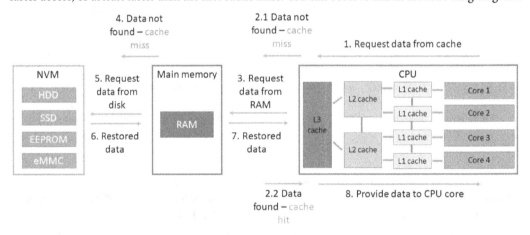

Figure 9.2 – Representation of temporal locality on the hardware level

As we mentioned with the **prefetching mechanisms** earlier, it's a known fact that having an object with multiple **cache hits** means that the data around it might also be referenced soon. This causes the processor to *request* or *prefetch* that additional nearby data from the RAM and load it a priori, so it will be there in the cache when it is eventually needed. This causes **spatial locality**, meaning accessing nearby memory and benefiting from the fact that caching is done in chunks, known as **cache lines,** thus paying for a single transfer and using several bytes of memory. The prefetching technique assumes that the code already has **spatial locality** in order to improve performance.

Both locality principles are based on assumptions. But code branching requires good design. The simpler the branch tree, the simpler to predict. Again, you need to consider carefully the data structures and algorithms to be used. You also need to aim at contiguous memory access and reduce the code to simple loops and small functions; for example, switching from using linked lists to arrays or matrices. For small-sized objects, the `std::vector` container is still the optimal choice. Additionally, we ideally seek a data structure object that can fit into one **cache line** – but sometimes this is just not possible because of the application's requirements.

Our process should access the data in contiguous blocks, where each one has the size of a cache line (typically 64 bytes but depends on the system). But if we want to do parallel evaluations, then it would be preferable for each CPU core (processor) to handle data in different **cache lines** from other cores' data. If not, the cache hardware will have to move data back and forth between cores and the CPU will waste time on meaningless work again and the performance will worsen, instead of being improved. This term is known as **false sharing**, which we'll now have a look at in the following section.

A glance at false sharing

As a rule, small pieces of data will be put together in a single **cache line** unless the programmer instructs otherwise, as we will see in the following examples. This is the way processors work in order to keep latency low – they handle one cache line for each core at a time. Even if it's not full, the **cache line**'s size will be allocated as the smallest possible block for the CPU to handle. As mentioned earlier, if the data in that **cache line** is requested by two or more threads independently, then this will slow down the multi-threaded execution.

Dealing with the effects of **false sharing** means getting predictability. Just as code branching can be predicted, so can the system programmer predict if an object is of the size of a cache line, and thus each separate object can reside in its own memory block. In addition, all computations can happen in the local scope and the shared data modifications take place at the end of a given procedure. Of course, such activities will lead to the wasting of resources at some point, but it's a matter of design and preferences. Nowadays, we can use compiler optimizations to improve this predictability and performance, too, but we shouldn't always rely on this. Let's first check the size of our cache line:

```
#include <iostream>
#include <new>
using std::hardware_destructive_interference_size;
int main() {
    std::cout << "L1 Cache Line size: "
        << hardware_destructive_interference_size
        << " bytes";
    return 0;
}
```

The expected output is as follows:

```
L1 Cache Line size: 64 bytes
```

Now that we know how to get the **cache line**'s size, we are able to align our objects in such a way that no **false sharing** occurs. In *Chapter 7*, we used `std::atomic` to guarantee a single modifier to a shared resource, but we also emphasized that this is not the full picture. Let's enrich the previous example with three atomic variables:

```
cout << "L1 Cache Line size: "
     << hardware_constructive_interference_size
     << " bytes" << endl;
atomic<uint32_t> a_var1;
atomic<uint32_t> a_var2;
atomic<uint32_t> a_var3;
```

Printing the addresses out gives the following:

```
cout << "The atomic var size is: " << sizeof(a_var1)
     << " and its address are: \n"
     << &a_var1 << endl
     << &a_var2 << endl
     << &a_var3 << endl;
...
```

The output is as follows:

```
L1 Cache Line size: 64 bytes
The atomic var size is: 4 and the addresses are:
0x7ffeb0a11c7c
0x7ffeb0a11c78
0x7ffeb0a11c74
```

This means that even when we have atomic variables, they can be fitted into a single **cache line** with high, albeit system-specific, probability. So, even if they are responsible for handling different shared resources, the hardware threads (or cores) will not be able to write in parallel due to the back-and-forth activity in the cache hardware. To keep the cache in line, the CPU implements different **cache coherency protocols**, including **MESI**, **MESIF**, and **MOESI**. None of them allow multiple cores to modify one **cache line** in parallel, though. The **cache line** can only be occupied by one core. Luckily, C++20 provides `atomic_ref<T>::required_alignment`, which allows the programmer to align atomics as per the current cache line size, thus keeping them well apart. Let's apply it for all atomics as follows:

```
alignas(hardware_destructive_interference_size)
    atomic<uint32_t> a_var1;
```

The output is as follows:

```
L1 Cache Line size: 64 bytes
The atomic var size is: 4 and the addresses are:
0x7ffc3ac0af40
0x7ffc3ac0af00
0x7ffc3ac0aec0
```

In the preceding snippet, you can see that the differences in the addresses are as expected and the variables are well aligned, which was always the system programmer's responsibility. Now, let's apply the `increment ()` method that you might remember from *Chapter 7*:

```
void increment(std::atomic<uint32_t>& shared_res) {
    for(int I = 0; i < 100000; ++i) {shared_res++;}
}
```

We increment an atomic resource, and as covered in *Chapter 8*, we know how to measure the duration of a procedure. So, we can analyze the performance for the next four scenarios. One remark – if you feel so inclined, you could play with the compiler optimization levels to spot the difference in the following values, as we are not using any of the optimization flags. The full code example could be found at `https://github.com/PacktPublishing/C-Programming-for-Linux-Systems/tree/main/Chapter%209`. Our scenarios are as follows:

- A single-threaded application, calling `increment ()` 3 times, doing 300,000 increments of an atomic variable, which takes 2,744 microseconds

- Direct sharing with one atomic variable, incremented 100,000 times by each of 3 threads in parallel, taking 5,796 microseconds

- False sharing with three unaligned atomic variables, incremented 100,000 times by each of the 3 threads in parallel, taking 3,545 microseconds

- No sharing with three aligned atomic variables, incremented 100,000 times by each of 3 threads in parallel, taking 1,044 microseconds

As we are not using a benchmarking tool, we cannot measure the number of cache misses or hits. We simply do the following:

```
    ...
    auto start = chrono::steady_clock::now();
    alignas(hardware_destructive_interference_size)
        atomic<uint32_t> a_var1 = 0;
    alignas(hardware_destructive_interference_size)
        atomic<uint32_t> a_var2 = 0;
    alignas(hardware_destructive_interference_size)
        atomic<uint32_t> a_var3 = 0;
```

```
jthread t1([&]() {increment(a_var1);});
jthread t2([&]() {increment(a_var2);});
jthread t3([&]() {increment(a_var3);});
t1.join();
t2.join();
t3.join();
auto end = chrono::steady_clock::now();
...
```

The **no-sharing** work is presented in the following diagram:

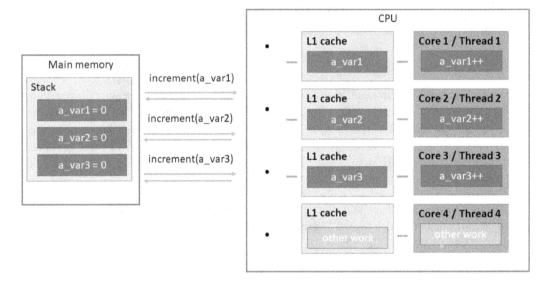

Figure 9.3 – Representation of no-sharing (correct sharing) of data on multiple cores/threads

> **Important note**
>
> It's obvious that we either have to align our atomic resources before we modify them in parallel, or use single-threaded applications for small procedures. The time metric could differ, depending on the system and the compiler optimization flags. Keep in mind that these speed-ups are great when you get the best out of your hardware, but going into so much detail might also lead to complex code, harder debugging, and time wasted on maintenance. It's a balancing act.

False sharing happens during multi-threading and can be fixed if the shared object is fitted into one cache line. But what happens if the object is larger than one cache line in size?

Sharing resources larger than a cache line in C++

The analysis here is relatively simple, as it is not so dependent on the language. Large objects, representing large data structures, are just... large. They don't fit into single **cache lines** and therefore they are not **cache friendly** by nature. Data-oriented design deals with this issue. For example, you could think about using smaller objects or share only small parts of them for parallel work. Additionally, it is good to think about optimizations in algorithms. Making them linear leads to better **branch predictions**. This means making conditional statements depend on predictable, not random, data. Complex conditional statements can be replaced with arithmetic solutions and templates, or chained differently, so it is easier for the CPU to predict which branch has a higher probability of occurring. Such operations, again, could lead to unreadable code and complex debugging, so proceed with them only when the code is not fast enough for your requirements.

As **branch misprediction** could be expensive and remain well hidden, another proposal is the so-called **conditional move**. It is not based on predictions, but on data. The data dependencies include both *condition true* and *condition false* cases. After an instruction that conditionally moves data from one register to another, the contents of the second depend on both their previous values and the values from the first register. As mentioned, well-designed branching allows better performance. But data dependencies require one or two CPU cycles to arrive, sometimes making them a safer bet. A probable trap is when the condition is such that the value taken from the memory is not assigned to the register – then it's just meaningless waiting. Luckily for the system programmer, the **conditional move** instructions in the instruction sets are typically close register-wise.

Cache unfriendliness is something you must consider when using excessively complex object designs or design patterns that spread the data around the memory. That doesn't mean you shouldn't think about improvements. If you rely on C++, the simplest and the most useful thing to apply quickly is to use contiguous containers in the code, such as `std::array` and `std::vector`. Yes, the vector could be resized, but it's still cache friendly, as the elements are next to each other in the memory. Of course, if you have to reallocate the vector due to constant resizing, then probably it's not the data structure you need. You could consider the `std::deque` container, which is efficient for modifications in the middle of the collection, or `std::list` as an alternative, which is a linked list and is not cache friendly at all.

> **Important note**
>
> Depending on the system, many reallocations (construction and destruction) of contiguous memory blocks could cause memory fragmentation. This can happen due to software algorithms for memory management, language standards, OSs, drivers, devices, and so on. It is hard to predict it until it happens. It might take a good portion of non-stop execution time for the memory allocations to start failing. There could be enough free space in the sum of the free memory blocks in the RAM, but not a single block big enough to hold the currently reallocated or created contiguous block. Excessive fragmentation could lead to poor performance and even denial of service.

A final remark on the topic is that there are many articles discussing optimal ways of using C++'s algorithms and containers efficiently. It deserves a book on its own and most of the time is very CPU specific – or at least when you get to the absolute performance. For example, the **conditional moves** lead directly to assembly code, which we don't have the opportunity to explore here. That said, the variety of solutions for different practical problems is enormous when it comes to algorithms and data structures.

Revisiting shared resources through the C++ memory model via spinlock implementation

We learned about atomic operations back in *Chapter 7*. In this chapter, you learned that the placement of atomic variables in the cache is crucial as well. Originally, atomics and locks were introduced because of correctness when multiple threads want to enter the same critical section. Now, our investigation will continue a bit deeper. There's one last piece of the puzzle of atomic operations. Examine the following snippet:

```
Thread 1: shrd_res++; T1: load value
                      T1: add 1
Thread 2: shrd_res++; T2: load value
                      T2: add 1
                      T2: store value
                      T1: store value
```

This was an example of a non-atomic operation. Even when we make it atomic, we still don't have a word about the order of the instructions. Until now, we used the synchronization primitives to instruct the CPU about which section of instructions has to be taken as a unitary context. What we need now is to instruct the processor about the order of those instructions. We do this through C++'s memory_order, which is a part of the C++ standard memory model.

Introducing the memory_order type in C++

With the memory_order type, we specify how atomic and non-atomic memory accesses are ordered around an atomic operation. The atomic realization of the snippet from the preceding section and the example using read-write locks earlier in the chapter could both suffer from the same issue: two atomic operations are not atomic as a whole. The order of instructions inside the atomic scope will be kept, but not around it. This is usually done after optimization techniques in the CPU and the compiler. So, if there are many reader threads, the order in which we (and the threads) expect to observe changes could vary. Such an effect could appear even during single-threaded execution as the compiler might re-arrange instructions as allowed by the memory model.

> **Note**
>
> We encourage you to check out the full information on `memory_order` here: `https://en.cppreference.com/w/cpp/atomic/memory_order`.

An important remark is that the default behavior of all atomic operations in C++ applies sequentially consistent ordering. The defined memory orders in C++20 are as follows:

- Relaxed ordering, tagged like so:

  ```
  memory_order_relaxed = memory_order::relaxed;
  ```

  This ordering is the bare minimum. It is the cheapest option and provides no guarantees, except of the current operation's atomicity. One example of this in action is the incrementation of the `shared_ptr` reference counter, as it needs to be atomic, but no ordering is required.

- Release-acquire ordering, tagged as follows:

  ```
  memory_order_acquire = memory_order::acquire;
  memory_order_release = memory_order::release;
  memory_order_acq_rel = memory_order::acq_rel;
  ```

  Reads and writes are prevented from reordering right after an atomic region when the release operation is in effect. The `acquire` operation is similar, but reordering is prohibited before the atomic region. The third model, `acq_rel`, is a combination of both. This model could really help in the creation of read-write locks, except there's no locking going on. The decrementing of the `shared_ptr` reference count is done through this technique as it needs to be synchronized with the destructor.

- Release-consume ordering, tagged as follows:

  ```
  memory_order_consume = memory_order::consume;
  ```

  The `consume` operation's requirements are still being revised to this day. It is designed to work as the `acquire` operation does, but only for specific data. That way, the compiler is more flexible in optimizing the code than the `acquire` operation. Obviously, getting the data dependencies right makes the code more complex, therefore this model is not widely used. You can see it when accessing rarely written concurrent data structures – configurations and settings, security policies, firewall rules, or publish-subscribe applications with pointer-mediated publication; the producer publishes a pointer through which the consumer can access information.

- Sequentially consistent ordering, tagged as follows:

```
memory_order_seq_cst = memory_order::seq_cst;
```

This is the exact opposite of the relaxed order. All operations in and around the atomic region follow a strict order. Neither instruction can cross the barrier imposed by the atomic operation. It is considered the most expensive model as all optimization opportunities are lost. Sequentially consistent ordering is helpful for multiple producer-multiple consumer applications, where all consumers must observe the actions of all producers occurring in an exact order.

One famous example directly benefiting from the memory order is the **spinlock** mechanism. We will proceed to examine this in the next section.

Designing spinlocks for multiprocessor systems in C++

Operating systems often use this technique as it's very efficient for short-period operations, including the ability to escape rescheduling and context switching. But locks held for longer periods will be at risk of being interrupted by the OS scheduler. The **spinlock** means that a given thread will either acquire a lock or will wait *spinning* (in a loop) – checking the lock's availability. We discussed a similar example of *busy waiting* earlier in the chapter when we presented **cooperative cancellation**. The risk here is that keeping the lock acquired for longer periods will put the system into a **livelock** state, as described in *Chapter 2*. The thread holding the lock will not progress further by releasing it, and the other threads will remain *spinning* while trying to acquire the lock. C++ is well suited for the implementation of the spinlock as atomic operations can be configured in detail. In low-level programming, this approach is also known as test-and-set. Here's an example:

```
struct SpinLock {
    atomic_bool state = false;
    void lock() {
        while (state.exchange(true,
                              std::memory_order_acquire){
            while (state.load(std::memory_order_relaxed))
            // Consider this_thread::yield()
                // for excessive iterations, which
                // go over a given threshold.
    }
    void unlock() noexcept {
        state.store(false, std::memory_order_release); };
```

You're probably wondering why we aren't using the already-known synchronization techniques. Well, keep in mind that all memory order settings here cost only one CPU instruction. They are fast and simple, both software- and hardware-wise. You should limit your use of them to very short periods of time, though, since the CPU is prevented from doing a useful job for another process.

An atomic Boolean is used to mark whether the state of SpinLock is locked or unlocked. The unlock() method is easy – when the critical section is released, the false value is set (store() is atomic) to the state member through the release order. All following read/write operations have to be ordered in an atomic manner. The lock() method firstly runs a loop, trying to access the critical section. The exchange() method will set state to true and will return the previous value, false, thus interrupting the loop. Logically, this is very similar to the semaphore P(S) and V(S) functions. The inner loop will execute the busy wait scenario without order limitations and without producing **cache misses**.

> **Important note**
>
> The store(), load(), and exchange() operations have memory_order requirements and a list of supported orders. Using additional and unexpected orders leads to undefined behavior and keeps the CPU busy without doing useful work.

An advanced version of the **spinlock** is the ticket lock algorithm. In the same fashion as with queues, tickets are provided to the threads in a FIFO manner. That way, the order in which they enter a critical section is managed fairly. In contrast with spinlocks, starvation is avoided here. However, this mechanism does not scale well. First of all, there's a greater number of instructions to read, test, and acquire the lock, as there are more instructions for managing the order. Secondly, as soon as the critical section is free for access, all threads must have their context loaded into the cache to determine whether they are allowed to acquire the lock and enter the critical section.

C++ has an advantage here thanks to its low latency. The full example is available at https://github.com/PacktPublishing/C-Programming-for-Linux-Systems/tree/main/Chapter%209.

First, we implement the TicketLock mechanism, providing the necessary lock() and unlock() methods. We use two helper member variables, serving and next. As you see, they are aligned to be in separate **cache lines** to avoid **false sharing**. Both the lock() and unlock() methods are implemented as in the SpinLock example. Additionally, an atomic increment is done through fetch_add(), allowing the lock to generate tickets. No read/write operations happen around it, so it is executed in a relaxed order. Instead of just setting the variable to false as with SpinLock, the unlock() method loads a ticket number value, again in a relaxed manner, and stores it as the currently served thread:

```
struct TicketLock {
    alignas(hardware_destructive_interference_size)
        atomic_size_t serving;
    alignas(hardware_destructive_interference_size)
        atomic_size_t next;
```

The methods for locking and unlocking of the `TicketLock` algorithm follow:

```cpp
void lock() {
    const auto ticket = next.fetch_add(1,
                                memory_order_relaxed);
    while (serving.load(memory_order_acquire) !=
        ticket);
}
void unlock() {
    serving.fetch_add(1, memory_order_release);
}
};
```

Now, a global `spinlock` object of type `TicketLock` is created. We also create a `vector` that plays the role of a shared resource. The `producer()` and `consumer()` routines are as expected – the first will create data and the latter will consume it, including clearing the shared resource. As both operations will be carried out in parallel, the order of their execution is random. If you want instead to create a ping-pong-like behavior for this, **conditional variables** or **semaphores** could be used as signaling mechanisms. The current implementation is limited just to the purposes of the **ticket lock**:

```cpp
TicketLock spinlock = {0};
vector<string> shared_res {};
void producer() {
    for(int i = 0; i < 100; i ++) {
        osyncstream{cout} << "Producing: " << endl;
        spinlock.lock();
        shared_res.emplace_back("test1");
        shared_res.emplace_back("test2");
        for (const auto& el : shared_res)
            osyncstream{cout} << "p:" << el << endl;
        spinlock.unlock();
        this_thread::sleep_for(100ms);
    }
}
```

And the consumer is similar to what you've already learned:

```cpp
void consumer() {
    for (int i = 0; i < 100; i ++) {
        this_thread::sleep_for(100ms);
        osyncstream{cout} << "Consuming: " << endl;
        spinlock.lock();
        for (const auto& el : shared_res)
            osyncstream{cout} << "c:" << el << endl;
```

Remove the contents of the vector:

```
            shared_res.clear();
            spinlock.unlock();
            if (shared_res.empty())
                osyncstream{cout} << "Consumed" << endl;
        }
    }
```

The output is as follows:

```
Producing:
p:test1
p:test2
Consuming:
c:test1
c:test2
...
```

The output shows that the production and the consumption routines are treated as a whole, although they are not called an equal number of times, which is expected. As mentioned previously, instead of pausing the threads for 100ms, you could also modify the code by adding a **condition variable**:

```
void producer() {
    for(int i = 0; i < 100; i ++) {
        cout <<"Producing:" << endl;
        unique_lock<mutex> mtx(cv_mutex);
        cond_var.wait(mtx, []{ return work_done ==
                                    !work_done; });
```

Proceed with the expected critical section:

```
            spinlock.lock();
            shared_res.emplace_back"test1");
            shared_res.emplace_back"test2");
            for (const auto& el : shared_res)
                cout <<"p" << el << endl;
            spinlock.unlock();
            work_done = !work_done;
        }
    }
```

With all of these techniques combined – memory robustness, synchronization primitives, cache friendliness, and instruction ordering awareness – you have the instruments to really sharpen your code's performance and tweak it to get the best performance on your specific system. We want to take this opportunity to remind you that such detailed optimizations could lead to unreadable code and hard debugging, so use them only when required.

Summary

In this chapter, we've gathered together the entire set of instruments required for optimal code performance with C++. You learned techniques on many different system and software levels, so it's understandable if you want to take a breather now. It is true that it would be good to spend more time on some of what we covered, for example, **branch predictions** and **cache friendliness**, or to implement more algorithms through **condition variables** and memory order. We strongly encourage you to use this chapter as a step in the direction of system improvements and more efficient work.

The next chapter is dedicated to one more significant improvement in C++'s features – **coroutines**. You will see that they are much lighter and, for some of the mechanisms discussed here, such as event waiting, they are much more preferable.

10

Using Coroutines in C++ for System Programming

We are almost at the end of our book. The final chapter is dedicated to a feature that is very useful for the purposes of system programming but is fairly new to the C++ standard. **Coroutine** objects found their application fast, becoming first-class state machine objects. Their power is in hiding logic behind the **coroutine frame**. Be advised that this is an advanced topic, and the coroutine interface of C++ is neither simple nor comfortable to use. It is well thought out but definitely not the most user-friendly in comparison to other programming languages.

In this chapter, you will learn the basics of using this facility. If you are new to it, then you'll spend some time understanding its requirements. You'll have an easier time with coroutines if you have previous experience with them in other programming languages. Still, we will use this chapter to propose their application in system programming.

We will present two practical solutions of previous examples related to **networking** and **shared memory**. You will immediately see the predictability and the clear execution path of the routines. We hope that you are impressed by the concurrent manner of execution without the use of synchronization primitives. Direct reuse in a real-world environment is possible; just make sure you have the required compilers, as the feature is still new. Without further ado, let's get to our final topic.

In this chapter, we are going to cover the following main topics:

- Introducing coroutines
- Network programming and coroutines in C++
- Revisiting the shared memory problem through coroutines in C++
- Final thoughts on coroutines and their implementations in C++

Technical requirements

In order to run the code examples, you must prepare the following:

- A Linux-based system capable of compiling and executing C++20 (for example, **Linux Mint 21**)
- The GCC12.2 compiler – `https://gcc.gnu.org/git/gcc.git gcc-source:`
  - With the `-fcoroutines`, `-std=c++2a`, `-lpthread`, and `-lrt` flags
- For some of the examples, you can alternatively use `https://godbolt.org/`.
- All code examples in this chapter are available for download from `https://github.com/PacktPublishing/C-Programming-for-Linux-Systems/tree/main/Chapter%2010`

Introducing coroutines

At the end of your journey, we'd like to remind you about the knowledge you received in *Chapter 1* and *Chapter 2* about **processes** and **threads**. If you remember well, a process is simply a running instance of a program. It has its respective address space, which is not shared with others, except through shared memory. Threads reside in a process, and they cannot exist outside of them, although both processes and threads are treated as **tasks** in Linux. They are scheduled in the same manner and have the same controlling structures on the **kernel** level. Still, threads are considered lightweight because the bigger overhead for the initial load of a program is taken by the parent process.

But this is not the full picture. There are **fibers** and coroutines as well. If the processes and threads are truly **concurrent** and working in parallel over shared resources, fibers are just like threads but are not **concurrency**-compliant. While threads often depend on **preemptive** time-slicing because of the task scheduler, fibers use **cooperative multitasking**. That is, they yield themselves to run another fiber while executing. They are also known as **stackful coroutines**. Meanwhile, coroutines in C++ are known as **stackless coroutines** and are not OS-managed. In other words, stackful coroutines could be suspended in a nested stack frame, while stackless coroutines can only be nested by the top-level routine.

Both facilities are considered implicitly synchronized, so all of the synchronization primitives and the **atomic** constructs from the previous chapters are needless. But you could picture the early example with reading from the file system – where the OS waits for the file to be opened, and the process-caller is signaled to continue its work. Imagine that the fibers and the coroutines are useful exactly for that reactive access, which does not need additional CPU processing. Actually, the networking and the file systems are the areas where the fibers and coroutines are considered most valuable. When a request is made, a fiber gives control to the main thread, and when the I/O operation is finished, the fiber continues where it yielded.

The coroutines technique is rather old. C++ introduced it recently, and it is very useful for network programming, I/O operations, event management, and so on. Coroutines are also considered executions with the ability to pause. Still, they provide multitasking in a cooperative fashion and do not work in parallel. This means that tasks cannot be executed simultaneously. At the same time, they are real-timw-friendly, allowing switching context between coroutines to be fast, and not requiring system calls. In fact, they are **hard-RTOS**-friendly because the order of execution and scheduling is controlled by the system programmer, as you will see later in the chapter. The coroutines in C++ are very useful for implementing task graphs and state machines, too.

Some of you are probably wondering what the difference between coroutines and standard single-threaded functional programming is. Well, the latter is considered a synchronous approach, while the former is an asynchronous approach with synchronous readability. But coroutines are really about reducing the needless (busy) waiting and doing something useful while a required resource or a call is being prepared. The following diagram is simple but reminds us of the respective differences between sync and async executions.

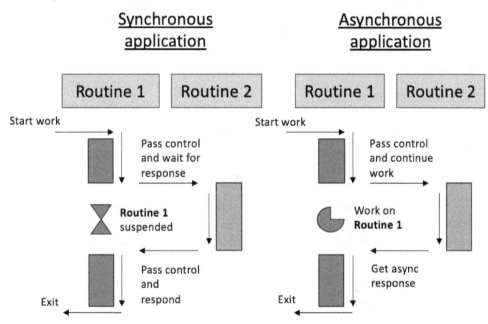

Figure 10.1 – Synchronous versus asynchronous application execution

A regular single-threaded execution is also limited in some ways. First of all, calling, suspending, or resuming a function is not traceable inside a program, or at least not through a reference. In other words, the control flow happens in the background and is implicit. In addition, the control flow has a strict direction – a function could either return to its caller or proceed inward toward calling another function. Each function call creates a new record on the stack and happens immediately, and once invoked, a method cannot be delayed. As soon as that function returns, its portion of the stack is cleared and cannot be restored. In other words, the activation is not traceable.

On the other hand, coroutines have their own lifetime. A coroutine is an object and can be referenced explicitly. If the coroutine should outlive its caller or should be transferred to another, then it could be stored in the **heap**. At the same time, control could be transferred to other coroutines in both directions – *up* or *down*. Coroutines add to the meanings of *function call* and *function type*. The int func (int arg) prototype would mean a function with the name func, receiving an argument, arg, of an integer type, returning an integer. A similar coroutine may never return to its caller and the value that the caller expects may be produced by another coroutine. Let see how this happens in C++.

The coroutine facility in C++

Initially, you can think about them like **smart pointers**. You already know they are wrappers to pointers and provide additional control for memory management. Coroutines work in a similar manner, but the code around them is more complex. This time, we need a wrapper of a function prototype. This wrapper is going to handle the data flow and the scheduling control. The wrapper itself is the coroutine. We define a Task exCoroutine () task (a task is different from the Linux definition of task) – it is interpreted as a coroutine if it uses one of the following three operators: co_await, co_yield, or co_return. Here's an example:

```
#include <coroutine>
...
Task exCoroutine() {
    co_return;
}
int main() { Task async_task = exCoroutine(); }
```

The wrapper type is currently Task. It is known on the caller level. The coroutine object is identified as the exCoroutine () function through the co_return operator. It's the job of the system programmer to create the Task class. It is not a part of the Standard library. What's the Task class then?

```
struct Task {
    struct promise_type {
        Task get_return_object()
            { return {}; }
        std::suspend_never initial_suspend()
            { return {}; }
        std::suspend_never final_suspend() noexcept
            { return {}; }
        void return_void() {}
        void unhandled_exception() {}
    };
};
```

> **Important note**
>
> This is a very generic pattern that is used in almost every coroutine example. You should initially refer to it at `https://en.cppreference.com/w/cpp/language/coroutines`.

We call a task a coroutine that executes a given routine but doesn't return a value. In addition, the coroutine is associated with a `promise` object – we spoke about that in *Chapter 6*. The `promise` object is manipulated on a coroutine level. The coroutine returns the operation result or raises an exception through this object. This facility also requires the **coroutine frame** (or **coroutine state**), which is an internal object on the heap, containing the `promise`. It also consists of the passed parameters – copied by value, a representation of the current invocation reference; the suspension point, so that the coroutine is resumed accordingly; and the local variables outside the scope of that point. So, what does our code do? Well, from a user standpoint, it does nothing, but there's a lot happening in the background. Let's observe the following diagram:

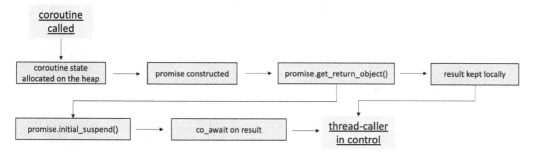

Figure 10.2 – Simple demonstration of a coroutine startup

Remember, by-value parameters are copied or moved in the scope of the coroutine, and the by-reference parameters remain as references. This means that the programmer should consider their lifetime in the task-caller, so no dangling pointers appear. Afterward, the `promise` is constructed and `get_return_object()` is called. The result will be returned to the task-caller when the coroutine first suspends.

Figure 10.2 demonstrates a case where the `promise` returns `suspend_always` and we have lazily started a coroutine. The `initial_suspend()` operation resumes and, without the knowledge or the context of how to continue, the coroutine will never be resumed and will leak. In order to handle this, we need... a `handle` object. You can think of the `handle` object as a view. Similar to the relationships between the `string_view` object and a `string` object, or a `vector` object and a `range` object with a `range view` object, the `handle` object is used to provide indirect access to `*this`. Through the `handle` object, we can call `resume()` to continue the coroutine's work. It must be suspended first, or the behavior will be undefined:

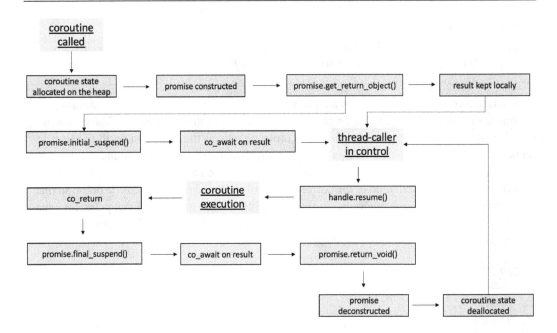

Figure 10.3 – Graph demonstrating a coroutine's creation and resumption

The initial_suspend() operation is called and the result is handled through co_await. This is done through the compiler generating additional code in the background around the suspend_never awaitable – the coroutine is not created in a lazy manner as with suspend_always, but is immediately started. Both are defined in the C++ Standard Library.

The current coroutine does a co_return keyword (in exCoroutine()). But that way, the coroutine body is exited. If we want to use it to produce constantly new or the next generated values, then we require the co_yield operator. We call such a coroutine a **generator**. We could express the co_yield operator as co_await promise.yield_value(<some expression>). Otherwise, if it simply calls co_await, it is a task, as mentioned earlier. Now, if we look at *Figure 10.3* again, using the co_yield operator will redirect the arrow from *thread-caller in control* to *coroutine execution*, thus providing the opportunity to coroutine to continue work. In other words, the co_return keyword will lead to execution completion, while the co_yield keyword will just suspend the coroutine temporarily.

Let's go a step back and take a look at **awaitables** and the `co_await` call. Their work is presented in the following diagram:

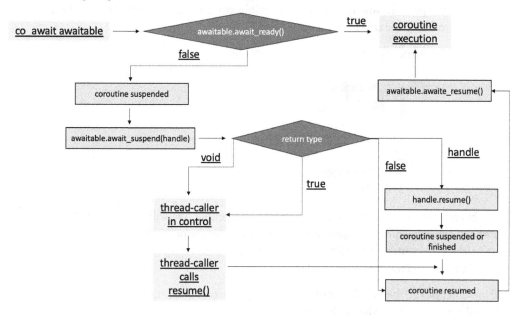

Figure 10.4 – Graph representing generated invocations after a co_await call

Now, a private variable of the `Handle` type is used to call the true `resume()` function. Let's check the code:

```
using namespace std;
struct Task {
    struct promise_type {
        using Handle = coroutine_handle<promise_type>;
        Task get_return_object() {
            return Task { Handle::from_promise(*this) };
        }
...
```

We will use the explicit specifier. In C++ 20, it allows you to be more restrictive on constructor calls. That is, it cannot be used for copy tnitialization or implicit conversions. Additionally, we keep our handle object private. Now, let's see how this might come in handy (markers {1} and {2}, while a wrapper is provided to the caller – markers {1} and {3}):

```
explicit Task (promise_type::Handle crtHdnl)  :
                              crtHandle(crtHdnl)  {}
void resume() { crtHandle.resume(); } // {1}

private:
      promise_type::Handle crtHandle;    // {2}
...
    auto async_task = exCoroutine();
    async_task.resume();   // {3}
```

Let's use this code structure to build a fully functional example. We will rename the Task struct Generator, and implement a coroutine with a generator functionality. The full code can be found here: https://github.com/PacktPublishing/C-Programming-for-Linux-Systems/tree/main/Chapter%2010.

We will increment a variable N number of times through the coroutine. That's why it needs to be able to yield, and we add the following to Generator:

```
...
    suspend_always yield_value(auto value) {
          currValue = value;
          return {};
       }
...
        uint32_t currValue;
    };
```

Then, getting the next element happens as follows:

```
int next() {
      crtHndl.resume();
      return crtHndl.promise().currValue; } ...
```

Proceeding with the coroutine body and its creation in the main thread. The increment will happen 100,000 times. This example allows the programmer to generate data lazily and not use a big portion of the RAM. At the same time, no separate thread is used, so the execution remains in the user space without extensive context switching:

```
Generator exCoroutine() {
    auto idx = 0;
    for (;;) {
        co_yield idx++;
    }
}
int main() {
    auto crt = exCoroutine();
    for (auto idx = 1; (idx = crt.next()) <= 100000; )
        cout << idx << " ";
    cout << endl;
    return 0;
}
```

The shortened version of the output is as follows:

```
1 2 3 4 ... 100000
```

Unfortunately, you probably already understand why it is not that trivial to create a simple coroutine application in C++. As a new feature, this facility continues to improve and there are new interfaces expected in upcoming C++ versions, which should simplify coroutine usage. But this shouldn't discourage you from continuing to use them. This example could be easily extended to other functionalities, and you could build up your knowledge step by step. In the next sections, we will do exactly this and get the discussion back in the area of system programming.

Network programming and coroutines in C++

In *Chapter 7*, you learned about the **TCP** and **UDP** communication protocols. We discussed their usefulness in network data transfer, but coroutines make them even more powerful. As mentioned, the code will behave in an asynchronous way, but we have control over the scheduling. Coroutines will be more efficient in **context switching** as they are executed on the user level. We'll continue with the `Generator` definition to match the type of the **coroutine**, as discussed earlier. Traditionally, that object is made move-only – this allows us to restrict the usage of the coroutine wrapper, but in general cases, coroutine objects are non-copyable and non-moveable, because the **coroutine frame** is a part of them, and some local variables can be references or pointers to other local variables. Thus, let's extend the structure accordingly:

```cpp
template<typename T> struct Generator {
    Generator(const Generator&)                 = delete;
    Generator& operator = (const Generator&) = delete;
    Generator(Generator&& other) noexcept :
        c_routine(other.c_routine) {
        other.c_routine = {};
    }
}
```

You'll notice that the `struct` object is defined as a `template` in order to be generic. We overload the `()` operator in order to be able to appropriately give the control back to the caller:

```cpp
    Generator& operator = (Generator&& other) noexcept {
        if (this == &other)
            return *this;
        if (c_routine)
            c_routine.destroy();
        c_routine = other.c_routine;
        other.c_routine = {};
        return *this;
    }
    optional<T> operator()() {
        c_routine.resume();
        if (c_routine.done()) {
            return nullopt;
        }
        return c_routine.promise().currValue;
    }
```

We also add a behavior during an exception – the application will be terminated:

```cpp
        void unhandled_exception() {
            exit(EXIT_FAILURE);
    }
```

In the main thread, we create and join two threads – a server and a client. Each of them will execute the coroutines for the respective domains. We provide a **UDP** example for shorter code, but TCP is similar as an approach, and you could take the pattern from *Chapter 7*. Initially, we create the **socket** and set it up. Afterward, we proceed with its binding and actual coroutine construction of the sender.

Time after time, the result will be printed out. Currently, it will be the number of bytes sent through the **UDP** socket (marker {9} in the following code):

```
auto sockfd = 0;
  if ((sockfd = socket(AF_INET, SOCK_DGRAM, 0)) < 0) {
      const auto ecode{ make_error_code(errc{errno}) };
      cerr << "Error opening shm region";
      system_error exception{ ecode };
      throw exception;
  }
  auto server = jthread([&sockfd] {
      struct sockaddr_in servaddr = { 0 };
      servaddr.sin_family = AF_INET;
      servaddr.sin_addr.s_addr = INADDR_ANY;
      servaddr.sin_port = htons(PORT);
      if (bind(sockfd,
          (const struct sockaddr*)&servaddr,
          sizeof(struct sockaddr_in)) < 0) {
          perror("Bind failed");
          exit(EXIT_FAILURE);
      }
      cout << "\nsend_to():\n";
      string_view message{ "This is a test!" };
      auto sender = send_to(sockfd, message,
          servaddr);
                                              // {9}
```

Inside the **coroutine** function, we invoke the sendto() method. We use a string_view object, the same way we did in *Chapter 3* – the reasoning is primarily the safety of the code and the compactness of the data and its size. At the end of the loop, we use co_yield value, thus providing the number of bytes sent to the main thread. The endless loop allows the coroutine to run until truly canceled by outer logic – in this, it's called 10 times, because of the for loop in the main thread (marker {10} in the following code):

```
for (int i = 1; i <= 10; i++) {
        auto sentData = sender();
        cout << i << " Bytes sent: "
            << *sentData << endl;       // {10}
    }
});
```

The client thread is implemented in a similar fashion:

```
auto client = jthread([&sockfd] {
    cout << "\nrecv_from():\n" << endl;
    struct sockaddr_in clntaddr = { 0 };
    auto receiver = recv_from(sockfd, clntaddr);
    for (auto i = 1; i <= 10; i++) {
        auto recvData = receiver();
        cout << i << " Message received: "
            << *recvData << endl;    // {11}
    }
});
server.join(); client.join();
close(sockfd); return 0;
}
```

The server-side coroutine has the following body:

```
Generator<size_t> send_to(int sockfd,
                          string_view buffer,
                          auto servaddr) noexcept {
    for (;;) {
        auto value = sendto(sockfd,
                            buffer.data(),
                            buffer.size(),
                            MSG_DONTWAIT,
                            (const struct sockaddr*)
                                &servaddr,
                            sizeof(servaddr));
        co_yield value;
    }
}
```

The client-side coroutines are implemented in a similar fashion:

```
Generator<string> recv_from(int sockfd,
                            auto clntaddr,
                            size_t buf_size =
                                BUF_SIZE) noexcept {
    socklen_t len = sizeof(struct sockaddr_in);
    array<char, BUF_SIZE> tmp_buf = {};
```

The coroutine function calls the `recvfrom()` system call. At the end, instead of the bytes received, the message coming from the socket is stored in the `currValue` member variable. It's then printed out in the main thread. We also use the `MSG_DONTWAIT` flag. The respective output will be printed out in different ways every time as the code is asynchronous. The last part is as expected:

```
for (;;) {
    recvfrom(sockfd,
            tmp_buf.data(),
            tmp_buf.size(),
            MSG_DONTWAIT,
            (struct sockaddr*)&clntaddr,
            &len);
    co_yield tmp_buf.data();
}
```

The merging or misplacing of text is to be expected, but it proves the useability of coroutines. The shortened version of the output is the following:

```
send_to():
1 Bytes sent: 15
...
10 Bytes sent: 15
recv_from():
1 Message received: This is a test!
...
10 Message received: This is a test!
```

The full example can be found at `https://github.com/PacktPublishing/C-Programming-for-Linux-Systems/tree/main/Chapter%2010`.

In the previous chapter, we also had the issue of synchronizing parallel threads, but the code was not truly parallel every time. For example, waiting for an event such as "the resource is accessible" is a matter of concurrency, not parallel execution. That said, coroutines are a powerful tool in the shared memory problem, too – let's check it out in the next section.

Revisiting the shared memory problem through coroutines in C++

One of the issues we had with **condition variables** was synchronization during process startup. In other words, for the producer-consumer example, we didn't know which threads were going to be first. We synchronized the code through a condition variable – its **mutex**, together with a predicate in order to handle the correct sequence of events. Otherwise, we would've risked losing information or ending in a **deadlock**. For a good portion of this book's example preparations, we got to this situation, which made the writing experience even better. But coroutines provide another way of doing it, which could be more efficient at times and simpler to use (after you get used to the interface of coroutines as it is not the easiest to grasp).

The next example is motivated by the **awaitable-awaiter** pattern. It is similar to the condition variable, but it doesn't use such synchronization primitives. Still, the notification signaling is dependent on an atomic variable. We'll get back to the Task coroutine. It will used for handling the receiver end. The full example can be found here: `https://github.com/PacktPublishing/C-Programming-for-Linux-Systems/tree/main/Chapter%2010`.

> **Important note**
>
> The example is inspired by `https://www.modernescpp.com/index.php/c-20-thread-synchronization-with-coroutines/`.

We reuse the code from the **shared memory** example from *Chapter 9*:

```
template<typename T, typename N>
Task receiver(Event& event, int fd, N size) {
    co_await event;
    ftruncate(fd, size);
```

We align the shared memory and set its size first, then we continue mapping the pointer to it:

```
    if (const auto ptr = mmap(0, size,
                         PROT_RW, MAP_SHARED,
                         fd, 0); ptr != MAP_FAILED) {
        auto* obj = static_cast<T*>(ptr);
        auto del = mmap_deallocator<T>(size);
        auto res =
            unique_ptr<T, mmap_deallocator<T>>(obj, del);
        if (res != nullptr)
            cout << "Receiver: " << *res << endl;
    }
    else {
        cerr << "Error mapping shm region";
    } }
```

It is really important that the address of `res` is accessible for dereferencing inside the coroutine. Otherwise, the code will crash with `Segmentation fault`, which is preferable to a dangling pointer. Another remark is that different compilers (or environments) will give you different behavior for this code. Before we get to the `Event` struct, let's see what the sender does – again, we step on our previous code:

```
template<typename T, typename N>
void Event::notify(T buffer, int fd, N size) noexcept {
    notified = false;
    auto* waiter =
        static_cast<Awaiter*>(suspended.load());
    if (waiter != nullptr) {
        ftruncate(fd, size);
```

Again, we make sure the shared memory is of the correct size and we map the pointer to it:

```
        if (const auto ptr = mmap(0, size,
                                  PROT_RW, MAP_SHARED,
                                  fd, 0);
                            ptr != MAP_FAILED) {
            auto* obj = new (ptr) T(buffer);
            auto del = mmap_deallocator<T>(size);
            auto res =
                unique_ptr<T, mmap_deallocator<T>>
                                            (obj, del);
        }
        else {
            cerr << "Error mapping shm region";
        }
        waiter->coroutineHandle.resume();
    }
}
```

Initially, the notification flag is set to `false`, meaning that the coroutine will not behave as a regular function but is going to be suspended. Then, the `waiter` object is loaded, which is `nullptr`, because it's not previously set. Its respective `resume()` operation is not called. The subsequentially performed `await_suspend()` function gets the **coroutine handle** and stores it, so it will be called later, when the **coroutine** is resumed. Most importantly, the `waiter` state is stored in the `suspended` member variable. Later, `notify()` is triggered and it's executed fully:

```
bool
Event::Awaiter::await_suspend(coroutine_handle<> handle)
  noexcept {
    coroutineHandle = handle;
    if (event.notified) return false;
    event.suspended.store(this);
    return true;
}
```

In the main thread, an `Event` object is required to synchronize the workflow. A shared memory region is defined as well. If `shm_open()` is called inside each coroutine, it will not really be shared virtual memory, as the file descriptor will access private regions for each of the coroutines. Thus, we will end up with `Segmentation fault`. There are two threads, representing the sender and the receiver ends. The aforementioned coroutines are called respectively after the threads are joined:

```
Event event{};
int fd = shm_open(SHM_ID, O_CREAT | O_RDWR, 0644);
auto senderT = jthread([&event, &fd]{
    event.notify<const char*, size_t>(message.data(),
                                      fd,
                                      message.size());
});
```

The receiver's code is similar, but the `event` object is passed as an argument:

```
auto receiverT = jthread([&event, &fd]{
    receiver<char*, size_t>(ref(event),
                            fd, (message.size())); });
```

The output is as follows:

```
This is a testing message!
```

This example gives you the flexibility to manage your shared resources in a concurrent manner. The notification mechanism of awaiter-awaitable will do the job without the need for synchronization primitives. We encourage you to try it out yourself. In the meantime, we'll proceed with some final notes on coroutines usage in system programming.

Final thoughts on coroutines and their implementations in C++

The examples earlier were practical, although not so simple. They were useful in understanding the sequence that a coroutine's execution might take. It is good to visualize the state graph of coroutines, although we still believe it would be confusing for inexperienced developers.

As presented earlier, *Figure 10.2*, *Figure 10.3*, and *Figure 10.4* pretty much cover what we've already explained through the code examples. It is useful to understand how much additional logic is generated around the coroutine and its members. Most of it happens in the background, and the system programmer only arranges the scheduling. In this chapter's examples, we did this through the `promise` object and awaitables. The fact that the aforementioned figures partially represent a coroutine's execution as a finite state machine should hint to you that this is another application where coroutines are useful. They transform state machines into first-class objects. Once the coroutine frame is defined, much of the logic remains there and it's hidden from callers. This provides the opportunity for system programmers to put aside the concurrent logic for a moment and just focus on calling the coroutines through short code snippets, as we did. The system behavior code and task scheduling will be simpler and more obvious. Thus, much of the power of managing algorithms, parsers, data structure traversals, polling, and so on could be interpreted by this technique. Unfortunately, we cannot cover everything here, but we believe it's worthwhile checking these things out.

Last but not least, we'd like to emphasize that coroutines are fairly new to the language. As the coroutine interface in C++ is still lacking comfort and simplicity, you can find many custom-made coroutine libraries on the internet. We advise you to rely only on the trustworthy ones or wait for the next Standard features of this facility. It makes more sense to apply those than to implement them anew yourself. As you can see, it's quite a complex concept, and there's a lot of research being done on the matter. For curious readers, we encourage you to spend some time learning about the evolution of coroutines in C++, especially in recent years. There are three techniques discussed in the C++ Standard – Coroutines TS, Core Coroutines, and Resumable expressions. Although just one is currently used in the Standard, the three of them deserve attention. A great summary and analysis has been done by Geoffrey Romer, Gor Nishanov, Lewis Baker, and Mihail Mihailov here: `https://www.open-std.org/jtc1/sc22/wg21/docs/papers/2019/p1493r0.pdf`.

Feel free to check it out. Many of the clarifications we gave in this chapter are presented in the document as a great visual comparison of the regular functions and coroutines. Meanwhile, we continue to the finish.

Summary

With this, we've covered all the topics of this book. With the upcoming improvements of C++23, coroutines and their evolution will be analyzed more and more, especially in the system programming domain – and applied there, of course. Although complex to understand at first, coroutines allow you to continue sharpening the usage of C++ and give you one more instrument to enhance code.

In this chapter, you learned how to apply them in your concurrent applications, but their usefulness is far greater. We are excited about what comes next. We expect the `modules` language feature, which we didn't cover in this book – intentionally – to be fully covered by the compilers and be broadly applied. Another interesting feature is `std::generator` – a view for the synchronous creation of coroutines in C++23. **Stackful coroutines** in C++26 are going to be a splendid system programming technique. In that version, you will also be able to obtain and visualize `std::stacktrace` from a thrown exception, which will help you in code debugging. And for easier printing, you'll be able to use `std::print` as well. The monadic interface of `std::expected` will allow you to store either of two values. In addition to all this, files will be loaded at compile time as arrays through `#embed`.

We'd like to use this opportunity to express our gratitude to you – the reader! We hope you found this book useful and will apply parts of it in your daily job. We also hope you enjoyed the experience the way we enjoyed writing the book. It was a tremendous journey for us, and we'd be glad to share future journeys with you. With this, we wish you good fortune in all your projects!

Index

packtpub.com

Subscribe to our online digital library for full access to over 7,000 books and videos, as well as industry leading tools to help you plan your personal development and advance your career. For more information, please visit our website.

Why subscribe?

- Spend less time learning and more time coding with practical eBooks and Videos from over 4,000 industry professionals
- Improve your learning with Skill Plans built especially for you
- Get a free eBook or video every month
- Fully searchable for easy access to vital information
- Copy and paste, print, and bookmark content

Did you know that Packt offers eBook versions of every book published, with PDF and ePub files available? You can upgrade to the eBook version at packtpub.com and as a print book customer, you are entitled to a discount on the eBook copy. Get in touch with us at customercare@packtpub.com for more details.

At www.packtpub.com, you can also read a collection of free technical articles, sign up for a range of free newsletters, and receive exclusive discounts and offers on Packt books and eBooks.

Other Books You May Enjoy

If you enjoyed this book, you may be interested in these other books by Packt:

Expert C++ - Second Edition

Marcelo Guerra Hahn, Araks Tigranyan, Vardan Grigoryan, Shunguang Wu

ISBN: 978-1-80461-783-0

- Go beyond the basics to explore advanced C++ programming techniques
- Develop proficiency in advanced data structures and algorithm design with C++17 and C++20
- Implement best practices and design patterns to build scalable C++ applications
- Master C++ for machine learning, data science, and data analysis framework design
- Design world-ready applications, incorporating networking and security considerations
- Strengthen your understanding of C++ concurrency, multithreading, and optimizing performance with concurrent data structures

Hands-On Design Patterns with C++ - Second Edition

Fedor G. Pikus

ISBN: 978-1-80461-155-5

- Recognize the most common design patterns used in C++
- Understand how to use C++ generic programming to solve common design problems
- Explore the most powerful C++ idioms, their strengths, and their drawbacks
- Rediscover how to use popular C++ idioms with generic programming
- Discover new patterns and idioms made possible by language features of C++17 and C++20
- Understand the impact of design patterns on the program's performance

Packt is searching for authors like you

If you're interested in becoming an author for Packt, please visit authors.packtpub.com and apply today. We have worked with thousands of developers and tech professionals, just like you, to help them share their insight with the global tech community. You can make a general application, apply for a specific hot topic that we are recruiting an author for, or submit your own idea.

Share Your Thoughts

Now you've finished *C++ Programming for Linux Systems*, we'd love to hear your thoughts! Scan the QR code below to go straight to the Amazon review page for this book and share your feedback or leave a review on the site that you purchased it from.

https://packt.link/r/1805129007

Your review is important to us and the tech community and will help us make sure we're delivering excellent quality content.

Download a free PDF copy of this book

Thanks for purchasing this book!

Do you like to read on the go but are unable to carry your print books everywhere?

Is your eBook purchase not compatible with the device of your choice?

Don't worry, now with every Packt book you get a DRM-free PDF version of that book at no cost.

Read anywhere, any place, on any device. Search, copy, and paste code from your favorite technical books directly into your application.

The perks don't stop there, you can get exclusive access to discounts, newsletters, and great free content in your inbox daily

Follow these simple steps to get the benefits:

1. Scan the QR code or visit the link below

https://packt.link/free-ebook/9781805129004

2. Submit your proof of purchase
3. That's it! We'll send your free PDF and other benefits to your email directly